Praise for *Libretto*

"What happens when talented young mezzo-soprano Jessica St. James puts herself completely in the hands of the obsessive and authoritarian singing teacher Svetlana Usova? The answer is disaster which is why I.V. Mazzoleni's disturbing novel, *Libretto*, should be required reading for all budding opera singers.
On a lighter note, Mazzoleni has clearly penned a *roman à clef* about the early years of the Canadian Opera Company and it is tantalizing to try and match fictional people with their real-life counterparts. Amid Jessica's career *sturm und drang*, Mazzoleni has her heroine relate some scandalous tales that make absolutely delicious reading."

>Paula Citron is a Toronto-based arts journalist who is a frequent contributor to the Globe and Mail, Classical 96.3 FM, Toronto Life and Opera Canada Magazine.

"Jessica's journey through the arduous world of opera rings true throughout this lovely book. Reading it brought back many early memories."

>Mario Bernardi, C.C., D MUS, LLD
>First Conductor National Arts Centre Orchestra, Calgary Philharmonic Orchestra 1984–1993, CBC Vancouver Orchestra (CBC Radio Orchestra) 1983–1993

"Mrs. Mazzoleni knows her stuff and her novel bristles with the truth about the world of opera and its beginnings in Canada. Although she insists that it's a work of fiction, music lovers will have a field day identifying the many colourful characters and situations in this lively *roman à clef*."

    Stuart Hamilton, C.M.
    Quizmaster, CBC Saturday Afternoon at the Opera

"*Libretto* is a novel about ambition, success, disappointment, tragedy, jealousy, melodrama. In other words it is about opera, an account of a singer's life and the world beyond the footlights, sensitively created by someone who was there.
For the opera fan out front, *Libretto* is a vivid and intimate look at the lives of singers offstage with all the high emotion of an operatic setting in real life. By turns amusing, revealing and tragic the novel provides a glimpse of the reality beyond the footlights."

    Carl Morey
    Professor Emeritus, Faculty of Music, University of Toronto

"Only a singer could describe so vividly and sometimes so hilariously the serious technical demands imposed on a student by an uncompromising diva teacher in the early 50's. For one who was there, separating fact from fiction is an intriguing puzzle—Thanks for the memories, I.V."

    Mary Morrison, C.C.
    One of Canada's eminent voice teachers

Libretto

Dear Andrea
   Many thanks for all your help with the typing. I hope, after reading the book you feel all your time spent was worth while.
      Much love
         Mummy

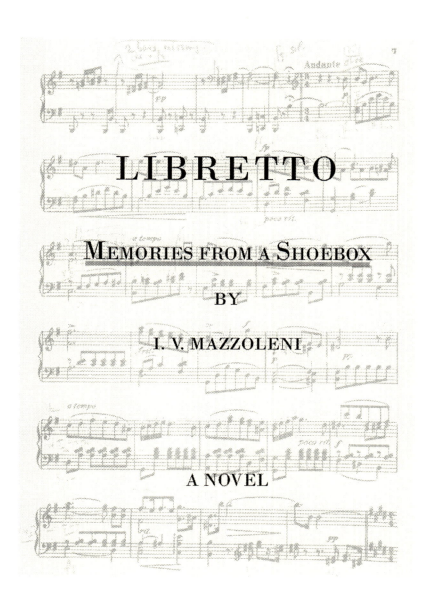

LIBRETTO

Memories from a Shoebox

by

I. V. Mazzoleni

A Novel

iUniverse, Inc.
New York Lincoln Shanghai

Libretto
Memories from a Shoebox

Copyright © 2007 by I.V. Mazzoleni

All rights reserved. No part of this book may be used or reproduced by any means, graphic, electronic, or mechanical, including photocopying, recording, taping or by any information storage retrieval system without the written permission of the publisher except in the case of brief quotations embodied in critical articles and reviews.

iUniverse books may be ordered through booksellers or by contacting:

iUniverse
2021 Pine Lake Road, Suite 100
Lincoln, NE 68512
www.iuniverse.com
1-800-Authors (1-800-288-4677)

Because of the dynamic nature of the Internet, any Web addresses or links contained in this book may have changed since publication and may no longer be valid.

The views expressed in this work are solely those of the author and do not necessarily reflect the views of the publisher, and the publisher hereby disclaims any responsibility for them.

ISBN: 978-0-595-43057-4 (pbk)
ISBN: 978-0-595-87399-9 (ebk)

Printed in the United States of America

Contents

Acknowledgements ix
Prologue   Discovering the shoebox 1
Chapter 1   May 27, 1952—First Meeting with Usova in New York 11
Chapter 2   Sailing for Europe 29
Chapter 3   Dashed Hopes in Bayreuth, Germany 38
Chapter 4   Continual Confrontation with Usova in Salzburg. 48
Chapter 5   Eva Arrives 57
Chapter 6   Disastrous Love Affair—Severed Relations with Usova 69
Chapter 7   New York—Back in Usova's Clutches. 81
Chapter 8   Toronto—Meeting the Future Husband 94
Chapter 9   Usova's Attempted Seduction in New York 102
Chapter 10   The Wedding 114
Chapter 11   Performance of Fledermaus in Toronto 124
Chapter 12   Robbed in Rome, Italy 133
Chapter 13   Primitive Existence in Sardinia 141
Chapter 14   Bayreuth—Arturo Meets Usova. 153
Chapter 15   Toronto—Arturo's Concert with Victor 167

Chapter 16	Preparations for Carmen Begin 172
Chapter 17	Usova's Master Class 186
Chapter 18	Ill-Fated First Performance of Carmen 203
Chapter 19	Carmen Redeemed 214
Chapter 20	A Burst Blood Vessel in the Throat 223
Chapter 21	Big Plans for an Opera Workshop 234
Chapter 22	Plane Crash 241
Chapter 23	June 1998—Return to Salzburg 251
Epilogue	A Stranger in the Mirror 269

Acknowledgements

The seed of LIBRETTO was sown years ago while watching a movie on television about a dictatorial and tempestuous piano teacher. It instantly triggered a distant memory. The seed simmered and festered for years and was finally brought to fruition by a creative writing class, master-minded by Prim Pemberton. Without the discerning advice of Prim and the encouragement of the group, this book would never have been written. I must also thank John Pemberton for cleverly coming up with a well-suited title for the book. A special thanks also to Barb Nahwegahbow, whose reading of the rough draft resulted in many helpful suggestions. Thank you Earlaine Collins and Ninalee Craig for your pertinent comments and your useful directives.

A particular thanks to members of my family: to my daughter Andrea Mazzoleni, for typing chapters of the book when in its infancy; to Gina McDonnell, for reading through the manuscript and pointing out overlooked discrepancies. Thanks also to my granddaughter, Erika Randlesome, for painstakingly proofreading the final product; and thanks to my grandson Chris Piller, for initially setting up my new toy, the computer, and for putting everything together for online-publishing, at the end.

My thanks also go to Walter and Emmy Homburger, for taking the time from their busy lives to help me with the sprinkling of German text, and for being such wonderfully supportive friends.

I am indebted to Peter Arblaster, whose patience, when continually called upon for his computer expertise, has been greatly appreciated; also, thanks and admiration for his striking design of the front cover.

I owe a huge debt of gratitude to my daughter, Clare Piller, who throughout, has held my hand and guided my purpose. If I have inadvertently omitted anyone, I ask their indulgence, for the writing of this book has been a long but enjoyable exercise.

Prologue

Discovering the shoebox

Toronto, Canada, June 1998

Last night I had one of my alarming dreams which used to recur with relentless regularity when I was singing professionally many years ago. Each nightmare differed but the outcome was always humiliation and terror. Sometimes I was in an opera house staring out at a sea of expectant faces, my mouth opening and closing like a fish at the bottom of a boat struggling to fill its lungs with air, and there would be no sound. Other times I was ready to go on stage and would suddenly realize I had learned the wrong opera. Though these nightmares had continued occasionally after I stopped singing, it had been many years since such a frightening and vivid one had disturbed my sleep.

I was in Madame Svetlana Usova's studio in Salzburg, Austria, having a singing lesson, when her phone rang. It was festival time and the director asked her if she knew of someone who could sing the Third Spirit in Mozart's The Magic Flute *that evening. Without a moment's hesitation she said, 'Yes' and immediately began teaching me the small role. I arrived at the Festspielhaus an hour before curtain, plenty of time to get into costume and makeup for I knew my first entrance would not be until at least half-an-hour after the opera began; time enough to get my staging instructions from the other two spirits. When I told the stage manager that I was there to sing the Third Spirit he shook his head emphatically and said, "You mean the Third Lady. You are on in half-an-hour." He turned and disappeared into the darkness of backstage.*

Third Lady—oh my God! I knew the ladies were on at the beginning of the opera and that the role was a much more important one. I would have to find a score and try to learn each sequence as the opera progressed. For the staging I would have to depend on the other two ladies to push me around the stage, and fake the rest.

No one had a score. I searched everywhere, taking up precious time. The overture began. I quickly got into my costume; I had no time to worry about makeup. One of the ladies handed me a spear and pushed me onto the stage. The lights went up and the curtain slowly lifted as a huge dragon lumbered toward me, spewing fire from each nostril. I took my cue from the other two ladies and raised my spear to strike—then all action ceased. The orchestra stopped playing; the ladies stared at me, frantically mouthing something I couldn't understand. The monster stopped in its tracks. I looked at the conductor who was waving his baton like a windmill in a hurricane. Then, with his left arm extended, he pointed his forefinger directly at me. Before I could take a breath, he bent his right arm back behind his head and, bringing it forward, released the baton. It streaked through the air like a dart at supersonic speed heading straight for my eyes. I instinctively turned to stave off its blow and felt the point of the baton pierce the flesh of my shoulder.

I awoke feeling a sudden jab of pain. I must have been thrashing about in my sleep and my shoulder had caught the sharp corner of my bedside table. I sat bolt upright in bed shaking from head to foot, drenched in sweat.

Strange that after all these years I should dream of Svetlana Usova! It was over forty years ago when Irma Mensinger, the world-renowned Austrian soprano, first told me of this woman who became the anvil on which my technique was forged. Perhaps it was time I returned to Salzburg to disperse the mists of the past, to relive those heady days of the summer of 1952, when I began my studies with the famous Russian mentor. For days I could think of nothing else.

First I would have to make sure my passport was in order and then make both air and hotel reservations. If I went before the Salzburg Festival began in July my chances of success would be greater. Flight and hotel reservations were always booked well in advance during July and August and it was now the beginning of June; I would have to work fast. The flight reservation was easy; I booked for June 12 returning June 29. Hotel accommodation was a different story. A friend recommended Hotel Mozart, close to the *Festspielhaus*. I called the hotel and found it could accommodate me for the first four nights only. I decided to book a room for the four nights anyway and take a chance on finding something suitable when I arrived.

I rummaged through a cupboard full of old travel information to see if there was something on Salzburg; a brochure with names of hotels and places to eat. The only thing I could find was a map of the city marked with addresses of where I had stayed and people I had met on previous trips. This, I thought, would come in handy as things were apt to change little in an ancient city like Salzburg.

Underneath the map was a shoebox marked 'Summer, 1952'. Inside was a bundle of letters held together with rotting rubber bands, the envelopes long ago discarded. The first letter was in the familiar hand of my mother. Most of the others appeared to be penned by me, written on both sides of thin airmail paper with a pen that had leaked dark blue spots of ink. Reading the letters wouldn't be easy, but I was curious to see if they might reveal something that would prove useful.

I lifted my mother's letter from the box.

April 20, 1952
Home

Jess, dear,
This is a hasty note to let you know that Irma Mensinger is to sing with the Women's Musical Club next Monday evening here in London. Isn't she the singer you were so taken with the summer before last at the Salzburg Festival? I phoned the manager to see if Madame Mensinger would like to stay with us and apparently she said 'Yes.' I tried to reach you by phone, but I guess you were on tour with Opera Backstage.
It is the last concert of the season and I thought you might like to both hear and meet her. Do try to make it; it's the evening of April 27. Hope this reaches you in time.

In haste,
Mum

Reading the letter, Irma's face came vividly into focus.

I had heard Madame Mensinger two summers before, in 1950, while studying in Salzburg. She had sung the role of Susanna in Mozart's *The Marriage of Figaro* at the Festival. I remember thinking she was one of the most gifted singers I had ever heard. The thought of not only meeting her but staying under the same roof was more than I could resist, no matter which rehearsals I would have to miss.

For the past two years I had been enrolled in the opera school at the National Academy of Music in Toronto. We were in the midst of preparing *The Old Maid and the Thief,* by Gian-Carlo Menotti, to take on tour in the fall. I was playing the role of the old maid, Miss Todd, and was expected to be at all rehearsals. I was sure that under these circumstances Maestro wouldn't mind if I missed Monday's rehearsal, but I would have to check. He agreed immediately. He would be conducting the CBC Symphony on the radio program, Wednesday Night Live, two days later. Madame Mensinger was to be the soloist.

Madame Mensinger was to arrive in St. Thomas on Sunday evening aboard the eight-thirty train from New York City. At that time the Grand Central Line went through Canada on its way from New York to Detroit and stopped in St.

Thomas, a small town about thirty miles south of London. I was expected to arrive home in plenty of time to meet her train.

It was one of those damp evenings in late April when the cold eats through to the bone. I was beginning to feel chilled and was about to retreat to the warmth of the station when I heard the approaching train. Eight-thirty; right on time!

My heart began to pound with excitement or nervousness, I wasn't sure which. What would I say to this famous woman I so admired? Did she even speak English? I began to hope the train wouldn't stop; that it would go straight on to Detroit.

I had no difficulty recognizing Madame Mensinger for she was the only passenger to get off the train that evening. She didn't look at all as I thought a diva should! She was taller than she appeared on stage. She had a round, friendly face and wore no makeup, which made her look young. I suspected she was about my age; in her early twenties. She had a smart short haircut which was covered by a plain navy beret placed on her dark hair at a rakish angle. She wore a beautifully tailored, forest green Austrian rain cape which perfectly suited her and the weather. She was not good-looking in the general sense, but the whole effect demanded attention, and she had the most marvellous smile that dispersed the cold damp air surrounding us. Her smile stretched from ear to ear on her wide face and looking at her was like bathing in the summer sun. All my nervousness dissolved. I waited for her to say something to see what language she would choose before trying my few words of German.

"Hello?" she said, raising her eyebrows, making the hello sound like a question. I nodded, still unsure which language to use. I tried to match her smile with one of my own while bending down to pick up the two medium-sized suitcases left by the porter.

"Hey, what are you doing? Those are much too heavy for you." She had only a trace of an accent and her voice had a ring to it that easily carried over the explosive sounds of the departing train.

With no red cap in sight we each carried a suitcase to the car. On the way back to London, I found myself chatting as though I had known her all my life; she was that kind of person. I told her how much I had enjoyed her singing of Susanna in Salzburg and that I had admired her work above all the other singers. I didn't mention that I was studying voice and was an aspiring opera singer on the bottom rung of a tall ladder to success.

By the time we reached the outskirts of London we were on a first name basis. The half-hour trip had sped by so quickly that in no time I was driving down our driveway and into the garage at the rear of the house.

The next day Irma slept until noon and, after a large brunch, I drove her to the local high school where the concert was to take place. She was to meet Edward Stewart, her accompanist, for a three o'clock rehearsal. He had the reputation of being one of the finest accompanists in the world. He was coming from Toronto where he had been staying with his brother and was expected on the two-thirty train.

Leading Irma through the school halls teeming with noisy teenagers, I thought I should apologize for our sad lack of the proper cultural facilities, but when I glanced at her face I knew it was unnecessary. She was smiling her wonderful smile and nodding a greeting to each teenager as we walked by. She seemed to be enjoying herself immensely and if she noticed the pungent odour of sweaty running shoes when we entered the gymnasium, already set-up with chairs for the evening concert, she didn't mention it. Without a word she strode onto the stage to the piano, opened the cover over the keys and, aided by a few chords, let forth with a series of scales. Each note was like a shimmering pearl strung to the others with a thread of silk. Glorious sounds echoed throughout the hall. I could feel them creeping under my skin. How did she make that sound? I should know; I should be able to analyze how, but I couldn't. I only knew that it was the purest sound I'd ever heard, and oh, how I envied her for it.

"The acoustics seem fine," she said between breaths. She had only time for a few scales when Mr. Stewart appeared at the back of the hall. He walked by without noticing me, removed his coat and hat and tossed them onto a seat in the front row before mounting the few steps to the stage.

"Sorry I'm late, but they don't seem to have taxis in this town. I'm Edward Stewart and you sound like Irma Mensinger." Before he finished the sentence, he was seated at the piano. He turned back the cover of Schumann's song cycle, *Frauen Liebe und Leben*, which Irma had left on the music rack. He struck the two opening chords of the first song and Irma began to sing. *"Seit ich ihn gesehen."* They performed as if they were one instrument. I found it incredible that these two artists had never met before. When the first song ended they talked, using an occasional music demonstration to determine how the other songs should be sung. The rehearsal was finished in less than an hour.

Afterward, I drove Irma and Mr. Stewart back to the house. He hadn't bothered to arrange for a hotel room for he was taking the night train to New York after the concert. It was four o'clock when we arrived home; just enough time for a light meal and a short rest before dressing for the concert. I remember wondering if this was the kind of life I wanted for myself. I would have to be at all times in top form, which would mean lots of sleep. In my case, I'd have to learn how to deal with sleepless nights and severe attacks of nerves before each performance. I was also not sure that I would like living out of a suitcase.

I sat beside my mother that evening while Irma captivated her audience with her interpretation of each song, whether in Italian, German, French, or English. I luxuriated in the splendour of her sound and would gladly have given up everything to be able to sing like that. I wondered how she had acquired her incredible technique in such a relatively short time. She seemed so sure of what she was doing. She would float the sound on her breath, colouring each nuance to perfection. The pianissimos floated over our heads, barely audible yet focused and clear. I never saw her take a breath yet each phrase was beautifully controlled, no matter how long or how demanding. It all seemed so effortless. The longer I listened the more aware I became of my own shortcomings. I was never totally relaxed when I sang. I could always feel tension in my neck, my shoulders and my back. My body seemed to be working overtime. I was constantly told by my teachers to relax. "I am relaxed," I would say, with my jaw seized as in a vice and the muscles in my neck bulging like ropes. I had never felt the sensation of singing without some form of rigidity. Listening to Irma, I realized how little I knew about the production of the voice. I had been coasting along on my ability to perform; my ability to 'put it across.'

When Irma finished, the entire audience rose to its feet, clapping and cheering.

Tuesday morning Irma and I made an early start for Toronto in my mother's car. Her afternoon rehearsal with the CBC Symphony was at three o'clock.

For the first few moments we were silent as we wove our way through the London streets and onto Highway 2. There were many questions racing through my mind, the foremost being, who had been her mentor? She must have been in expert hands to sing as she did.

It was Irma who broke the silence. "Your mother tells me that you also sing. Who do you work with?"

How flattering of her to use the word *also*, intimating that I was in the same category as she was.

I laughed! "That's exactly the question I was about to ask you."

"I have worked with only one woman so far. She is the mother of one of our most famous singers in Vienna and a fine teacher. She guided me rather than instructed me and for this I am grateful. My voice from the beginning was correctly placed; she only brought out the natural sound. She made the voice larger and more secure, that's all. There can be danger in this, however," she warned, "for sometimes when the voice is naturally in the right place, if you get into trouble, you won't know how to correct it."

Irma told me of a Russian teacher who lived in New York City. Her roster of students included many of the 'who's who' in the world of singing. She was noted for being able to patch up voices of established artists who had fallen by the wayside. According to Irma, this woman was able to successfully put these artists back into circulation.

"She's a fascinating person, but to tell the truth, I have stayed away from her. She frightens me a little."

"Why?" I asked.

Irma told me that she had met the Russian teacher, Madame Svetlana Usova, a year ago through her star pupil, the American bass baritone, Richard Alexander. Richard had made a sensational debut in 1950 at the Vienna State Opera in *Boris Godunov*. Vienna was full of Russians five years after the end of the Second World War and still occupied by the four powers: the United States, England, France, and Russia. Madame Usova had coached Richard to sing the role of Boris in its original language, Russian. Richard was in Vienna at the right time and at the right stage of his career. The Boris of the moment became indisposed and Richard was ready and waiting in the wings. His Russian, as well as his portrayal of the role, was flawless. The Russians in the audience flocked backstage after the performance to congratulate him, believing him to be one of theirs, though he spoke not a word of the language. He instantly became famous throughout the opera circles of Europe. Madame Usova rode victorious on the crest of Richard's fame and she became as sought after as a teacher as Richard was an artist.

A year after his triumphant debut, Richard and Irma sang together in *Figaro*, and Richard introduced her to Madame Usova. Irma said that Madame Usova immediately went to work on her, saying she needed her help. Irma did acknowledge that she thought Svetlana Usova knew more about training the singing voice than anyone she had ever met for she had listened to one of Richard's lessons and had come away convinced.

"But surely you now are so secure in what you are doing you need only to work with a coach,"

"You'll find," she said earnestly, "that throughout your career you will need, or at least should have, someone whom you can trust, who can point out the pitfalls before they happen. Only then can you stay away from vocal problems."

"Why are you afraid of Madame Usova?" I prodded. "Do you think you'll ever go to her?"

"I expect I'll probably weaken sooner or later, but at this moment, well, I'm still not sure." She hesitated, frowning, obviously searching for the right word in English to describe her feelings. "I think it's her personality. For some reason I find it too—uh—too overpowering."

"How did Richard Alexander happen to find her?"

Irma laughed, and the sound had the same bell-like quality as her singing voice. "It's always so strange in life how people find each other, don't you think?"

She went on to say that Mr. Alexander had heard of Madame Usova through Usova's husband, Wolfgang Swartz, who was the accompanist for a group from Los Angeles called, the Bel Canto Group, with whom he had sung. Irma supposed that Wolfgang must have told Richard that his wife could make him a star, which of course, she proceeded to do.

"Irma," I began tentatively, for I wanted to share with her my doubts about my own voice with the hope that she might steer me in the right direction, "I have been studying for the past two years with an incredible woman who is not only my teacher but a dear friend. She spends her summers teaching in Salzburg. It's sort of back home for her. It was with her that I first heard you sing."

I paused, not sure how to tell Irma my real problem. It was that my teacher was a *Kunst* mentor who coached me on how to interpret a song, when I needed a *Stimme* mentor; someone who could show me how to properly use my voice.

I began again. "The thing that worries me most is, that when I practice for over an hour, my voice feels tired. I complain to my teacher time and time again but she always tells me to search within and my talent will make the right sound for me. Honestly, I can search 'til the cows come home and I'm still never sure whether the sound I get will be the one I want"

I glanced sideways and saw that Irma was smiling.

"No, I mean it. She's a remarkable teacher, really," I insisted. "She brings to life the songs of Schumann, Schubert, and Hugo Wolfe. Although she's done little for my voice, my time with her hasn't been wasted for she has kindled in me a love and understanding of the *German Lied* that no one else could have given me. I'm not ready for her yet, I guess. My great concern is that she won't be alive when I am ready."

"Don't be silly." Obviously Irma thought I was jesting.

"I couldn't be more serious," I said sadly. "I wish it weren't so, but I'm afraid she's living on borrowed time. She's in her mid sixties and had a serious cancer operation before I began studying with her. Unfortunately, the cancer wasn't discovered in time and has recently recurred."

There was another long pause and then Irma asked, "I'm curious. What's her name?"

"She's a compatriot of yours; her name is Eva Stein. You perhaps know of her for most of her career was in Austria before the war."

Irma nodded her head. "She's one of the people I'm to look up while in Toronto. Yes, of course I've heard of her. She still has a large following in Austria."

All this time we had been driving past typical south-central Ontario scenery with its undulating landscape and prosperous-looking farms. It was 1952, before Highway 401 had been built and we had to pass through several small towns: Ingersoll, Woodstock, and Paris. This made the trip considerably longer than it would take in 1998.

We arrived in Toronto via the Queen Elizabeth Highway, driving along the shore of Lake Ontario. It was a beautiful sunny day, but for me it made no difference. I had been so intent on our conversation that had it been pouring rain, I wouldn't have noticed. We arrived at Irma's hotel close to noon, giving her time to freshen up and to have a bite to eat before being picked up for her rehearsal at three o'clock.

I saw Irma once more before she left for New York. She had said she always wanted to see Niagara Falls and, as I still had my mother's car, I said I'd be delighted to show her one of North America's greatest tourist attractions. The day after her radio broadcast we left mid-morning for the Falls, discussing Svetlana Usova most of the way. She urged me to go to New York and sing for her. She felt sure that Usova could give me a solid technique. I promised I'd think about it but would have to wait until the opera school closed in mid-May. After that, there would be daily coaching lessons for I was preparing to sing the role of Carmen in July in Massachusetts with a semi-professional group.

Before we parted, Irma insisted on giving me Usova's telephone number. "I'll be seeing her when I'm in New York. I'll tell her to expect your call; she'll be leaving for Europe in mid June so make sure you call her before then."

I worked hard on Menotti's *The Old Maid* and Bizet's *Carmen* over the next month. I carried Madame Usova's telephone number in the back pouch of my wallet where I had put it the day Irma gave it to me, just in case I mustered up my courage. Every time I passed a telephone I could feel the number tugging at me, urging me to make the call. I always rationalized that I should be more patient. Perhaps my voice was improving a little. I had been told that it would take time and that eventually my upper register would magically open up. My voice would leap out of my throat and into the mask of my face, resonating in the sinuses and behind the cheekbones where it ought to be. Besides, why should a teacher as famous and as sought after as Svetlana Usova take on the likes of me? What made me think that I had sufficient talent for her to give me the time of day?

I think what bothered me most was, what could I say to my teacher, Eva, if I was accepted: "I love you as a friend, but as a teacher you have failed me." Day and night I thought of little else. Finally, I took myself in hand. "Stop wasting your energy; to worry about something over which you alone have control is ridiculous. As my brother would say, in his usual down-to-earth fashion, 'Sis, pee or get off the pot!'—Either make the phone call or rip up the number."

I called! The phone must have rung ten times before it was answered. I was about to hang up, thinking at least I tried, when a deep resonant man's voice said, "Yes?" There was a soprano in the background singing a phrase, stopping, then beginning again.

"Could I speak with Madame Usova, please? I'm calling long distance from Toronto, Canada."

I could faintly hear what must have been Madame's voice speaking with a broad Russian accent. "Tell whoever it is to call later. I'm busy."

"It's from Canada," said the rich, baritone voice.

There was a moment's pause and then a curt, "Ello."

I swallowed hard. "I hate to bother you, Madame Usova," I began and then launched into my well-rehearsed *spiel,* making it sound as if it was all Irma's fault that I was disturbing her in this way.

"You needn't apologize to me for making the call, darlink. I knew I'd hear from you," she said with complete assurance, sounding as if she was pouring oil through the phone. "Now, this week is out of the question, but next week? Let me see, Richard darlink, bring me my book, that's a love." There was a long pause and I could hear the rustle of paper as she turned the pages of what must have been her date book. "Yes, next Wednesday, May twenty-seventh at ten o'clock in the morning, you will come to me and I will see what you can do." She spoke slowly and deliberately with a heavy Russian accent and I detected a slight lisp. She went on at some length about the weather and how wonderful it was and to be sure not to bring my nasty Canadian weather with me. She terminated the conversation with an abrupt, "Velcome into my clutches!" and hung up.

When I put down the phone I didn't know whether to laugh or to run for my life. I decided to do the former and take my chances. I'd tell Eva later if Madame Usova decided I was good enough material to teach.

1

<u>May 27, 1952—First Meeting with Usova in New York</u>

The next letter in the shoebox was in my handwriting, written on foolscap with frayed edges. The last pages were missing.

May 27, 1952
New York
(Park Ave, no less!)

Dearest Folks,
  I'm sending this c/o Dad's office in hopes that his secretary will forward it to wherever you are.
  I've got 'beaucoup' to report, and I want to put it all down before I forget it.
  I'm writing this from friend Joyce's apartment. (Remember, she was in Salzburg with me summer before last, studying with Eva). I'm staying with her until my trial with Usova is over. I'd love to describe her set-up to you 'cause it's worth at least five pages, but there's too much else to tell you so it will have to wait until I see you next.
  The trip down had its usual problems at the border. If it hadn't been for a student friend travelling with us as far as Niagara Falls, I doubt whether Joyce and I would have made it across—at least if we had, it would have been on foot. (Remind me to tell you about that, too, when next we meet.)
  Today I sang for the 'Great Madame'. (I told you about our phone conversation where she ended "Velcome een to my clawtches.") Needless to say, I was full of trepidation as I stood waiting for a good five minutes in the vestibule outside her door, when this gorgeous hunk of man walked in and asked me what I was scared of and rang the bell. Madame promptly appeared, and by God that's exactly what she looked like, a madam. If I hadn't heard the singing on the other side of the door, I would have sworn I was in the wrong place.
  I sang a few scales for her and when I finished, she said with a ...

Reading, the words arranged themselves into vivid pictures before my eyes; little scraps and shards collected from the dust of time.

It was early on the morning of May 25th when I set off for New York. I had recently purchased a small canary-yellow Austin convertible; a car for my summer in Massachusetts was a must! With me were two fellow students. Joyce had an apartment in New York, where she had been studying voice for the past year. She graciously offered me a bed until my ordeal with Madame Usova was over. Hank was a student of architecture at the University of Toronto who often assisted as stage manager at our opera school performances. He would be going with us only as far as his home in Niagara Falls.

We had chosen a bright sunny day for our trip, which was a good thing, for my car had a tendency to leak when it rained. When we reached Niagara Falls, I dropped Hank off at his house, and Joyce and I headed for the border. I was travelling on an American permanent visa which I had acquired with great difficulty. At the end of World War II, I had begun to study singing privately in New York City and was enrolled in the opera school at Columbia University. In order to help pay for my studies I needed to get a job. To get a job, I had to have a permanent visa. This necessitated my finding an American who would both hire me and vouch for me under all circumstances. The only person I could find was a business acquaintance of my father's who was willing to hire me to do little more than run errands and lick stamps.

Though it had been two years since I had resided in the States, I thought it best to keep up my visa in case I should ever again want to work south of the border. Little did I know what trouble this would cause! In my innocence, I brandished the visa at the immigration officer as we were about to cross the border.

"Your licence and car-ownership, please!" said the immigration officer. He had noticed that the car had a Canadian licence plate. "I think you'd better pull in over there." He pointed to the customs office. "As a resident of the United States, you are importing your car and will have to pay twenty per cent duty on it—in cash."

"How much did you pay for the car?" was the first thing the customs officer asked.

"I don't remember," I lied. "I bought it secondhand." I had paid two thousand dollars, a fortune for me in those days, and the car was less than a year old.

The officer was kind. It was obvious to him that Joyce and I were students, for the back of the car was loaded with her mother's old pots and pans. She was taking these to New York to supplement her apartment's limited stock.

"OK, let's see; the car's worth about five hundred bucks and twenty percent of that, well, let's say you owe Uncle Sam one hundred dollars."

I certainly didn't have one hundred dollars in my pocket and I doubted whether I even had it in the bank. I told the officer I had a friend in town that might be able to bail me out. I left Joyce at the border as collateral, and set off to find my friend Hank. His father was a respected lawyer in Niagara Falls, which gave Hank clout as far as the banks were concerned. After cashing my cheque at Hank's bank, I returned victorious, waving the hundred dollar bill at the customs officer. By now it was eleven in the morning and we had a long way to go. Thankfully, the remainder of our trip was without incident, and we arrived in New York City shortly before midnight.

Joyce lived on the top floor of an old Park Avenue mansion in midtown Manhattan. Exhausted after our long drive, even though Joyce had shared much of the driving, I could hardly wait to collapse onto a bed. I stopped the car outside the main entrance while we unloaded our suitcases and the pots and pans. Joyce parked the car, thinking it would be easier than giving me directions, and I waited for her in the spacious entrance. It gave me time to look around. The hall appeared elegant in the dim light. This surprised me for Joyce had always intimated she lived close to the poverty level.

The floor was covered with large black and white marble squares. There was a wide, curved, grand stairway leading up to the first floor, and tucked at the bottom of it was an oversized, gold Louis XV1 chair with dark red velvet upholstery. Actually, it looked more like a throne than a chair. This was the only piece of furniture I could see.

Most startling, however, was a mammoth parchment lamp shade, four feet in diameter, floating in the centre of the hall about ten feet off the ground. There was nothing holding it up that I could see; nothing above it or below, and it provided the only light in the hall. Covering the shade were beautifully painted, large butterflies flying in all directions. This floating lampshade and the shadows it cast gave an eerie feeling to the whole area. I looked up and saw four flights of stairs circling above the hall and realized that we would have to climb them several times to get all of our belongings to the top floor where Joyce lived. Maybe I could curl up under the lampshade and sleep until morning! The shade should have been an indication to me of things to come, but I was totally unprepared.

Joyce reappeared after a few minutes.

"Your apartment's at the top?" I queried. She nodded. "There's no way I'm carrying all this stuff up four flights tonight," I said firmly.

"Don't get excited!" she said, impatiently," I'll put the pots and pans beside the chair, here. We'll only take the suitcases up tonight."

We started to climb. Each step seemed steeper than the last. I was sure I'd never make it to the top. I was sufficiently awake, however, to notice the "creepy crawlies" on the wall as I went up. I shuddered and hoped that they wouldn't have the strength to climb the four flights to Joyce's apartment. On the way up I investigated the stairwell, for I was curious to see what held the lampshade in place. I reached over the banister of the first landing. Waving my hand back and forth over the space, I felt something cut across my forefinger; at the same time the lampshade below began to sway. I looked up. It was suspended by an electric cord attached to the ceiling of the top floor. At the lower end, inside the shade, was a large clear light bulb.

By the time we reached the last flight of stairs I was sure I had dislocated my back from the weight of the suitcase. We were almost to the top when I became aware of a shadowy figure at my side. Joyce heard my gasp and started to laugh.

"Oh, that's Annie, the local ghost." I looked again, more carefully this time. It was a life-sized figure painted on the wall, mounting the same step as I was. The step was cleverly painted in perspective, continuing onto the wall from the end of the actual step. The figure was dressed in a long white nightgown and was carrying a lighted candle which seemed to glow and flicker in the dim light. She had long, flowing, light brown hair, and on her face was an expression of utter exhaustion; exactly the way I felt at that moment. I was too tired to ask any questions about her. I'd do that in the morning.

Finally we arrived in front of the apartment door. I could hardly wait for Joyce to unlock it so I could fling myself onto the nearest piece of furniture. Once inside, I dropped my suitcase, and was about to collapse onto a chair close to the door, when I heard her yell, "For God's sake, watch it. Don't sit there."

At the sound of her voice I stumbled and fell against the wall, sliding down into a sitting position on the floor beside an elegant little chair. At close range, I could see why she had warned me. The chair had only a seat, with two front legs standing out from the wall. The back of the chair and the two back legs were exquisitely painted on the wall, complete with shadows. It was a remarkable piece of illusion. It looked like a beautiful Chippendale chair. I glanced around the spacious room and counted six such chairs.

"The man who owns this place is an artist," Joyce said. "Did you see all the bugs as you were going up the stairs, or was it too dark to notice them? There's every insect known to man crawling over these walls."

I marvelled that such fine workmanship could be found on the grimy walls of a decaying Park Avenue mansion-turned-apartment building.

"How on earth did you find this place? Does the artist live in this building as well?" I asked.

"I took over from an actress pal who's seldom in New York. We share when she's in town. As for our artist, you'll find it difficult to distinguish between him and what he paints, if you see him. He's always in paint-covered overalls with brush in hand. You can't miss him; he sort of slithers around the corridors, going from corner to corner. As you can see, in this house he'll never run out of walls to paint on. By the way, you can sleep in the bedroom. When my pal's here, I always sleep on the couch in this room."

I hoped, as she led me into the room, that the bed wouldn't be an illusion as well, masterfully painted in full perspective so that the only things protruding out from the wall would be the two front legs and a few inches of mattress. I needn't have worried; it was a real bed, although not a very comfortable one. I gratefully threw myself onto it without bothering to remove my clothes.

The next morning I took a good look around. The main room was pleasant enough but sparsely furnished. With the exception of the six half-chairs, the only thing to sit on was the couch-bed where Joyce had slept. There was, I was glad to see, an upright piano. The sun was streaming through the two dormer windows, side by side on the south wall, giving the room a warm and cozy feeling. I was relieved not to see any more creepy crawlies, real or otherwise.

Our day began with morning stair exercise, going up and down four flights to collect the pots and pans. On the way down I was able to get a closer look at the walls. Each fly was painted life-size. I could see the veins on the wings and tiny hairs on each leg. It was the same with the ants, spiders and even the cockroaches. The walls were covered with these insects, both in groups and alone. I wondered why our artist stopped with bugs; just think what he could have done with rodents. When Joyce and I bent down beside the stairs to load up with the kitchen utensils, I saw that the golden throne of last night was also an illusion. It was nothing more than two gold-leafed front legs and a large padded red velvet seat. The back was so cleverly painted on the wall that I had to touch it to find it wasn't real velvet surrounded by a gold ornately carved wooden frame.

The rest of the day I lay low, vocalizing a little, reading a little, and walking a lot. I walked and walked the streets of New York, taking in nothing, while nervousness and uncertainty increased with each step. What was I doing here when my career was beginning to take off at home? Engagements were coming my way bit by bit, and I loved my lessons with Eva. Why should I bother to sing for this woman? Irma had said that Usova taught only the best. I supposed the worst that could happen was that she'd say, "Darlink, why are you wasting my time? Isn't there something else you could do with your life?" Worse still, if she did accept me, what could I say to Eva without hurting her?'

As usual, I began to rationalize. Maybe I could study with them both; after all, that's what Joyce did. She worked technique with a woman here in New York and went frequently to Toronto for sessions of *German Lied* with Eva.

I slept little that night, endlessly tossing and turning, wishing I was tucked safely in my bed in Toronto; wishing too, that the next day would never come.

Ten o'clock sharp, Wednesday morning, May 27, I stood in front of Madame's door on West Seventy-Second Street. It was a typical five-floor narrow brownstone house, wedged between two large apartment buildings. My heart was pounding in my constricted throat when I mounted the stone steps. I kept telling myself to relax, that it wasn't a performance I was about to give; I was only going to sing for a teacher. I peered through the long narrow window beside the door to see if there was an inner hallway for I wasn't sure whether Madame Usova occupied the entire building. Because there was no bell, I tried the door; it was unlocked. Entering, I heard a soprano voice swooping up and down in a series of fast arpeggios behind the large double doors to my left. I must have stood there for five minutes waiting for the sounds to diminish. I had been straining my ears to hear what was going on inside and hadn't noticed that there was someone at my side.

"What are you frightened of? The sounds you hear are made by a human voice." He began to laugh. "It's no animal in distress; it's just my wife. She's one of Usova's victims," he said, ringing the doorbell.

The man was over six feet tall with strawberry-blond, curly hair and freckles. He was good looking in a soft kind of way, and his eyes danced with laughter. I was about to say something when the door opened a few inches, just enough for me to clearly see the figure behind it.

"Lana, here is your latest victim," said the man at my side.

Madame Usova was less than five feet tall and about the same in width. Her brightly hennaed hair was piled on top of her head in tiny curls. The brightness of the hair made her face look very pale. The red curls fell loosely over her narrow forehead, and below it was a pair of the most amazing eyes I'd ever seen. They were slightly bulging; the lids seemed too tired to open above half-mast. They were coated with a metallic green eye shadow which picked up the colour of her large emerald earrings. She wore a bronze, taffeta, floor-length housecoat that matched her hair. The garment had a high V neckline that framed her short neck and was tightly nipped in at the waist under her ample bosom. While she opened the door wide, a slow smile spread over her fleshy face, revealing slightly protruding teeth.

"Goodness, does it never stop?" she lisped in her broad Russian accent. I guessed she was referring to my height, for, beginning at my toes she thoroughly looked me over until her eyes met mine. I had imagined a much taller and more impressive-looking woman to match the strong dark voice I had heard over the phone.

"How long have you been outside my door, little one?" She emphasized the "little," for at five-foot-ten, I towered over her. I mumbled something about thinking that I should wait until the singing finished.

"Ray, darlink, you were naughty not to bring her immediately into my lair." When she spoke, the enigmatic smile never left her face.

Ray Darling immediately took my arm and pulled me through the door. Madame turned and walked toward two women standing by a concert grand piano.

"Go for it, kid. Good luck," he whispered. He let go of my arm and went over to join the group.

I stood glued to the spot, my stomach vibrating like a tuning fork. The room became alive with activity; *Ray Darling* collected his wife and she collected her music. I recognized the other woman but didn't know from where. Everyone began talking at once while Madame made sure they met her latest victim.

While the three were busily making arrangements with Madame Usova, my eyes began to survey my surroundings. The studio looked undernourished and unloved, as if the furnishings were part of a rental agreement. A shabby carpet, worn along the seams so the backing showed through like a person's scalp, covered the floor. A few nondescript chairs cluttered the room. In one corner I noticed a hard and uncomfortable-looking faded blue couch. Facing the entrance on the opposite wall was a small, iron-grated gas fireplace with a heavy dark wooden mantle. Above it was a wide built-in mirror—a mirror I would soon grow to hate.

The concert grand piano dominated the room. It was covered by an ornate, multi-coloured Russian shawl with a long burgundy fringe. Resting on the shawl were photographs in silver frames of Madame Usova in the many roles she had sung when younger—and certainly a lot slimmer: Usova as Marina in *Boris Godunov*, as Tatiana in *Eugen Onegin*, as Lisa in *The Pique Dame*, the princess in *Turandot*, and *Tosca* in the opera of that name. Tucked in between these photographs were two of the great Russian bass, Chaliapin, with long inscriptions in Russian. The other photographs were of Richard Alexander: Richard as Amfortas,

Richard as Scarpia, Richard as Boris, Richard as the count in *Figaro*, all inscribed, "To my beloved teacher, Lana, from your grateful and always devoted Richard." I had just finished reading the inscriptions when I looked up to see Mr. Alexander in person, standing under the arch leading from the studio to the rest of the apartment.

"Lana, darling, what did you do with the shirts that came back from the laundry yesterday?" He had been staying with Madame, as he frequently did when he was in New York for only a few days. He was packing to leave for Bayreuth. I found myself wondering about their relationship. However, observing their affectionate but seemingly platonic farewell, I decided they were like mother and son.

Realizing I was in the company of greatness, my nervousness returned in spades. It would soon be my turn. What was I doing here anyhow? What made me think I would be accepted into this exalted group? My eyes rested on the wall behind the piano, which was covered with photos of the famous faces of her pupils. Usova's *Wall of Fame,* I later learned she called it. My throat tightened and went dry.

Finally, the door closed behind Richard and the others.

"Now, let me see what you have to show me, little one," she said.

At the sound of Usova's voice I was brought quickly back to reality. She must have seen my eyes darting from photo to photo with a look of terror on my face.

"Darlink, have courage. Though my wall has many eyes, they are the eyes of the humble, for they have all suffered Lana's inquisition; and see, they are still smiling." As she spoke, her arm, with one sweeping gesture took in the whole wall. She turned, walked to the piano and sat down.

"Now, my little one, let me see if you too will be famous and have your picture on my wall." Did she keep referring to me as "little one," because of my height or because she didn't remember my name?

Madame played a simple arpeggio, F, A, C, A, F, and beckoned with a nod of her head for me to repeat it. Without changing the expression on her face, she guided me up and down the full range of my voice, sometimes with fast scales, sometimes directing me to hold the note, enlarging and diminishing the sound. At the end of each long phrase, as the sound diminished, I could feel my throat restrict in an effort to hold on. She certainly wasn't making it easy for me; and always those piercing eyes were upon me, scrutinizing my face through their half-opened lids. I found their gaze so unsettling that I lowered my head and fixed my eyes on the threadbare rug, studying its faded design.

"Darlink, why do you look at your feet when you sing; what help can they be to you? You must stand tall as though suspended by a cord from the top of your head to the ceiling above. Your body is your instrument. Would you want to play on a violin with a crooked neck? No! Your posture is an important part of your voice. You cannot perform on an instrument which is bent and misshapen. You are your own instrument, never forget that," she repeated. "You have a strong and healthy body. You have a wonderful throat to work with, beautiful vocal cords, but, little one, you have no idea how to breathe. It is obvious that you have never been taught this most necessary function. You are lucky, however, in the teaching you have had, for at least the voice is not r-ruined." The 'r' in ruined sounded like the roll of a drum. She got up from the piano and walked toward the arch where Richard had stood. "Now you will sing something for me to see if you can carry a tune. Wolfgang," she called through the arch, "I need you." She turned back to me. "My husband will play for you. Show me what you have to sing."

I went over to the uncomfortable couch where I had left my briefcase when I entered the studio and took out my score of *Carmen*. Madame's husband appeared at the doorway with his mouth full of bagel and a cup of coffee in his hand. His pale face bore an expression of annoyance at having been taken away from either his breakfast or lunch, I wasn't sure which. He was a short man who seemed to disappear in front of the beige walls of the studio. He was non-colour from head to foot. His bald head was beige; his face was beige; his shirt and trousers as well. I had a feeling he was there only to perform a function and would vanish again into the walls when his usefulness was completed. There was no sign of intimacy or affection between them. Like many couples who have thrown in their lot with destiny, they seemed resigned to a life together, bound by mutual dependence and usefulness to each other.

"So it is *Carmen*, is it?" Madame asked. Then, with a deep sigh, "It usually is. Wolfie, this is my latest victim. Darlink, this is my husband, Wolfgang Swartz."

He had already taken his place at the piano like a well-trained chimpanzee. His expression never changed as I placed my score in front of him and opened it to the third act card scene. I felt comfortable with this aria; I had performed it often while touring with a small group called Opera Backstage. When I began to sing, all my nervousness vanished. I was far too absorbed with the drama at hand to be self-conscious.

"*Carreau! Pique!*" I was surprised how easily the sound came out; it felt good. My hands began moving, dealing out my imaginary cards. I was caught up in Carmen's surrender to her fate. I cared not, nor even noticed if those penetrating eyes were upon me. "*Encore! Encore! Toujours la mort.*" I felt myself shudder with dread as those last chest notes poured from my throat. Silence! No sound came from Madame Usova. Her husband stood up and disappeared again into the beige wall to finish his brunch. I searched Madame's face for a sign of either satisfaction or rejection, but there was none; her face was like a mask. Slowly, she nodded her head.

"You obviously have gifts that a teacher could never give you, but they must be carefully developed. You are a good performer. You have a good voice, looks—in other words, enough artistic talent to have a serious career."

Relief swelled over me like a tidal wave. She liked me; I couldn't believe it. And then it came.

"But darlink, why do you do all those strange things when you sing? Why do you flail your arms about like a wind machine? Why do you sway from side to side as if demented? Do you really think this is emotion? No, it surely is not. It is cheap and not worthy of your talent."

"I sing it that way because I feel it that way," I said sharply, instantly on the defensive.

"You will learn to feel as I tell you to feel," she shot back. "You will learn to feel what the composer wants you to feel, and you will learn to sing things as they are written. You will learn to deal your cards with your eyes, to suffer with your body still and relaxed, your arms quietly by your sides. Your voice alone will speak for you. You will learn to trust Lana, and she will make you famous. Oh, yes, my little one, you have much to learn, and learn you will. We will begin tomorrow morning at ten o'clock, and you will come to me each day this week at the same time. After your lessons you will stay to listen to my other victims go through their torture. We will not sing; we will just breathe. I will charge you for half-an-hour lesson, but I seldom teach under an hour, and you will leave the money on the piano before you depart."

I was in, but my feelings of relief were mixed with fear. I could see working with Madame Usova wasn't going to be a joy ride. I knew she was right in everything she said, but it made me apprehensive the way she demanded everything. This was an authority to be reckoned with.

The next morning at ten I was again at Madame Usova's doorstep. I rang the doorbell with much more courage this time. The same soprano sounds were drifting through the double doors. Madame opened the door and beckoned me to come in. She pointed to the couch for me to sit down, as the singing continued undisturbed. I smiled my greeting and nodded, and was about to tip-toe to my designated corner and await my turn, when suddenly she was there in front of me, blocking my path. She reached up and took hold of my chin, pulled my face down to hers, and firmly planted a moist kiss directly on my mouth. I didn't like it! In fact, I found it so unpleasant that I could feel my face becoming warm, and I knew I must be blushing. Madame was already on her way back to the piano, so hopefully she hadn't noticed.

The lesson continued for some time. I sat on the blue couch watching with rapt attention what would soon be my fate. Wolfgang was at the piano accompanying the woman, while Usova jabbed at her, wrenched her shoulders back and jerked her head straight. She even squeezed her around her middle with such force that the poor woman broke on a high sustained note. The recipient of this onslaught was vainly trying to sing the beautiful Countess's aria, *"Dove sono"* from Mozart's *Marriage of Figaro*. I was fascinated by the way she accepted her fate without complaint. The lesson came to an end with the ringing of the doorbell. It was Ray, arriving to pick up his wife. This time, he greeted me as an old friend, hugging me around my shoulders. Then, with a wicked wink and a knowing smile to Madame, he gave me his condolences.

"Come, darlink, it is time for your torture," Usova said. Wolfgang had vanished into the woodwork, the others had left, and we were alone. She came toward me, talking as she walked.

"It is the breath that is of primary importance in singing. Without knowing how to breathe, you cannot produce a controlled sound. Like a violin or cello, without correct bowing you can never acquire a perfect technique. It has to be an unbroken flow of air over the cords: an unbroken draw of the bow over the strings."

She took hold of both my hands. She briskly shook my arms.

"Relax, little one, relax," she said, feeling the resistance in them. "Lana will not eat you." When she was satisfied that my arms were limp enough, she took them and, standing close in front of me with her back facing me, she wrapped my arms around her body below her ample bosom. "Darlink, are your hands always this cold and clammy? You needn't be so nervous; I am not going to make love to you. Oh, you English, you are always so—what should I say?—so reserved." (As far as she was concerned, we Canadians and we English were one and the same.) "Now, feel my rib cage while I take a breath." Her breasts covered her ribs on both the front and sides of her torso, and it was impossible to find even the bottom rib without having to explore the generous covering, so I settled for her waist instead. With her hands still on mine, she pushed them up as high as she could under her breasts and took a deep, low breath. When she inhaled, she made a half-growl, half-snore sound, which seemed to come from the back of her throat. She turned sideways, still holding my arms around her, and repeated the exercise. While she shifted my hands around her body, I was able to feel the expansion of her lower rib cage, particularly from the back. Each time she took a breath she would make that strange sound, always breathing through her nose with her mouth closed and her nostrils flared. The expression on her face was as if she was smelling a disagreeable odour. I hoped it wasn't me.

"Now, darlink, it is your turn." She led me over to the mirror above the fireplace. "Breathe," she commanded with her hands on my ribs. "Now we will learn to open the throat when you breathe in," she said, facing me toward the mirror. It took the better part of an hour before I was able to master the growling snore sound to her satisfaction and before the expression on my face was sufficiently unpleasant to convince her that everything was open behind my cheekbones and, most particularly, my throat. I would have found it easier to concentrate on opening what I was supposed to open if I hadn't been forced to confront my sneering reflection in the mirror.

"Please, Madame Usova," I queried, "am I expected to make that strange face and sound when I breathe?"

"Darlink, what is with this Madame Usova? It is Lana, please." Then she added, in her usual authoritative way, "You will always prepare in this manner with each breath and each phrase."

"I don't understand," I insisted. "When Richard Alexander sings, he doesn't make a face like that, and I have never heard that growling sound come out of his throat."

She frowned. "There you are again, doubting me. This I will not have!" she snapped, "Richard does not have to make that face, for that is his face. He has large nostrils which are always flared. His cheek bones are wide and high. You have a narrow face and a long thin nose like the English. You will have to learn to make your face work for you and not against you. Now you will leave Lana, for she is going out for lunch. You will come tomorrow at two o'clock in the afternoon. There will be two lessons before yours. Then after your lesson, we will go to the NBC studio together for the TV broadcast of 'The Firestone Hour'; one of my children is singing, and it would be good for you to see what goes on."

Her child, as it turned out, was a famous Italian tenor who had enjoyed a great success at the Metropolitan Opera the past season. The only thing I learned from attending the broadcast was that it was not a good idea to copulate before singing in front of an audience of several million people.

In the middle of his first aria Madame leaned over and whispered in my ear, "He sings as if he just fell out of bed and it wasn't his own. *Lieber Gott*, why can't that man wait until after the performance?"

The next day she took me to a dress rehearsal of the new production of *Sampson and Delilah,* which the Met was taking on tour. Another student was singing the role of the High Priest. When we went backstage afterward, everyone seemed to know Lana. I was intrigued as she switched languages as easily as changing channels on the radio. While watching her with the other artists, I became curious about her own career. Making our way back in a taxi to West Seventy-Second Street, I asked Madame where she had sung and what had made her retire from the stage.

"When we get back to the apartment, I will play for you a record. Then you will hear for yourself what your Lana was."

Entering her studio, she went directly to the shelf where her opera scores were kept. She took a seventy-eight record from the shelf, lovingly dusted it off, and slipped it onto the turntable of her old-fashioned record player. I recognized the music instantly. It was the "Drinking Aria" from Offenbach's opera, *La Périchole.* I had recently heard it sung by the French Canadian soprano Jennie Tourel. Any similarity in the interpretation of this aria by the two divas ended with its title. Madame Tourel sang it well, but Madame Usova created it. The voice was not a great one, but what she did with it was remarkable. She was delightfully drunk but at no time was it excessive. She seemed to swim through each note, touching the pitch sufficiently to keep the aria within its noted structure. I had a vivid picture of an enchanting little creature weaving around the stage.

When the singing had finished, I looked up to see Madame's green-lidded, half-opened eyes carefully scrutinizing my face for any telling reaction.

"Well?" she asked.

I instinctively knew that *well* signalled danger. Presuming I was expected to comment intelligently on both the voice and the interpretation, I avoided falling into the trap by asking if the record was available in the United States.

"I would love to own one," I said sincerely.

She shook her head. "No, darlink. It was recorded privately by a friend during my last performance in Moscow. A week later Lana was struck over with pneumonia in both her lungs."

Turning abruptly, she lifted the record from the player and carefully put it back into its cover, heaving a deep sigh. "She never sang again!"

With her back still toward me, she said with finality, "You now know all that is necessary to know about Svetlana Usova's past."

I spent the rest of the week meeting some of the greats and soon-to-be greats of the singing world who came in and out of the studio to pay homage to

Madame. For me, it was like being transported to a different planet or reincarnated into a new existence. My friend Joyce was my only link to the real life away from Madame. I would go back to the apartment after each session with Usova and relate such tales to her that she would invariably accuse me of making it all up. I could tell that she was green with envy.

When I told Joyce of Madame Usova's record, she casually said, "I have that record. I bought it because it has the Don Cossacks on the other side. So that's Svetlana Usova! You're right," she said with enthusiasm, "she's great." Then she added, "Now I come to think of it, the label says Madame Usov. That's the masculine of Usova, which makes no sense."

"Impossible," I said with annoyance. "You can't have it as it's not a commercial recording."

"Betcha," she countered. "I'll prove it when we get home."

It wasn't until my last lesson that I was allowed to complete even the simplest scale. On the previous days, over and over again I would breathe deeply to begin a note and, before the sound emerged from my throat, Madame would say, "No, no, no, darlink. That is simply not good enough." It was frustrating, particularly as I dared not ask her why. I knew if I did I would be accused of "having no faith in Lana."

She was right, of course, for by the time she had finished with me that week, she seldom had to correct my breathing. I knew how to stand erect but not stiff; how to keep my rib cage extended and never let it collapse; how to work my diaphragm; and, above all, how to stand still. I could even make that ghastly face and sound at the back of my throat to Madame's satisfaction, but I was never able to face, without dread, the mirror she always insisted I stare into while singing.

"Darlink, I am so proud of you," she told me. I learned later that this was her way of terminating each lesson. As she so aptly put it, "It keeps you coming back for more."

"Next week I leave for Rome," she said. "I go to the Bayreuth Festival at the beginning of July to help my children through their rehearsals, and you will meet me there. Richard will find you a room. We will have a week there together and then to Salzburg, where you will study with me until I leave for New York at the end of August."

I was stunned. I had never thought past this first week. I frankly wasn't sure I could survive another dose of Madame's torture so soon. I was counting on having the summer to try out the new breathing and to think. Besides, I had turned down my teacher Eva when she asked me to go to Salzburg with her for July and

August to study. I told her I had accepted to sing Carmen in the States and felt it too good an opportunity to pass up.

"Madame Usova—I mean, Lana," I stammered. "I can't meet you in Europe. I am engaged to sing Carmen in Massachusetts, but when you return in the fall …"

She cut me short. "Darlink, you sing Carmen this summer, and we say goodbye forever. I want nothing more to do with you. You have wasted a week of my time." Her eyes were cold as steel as she glared at me through her green lids. "You are far from ready to sing Carmen anywhere. If you want a serious career," she went on, "you will do as I say."

Though at that moment I was strongly tempted to tell her I'd go my own way and take my chances without her, I knew she had again spoken the truth; I wasn't ready. Carmen is one of the most demanding roles a mezzo can sing, and I realized I had many ladders to climb before I dared tackle that one.

When I nodded, for I could think of nothing to say that wouldn't sound like an argument, her eyes softened.

"Now that that is settled, you will call me next Friday before I leave for Europe so that I can tell you where you are to stay and what day you will arrive in Bayreuth." With that, she planted a wet kiss on my mouth and eased me out the door.

I understood then that Madame Svetlana Usova's studio could be in New York, Vienna, Salzburg, Bayreuth, or wherever she happened to be at a given time.

When I left for home the next day, I was sick at heart yet strangely elated. I was excited at being accepted by the great Svetlana Usova but I dreaded telling Eva that I was casting her aside like an old worn-out shoe because I would be studying in her beloved Salzburg, ensnared in the clutches of another diva.

Throughout the long drive back to Toronto, I agonized over what I would say to Eva. Finally, I decided to take the cowardly way out and say nothing. I would tell her that I was going to sing Carmen as planned and hope I wouldn't run into her during the summer in Salzburg; then in the fall, who knew what would happen?

For several days after my return, I put off seeing Eva. I couldn't face her as yet, for I was sure that my feelings of guilt would give me away. Finally, a fellow student who shared my apartment, told me that Madame Stein was asking after me and wondered if I was back from New York. I knew then that I could procrastinate no longer.

The next day, when Eva opened the door, I thought how old and tired she looked. A slow smile lit up her beautiful face when she saw me. It wasn't so much her features that made her appear beautiful—it was the woman behind the face that gave it the aura of beauty. If one were to paint her, it would have to be while she was talking or demonstrating a song for, when still, which was seldom, she looked like an ordinary *Hausfrau*. She motioned for me to come in.

"Go fix us a cup of tea, there's a good girl," she said in her slight German-British accent.

When I came out of the kitchen with the tea, I put the tray on the coffee table in front of her. She was sitting in her usual easy chair, and I pulled a small chair up beside her so that our knees were almost touching.

While she poured the tea, she said, "Now tell me everything. What did you see in New York?"

I started by describing Joyce's apartment in detail. I told her about the rehearsal at the Met and what I thought of the tenor on the "Firestone Hour" while we sat sipping tea. When I ran out of unimportant things to talk about, I fell silent, keeping my eyes on my teacup.

"Now that that's over with, you can tell me what's really on your mind," Eva said.

"What do you mean?" I asked, not daring to look at her. She waited while I turned my cup several times on the saucer. I knew she would wait me out. I knew I was cornered. I started haltingly, with no expression in my voice. I still couldn't look at her for I was ridden with guilt. I began by telling her that for some time I had been worried about the tired feeling in my throat after singing; that I never knew why sometimes I sang well and another time it would be ghastly. I told her how Irma Mensinger had suggested I go to New York to sing for Madame Usova. The hardest part was telling her about Salzburg.

When I finished, she took both my hands and looked hard into my eyes. "My dear girl," her voice was gentle and soothing, "If you think this Madame Usova is right for you, then it is right. The time has come for you to move on. I have little strength left, and you now need someone strong enough to properly shape your voice." She paused and gave my hands a squeeze. "You are very special to me," she said softly, "and I want only what's best for you."

I looked down quickly, for I could feel my eyes filling with tears.

She went on. "I'm glad you'll not sing Carmen this summer. Your madame is correct, you are not ready. It will be at least another few years before you should tackle that lady on stage. I'm sure by then she'll be right for you."

While she talked, I felt ashamed, not because I had turned to someone else but because I had so misjudged her. I was obviously far more disturbed about leaving her than she was. How could I have thought a woman as secure as Eva would be hurt by a pupil choosing a new way? She knew who she was and how much she had given to us all.

"It's a silly mother who won't allow her children to grow up and move on," she continued. "Things often work out for the best when you allow them to happen. We could go to Europe together. I have a reservation on the S.S. Atlantic which leaves Montreal on June 18. I will be spending two weeks in England with friends first. I hope to be in Salzburg by July 11. If you like, you could sing for me there from time to time. Then I could be sure you are in the right hands."

I left Eva's studio that day floating on air. The weight which had borne down on me those past weeks had miraculously disappeared. I was full of admiration for this dear and most cherished woman.

Before another day passed, I knew I would have to cancel my engagement to sing in Massachusetts. I had been putting it off, for it would require all the diplomatic skills I could muster. I had to make sure not to jeopardize my chances of working with this group in the future. Should I plead ill health; something contagious and long-lasting, or perhaps a broken blood vessel in one of my vocal cords? Eventually I opted for the truth. With dread and consternation, I made the phone call. The director was incredulous when I told him Usova refused to teach me if I sang Carmen in the summer.

"You say you want a career in opera, and you'd turn down an opportunity to sing a major role with my company because of some lousy singing teacher? Impossible!" By the time he had finished, he was shouting.

"She says I'm not ready, and she's not a lousy teacher." I spat back.

"Bull!" he exploded. "You turn it down, and you won't be asked again."

"I'm sorry you feel ..." I began, but it was too late; he had hung up. So much for my diplomatic effort!

I felt my stomach tighten. Had I done the wrong thing? I had sung with this group the previous summer, and it had been a marvellous learning experience. The orchestra and singers were all students of a high caliber. It was a chance to perform in a semi-professional climate, in a good theatre and, most importantly, in a small farming village under no pressure. If I laid an egg, it would be hidden under a mound of straw.

o available space for me on Eva's ship, the S.S. Atlantic. A week   sail, I was able to get an upper berth in a cabin for four in the bowels of the Empress of Scotland, leaving Montreal June 20.

The night before she left, I phoned Eva to tell her my plans. "How are you feeling?" I asked.

With a hollow laugh she answered, "As long as I'm flat on my back, I'm fine."

I wondered anew at the wisdom of her making the trip when her health was so fragile. Could it be she felt a compulsion to see her beloved Austria for the last time? I wished she would cancel her trip, but I hadn't the heart to say so.

"Goodbye. See you in Salzburg," I said with forced cheerfulness.

A few days before I was to leave for England, I invited Joyce to my apartment for dinner, on the understanding that she would bring the record of Usova she claimed she had. I still wasn't convinced it was really Madame.

Listening to that intoxicated voice weaving its way through the speakers of my hi-fi, I knew it had to be Usova. Because she had said it was recorded privately during a performance in Moscow, I knew the recording must have been pirated. Joyce had purchased it in Toronto on College Street. The Don Cossacks on the other side of the record were a popular item in the fifties. The next day I bought the last three copies the record store had. I would take one with me to Europe for Madame.

With a sparsely filled suitcase containing an outfit for rain and cold and one for sunshine and heat, accompanied by a generous array of scarves, belts, and costume jewelry, which I hoped would shock and awaken the dreariest of clothing, I departed by train for Montreal, full of excitement and anticipation. It was the beginning of an adventure I felt sure could end in a brilliant career on the operatic stage. As Madame had said, "Darlink, why waste your time being a big fish in a little pond? You study with Lana and she will make you a killer whale in the oceans of the world."

2

Sailing for Europe

The next letter was almost illegible having been written on airmail paper closely resembling French toilet paper, now yellow with age. At the top was an impressive red shield with Canadian Pacific printed on it, a fat brown beaver resting above. The pages were generously dotted with blotches of ink; however, undaunted, I took up the challenge with curiosity.

June 24, 1952
Empress of Scotland

Dearest Folks,

Four days out to sea and so far the meals have stayed down, which for me, as you know, is a miracle. The ship is a beauty; the food and service both excellent. I'm travelling steerage in the bowels of the ship in an upper berth, sharing a minuscule cabin with three other women. The two in the lower bunks are both crowding sixty. The woman from Liverpool is always last to bed at night. (She's the kind who measures having a good time by the number of hours she works at it.) The other, a sweet little Jewish lady from the Bronx, has to give herself a shot of insulin (at least I presume it's insulin by the looks of her) at five o'clock every morning. The other "upper bunker" is a youngish gal in her early thirties and a sympathetic spirit.

The first morning, around sun-up, the Liverpudlian staggers into the cabin very much the worse for wear. She slams the door shut and turns on the lights, jolting both us "upper ones" out of a sound sleep. She loudly begins a conversation with the lady from the Bronx, who has just given herself a shot in the arm. She wants to share her night's escapades with anyone sufficiently awake to listen. As the little Bronx lady is hard of hearing, I suspect they could hear these intimate indiscretions in the cabins on either side of us as well. The dialogue began much like this:

Liverpudlian: "These Canadian men sure are something."
Bronx Lady: "What?"
Liverpudlian (yelling): "I said I LIKE CANADIAN MEN, DON'T YOU?"
Bronx Lady: "Yes, this boat's very nice."

> The fun-loving lady then goes on to tell us at great length what fantastic lovers French Canadians are—particularly one ship's officer, and what she has in mind for him in the future.
>
> We've had an update each sun-up since. If this keeps up, I'll be a wreck by the time I get to England. Otherwise, so far it's been a dull trip, except for the captain's party the first night. I was well-attended by a Mr. McDonald who, according to him, is some high muckety-muck in Canadian Pacific Shipping. He's frightfully frightful—"what, what!"—and drops names like a slot machine disgorges coins—but a good dancer. Oh, well, you can't have everything!
>
> During the daytime, which thank God so far has been fairly calm, I circle the deck for hours, practicing my Usova breathing. Remember, Mom, I showed you how to take a low deep breath with a sneer on your face and a growl in the back of your throat; then exhale with a loud shhhh, keeping the sound as even as possible. Well, I synchronize this with my stride—five steps, inhale; twenty, exhale. I sure get stares from other passengers as I snore, sneer, and shush my way around the deck. This hasn't helped to form any close friendships, as you can imagine.
>
> Four days later.
>
> I'm writing this as we sail into the mouth of the Thames, past Gravesend. In an hour or so we dock on the outskirts of London. I hope Rob will be there to meet me.
>
> Love to all,
Jess
>
> P.S. Thanks "ever so" for the lovely corsage, which is still gloriously alive—and your telegram asking me to write often. As you see, I'm writing.

I can remember being greatly relieved to see the familiar figure of my brother leaning against a baggage cart smoking a cigarette, while we slowly maneuvered into the dock in London. We established eye contact, and I managed a tired wave before going below to disembark. First I had to go through Customs. In Customs, I was told to step aside and wait. An hour went by. Everyone's baggage had been cleared; everyone's, that is, but mine. I could see Rob impatiently pacing back and forth along the dock on the other side of the barrier with a scowl on his face. I watched while he stopped every official-looking man he could find, the scowl deepening as his face became redder and redder. I could see the veins in his neck bulge when he yelled at some poor official, furiously gesticulating and pointing in my direction.

Finally, a customs officer turned to me and rudely ordered me to open my suitcase. He took a knife from his pocket and, with one adroit stroke, slashed through the lining of the lid, an action he had obviously performed many times before.

"Hey, you can't do that," I protested. Ignoring me, he slid his hand inside the opening, feeling his way from corner to corner.

"Remove all this stuff," he ordered, picking up and dropping my clothing as though contaminated.

I carefully lifted everything out and put the clothes on the grubby table beside the suitcase, disturbing as little as possible. He then took his knife to the lining on the bottom of the case, slashing it as well. He felt around every little tuck in the cloth looking for whatever it was he thought I had. Satisfied there was nothing there, he gestured with a flip of his hand for me to put my things back into the suitcase. For a moment, I contemplated grabbing the knife from his hand and slashing him with the same skillful stroke.

"This is a new suitcase," I burst out. "You have no right to butcher innocent people's property like that, no matter what you're looking for."

"You can go now," was his curt reply.

I stood motionless like a broken vase, animosity searing through the cracks. Near tears, I tried hard to swallow my rage.

"You might at least have offered an explanation," I yelled at his retreating back, but my complaint fell on deaf ears. With the aid of a few deep breaths, I slowly gained control, gathered my scattered belongings, and put them back into the ravaged case.

Rob told me later that he could see I was having problems, so he began asking questions of the authorities, as only he can. As usual, he fared better than I. They were looking for drugs and had been tipped off that someone answering my description was on board with a contraband substance.

My four days in London were mostly spent acquiring the proper documents. My aunt had left her car in England for me, while she had the use of mine, when in Canada for the summer. This meant, as well as requiring a visa for Germany and Austria, I would need an international driver's license. It was a great idea in theory, but in reality it proved to be loaded with difficulties for the real challenge was how to get permission to take my aunt's car to the continent. I decided to leave this challenge to my brother for I was sure, if he had to, Rob could get manure from a rocking-horse.

My first afternoon, despite my plea of exhaustion, Rob dropped me off at the British Automobile Association, complete with car documents and instructions on how to proceed. Once inside, I was directed to take a number and wait my turn.

An hour later, a formidable-looking gentleman with a huge handle-bar moustache beckoned me to his desk and asked, with a mouthful of marbles, what he could do for me. Producing the documents, I explained that I wanted to take my aunt's car to the continent. Casually flipping through my papers, he shook his head and said emphatically, "I'm sorry but it simply cawn't be done."

I was too tired to argue with him, and my patience was wearing thin after the long wait, so I said with exaggerated sweetness, "Would you mind phoning this number and telling the gentleman who answers what you've just told me?"

"It won't help. Regulations are regulations."

"Please," I pleaded, "It can't do any harm."

My brother could cast fear into the stoutest of hearts. My father knew well what he was doing when he sent his son to start a branch of his business in London, England. Rob could cut through the English bureaucratic red tape with a butter spreader. The man grudgingly picked up the phone. I watched, fascinated, while he spoke, or rather tried to speak with my brother, his face a moving picture of changing expressions. His eyebrows knitted, then they went up and down separately and together. His face turned beet red. I guessed what Rob must have been dealing out at the other end of the line and I was enjoying every moment, for I knew the man didn't stand a chance.

Finally, with a nod of his head in a gesture of defeat, he said quietly, "Yes, sir, of course. I'll see what I can do," and hung up.

He collected my papers and, without so much as a glance in my direction, disappeared. Again I waited. When he finally returned, it was with my new documents enclosed in a bright blue plastic case. "A very persuasive man, your brother," he said with a twirl of the end of his moustache.

The day after I arrived in London, Rob decided to give a cocktail party so his new business acquaintances could meet his little sister. I wasn't exactly looking forward to the occasion, but he'd done so many favours for me, I owed him one. I had always hated cocktail parties but over the last few years, I had developed a formula which allowed me to get through them gracefully. I pretended I was on stage and worked myself into performance mode. Usually, by the end of the party my adrenalin was on fire and I could go on forever.

Because it was a weekday, most people left early. There was, however, one last straggler I saw struggling with his coat. I went over to help him into the second sleeve. Taking his hand as if he were my most intimate friend, I leaned over and gave him a peck on the cheek. Looking earnestly into his eyes, I thanked him profusely for coming and said I hoped to see him again very, very soon.

When my brother passed me on his way to open the door for the man, he whispered in an exasperated tone, "Cool it, Sis, he's the bartender."

A couple of days before I was to leave for the continent, Eva called. She had been given two tickets to *Le Nozze de Figaro* at Glyndebourne that evening; would I and my car be available to join her? She would supply the picnic dinner.

In 1950, I had spent the summer in Salzburg studying with Eva and, when we stopped over in London on our way to Austria, she had taken me to a performance of Mozart's *Cosi fan Tutte* at Glyndebourne. There are few cherished moments in life that shine through like beacons never to be forgotten, and that evening was one of them. The performance was perfection, a standard achieved by weeks of rehearsals. The conductor was Fritz Busch, and in the cast were Erich Kunz, Sena Jurinac, and Blanche Thebom, all world-class performers. The quality of ensemble singing was flawless. Small wonder I jumped at the chance to again visit Glyndebourne.

There is a special magnetism about Glyndebourne which guarantees that each visit is an experience. It is one of the most prestigious opera festivals in Europe. It is set in the beautiful English downs near Lewes, south of London.

The first house on the site was built in the early fifteenth century. It was substantially altered during the reign of Queen Elizabeth I. Three centuries later, it passed into the hands of the Christie family. In 1931, John Christie married a young English opera singer, Audrey Mildmay, and the transformation from an English estate into a three hundred-seat opera house began. The Manor House is still lived in by John Christie's son George and his family.

With the help of a landscape gardener, the nearby downs were transformed into lawns and gardens that became part of the unique atmosphere of Glyndebourne. Over the subsequent years, the theatre was upgraded, enlarged, and finally completely rebuilt.

From the beginning, evening dress was the tradition as a compliment to the artists. Not having packed in my one small suitcase anything remotely resembling dressy, I quickly went out and purchased a simple black gown which purists might have labelled a slip. I loaded myself with as much costume jewelry as space allowed, hoping to deflect attention from the dress's simplicity. Over this, I draped my largest and most colourful scarf.

"You look very nice," was Eva's comment when I picked her up. Relieved I had passed the test, I knew at least I wouldn't be an embarrassment to her.

The performance again was impeccable; the singers young and believable with superior voices. Most were to become, if not household names, at least well-known among the opera-going public.

It is the custom at Glyndebourne to break for dinner after the first act. Because the opera commenced at five o'clock, it was still sunlight when I went to the car to collect the picnic basket. Most of the audience ate in one of the two well-appointed dining rooms called Wallops, but on a hot summer evening, a picnic was the right choice. Rob had suggested I take one of his folding chairs for Eva, for sitting on the damp grass at her age and fragile health wouldn't be a good idea.

The expansive lawns were dotted with elegantly attired patrons strolling leisurely about or sitting on their spread-out blankets, daintily eating squab and sipping champagne. We found a partially shaded spot in front of a clump of flowering trees and bushes. I unfolded the chair, spread my car rug over the grass and sat at Eva's feet like a well-trained puppy, ready to lap up any morsel of wisdom dropped from the full to overflowing plate of her rich past.

Eva had brought a generous array of sandwiches and fruits which we downed with red wine, a perfect repast for such an occasion. Sitting in the rose glow of the setting sun, my nostrils drinking in the heady aroma of the surrounding blossoms, I found myself wishing time would suspend in an outstretched hand and that every tree, every leaf, every stem, every flower, even the sheep grazing in the distant verdant rolling hills, could be locked into place. In this rarefied atmosphere of beauty and tranquility, Eva told me about the magic of the first performance at Glyndebourne, May 28, 1934. She had been one of the lucky fifty-four people in the three-hundred-seat theatre. The opera was Mozart's *The Marriage of Figaro*. Though the critics resented having to travel fifty-some miles by special train in evening dress just to listen to a rich man's folly, by the end of the first week, there were full houses every night and raves from the audiences.

While Eva spoke, I couldn't help but think there would be few such moments left for her. Her voice sounded tired, as if some of its valves were shut down. A weary sadness seemed to flow through every cell of her body. The cancer had broken out again, and she was undergoing more treatments while in London. She must have read my thoughts, for she suddenly broke off, changing her course of reflection. She leaned forward in her chair and gently put her hand on my shoulder.

"*Liebling*, don't look so sad. In my long, and so happy …" she paused, seeming to dredge up unwanted recollections, "… and so *un*happy life, I have gathered a bouquet of rich and rewarding memories. Through Brahms, Schumann, Schubert, and Hugo Wolf, I have lived many lives and, with the gifts the good Lord has bestowed upon me, have been able to share these lives with others." Her hand dropped from my shoulder, too tired to remain there longer. I turned to see if she was all right. Her eyes seemed unfocused, gazing past the green meadows, past the grazing sheep, penetrating deeply into the rose-tinted sky.

"Last year I felt myself dying until I was talked out of it by one of my clever doctors. 'You have to go on with your work. You still have much to give to your pupils,' he said very sternly, and he was right. I must pass on to you all the knowledge that has been given to me before I leave you for good." She extended toward me her hand that held her empty wine glass."I think I could do with a little more of that wine you're hoarding in the basket."

I filled her glass, and she closed her eyes, enjoying the essence of the liquid before taking a generous sip. "There. That's better."

She began again, her eyes directly engaging mine to make sure I absorbed fully what she was about to tell me. "My good fortune enabled me to live among the finest writers, painters, and composers of the day. It made me understand the style of their time, of our time. The greatest artists in Austria took over my education as a human being: Schönberg, Alban Berg, Anton von Webern, Rilke, and Hoffmanstahl. Painters like Paul Klee, Kandinsky, Kokoshka, and many others. What a rich time that was for me. They taught me how to train, how to use my senses, how to see the beauty in nature and art, the composition and colour in paintings, the form and material of sculpture. Our noses must take in the different fragrance of flowers and trees and connect it to the sense of touch, then connect all these things to the melodies and harmonies the great composers have given us. When I sang for these great artists my art was lifted to their level. Singing for Thomas Mann, Rilke, and Hoffmanstahl gave me much more than reading about voice production." A low-pitched, mirthless laugh escaped her throat, clearly dismissing the need of training the voice to produce sounds which can only come from deep within.

"Of course, on those occasions, my stomach was full of butterflies, but my soul was full of prayer that I should sing well. Sometimes I succeeded, but each time it meant one step further in my development. I remember singing for Schönberg. During the First World War, he was drafted as an ordinary soldier. One day he asked if I would sing 'The Song of the Wood Dove' from his *Guerrelieder*. We were in a large restaurant where the soldiers of his regiment were being given a farewell dinner before going to the front; the general wanted to hear Schönberg's music. The place was full of smoke and smelled of food and beer. I insisted on having the window open and asked for silence." She stopped, nodded her head slowly, and, with a dry chuckle, went on. "Believe me, there *was* silence during our performance. Afterward, when the general patted Schönberg on the back and said, 'You're not only a good soldier but a good composer as well,' I wondered to myself if that general knew how much better a composer Schönberg was than a soldier. He was already famous." She paused, trying to regain strength to go on. "I tell you of this episode in my life because when I sang for Schönberg, I was to sing better than ever before. I was led on by his spirit: *great step forward!*" She emphasized each of the last three words to make sure I hadn't missed their importance.

Eva slumped into her chair as if she had finished all she had to say, her head falling back, her eyes closing. I thought she had exhausted herself, but she must have been searching for another valuable memory which lay secreted deep within her endless supply, for she slowly raised her head and began again. "We singers need six senses to do justice to the music we have been given by the composers. Remember how I often said to you, inhale the perfume of the song. If you feel a smile, then sing it. If you feel a shiver in your body when singing *Gretchen am Spinnrad*, please don't think of darkening your voice, but say it. Say it with all your trembling soul." She then spoke the first words of the Schubert song, "*Meine Ruh is hin, meine Herz ist schwer*" (My calm has gone, my heart is heavy). Her eyes had closed again, and her words, barely audible, seemed wrung from her body with such anguish that I worried she was actually suffering pain. I was still sitting at her feet, and there was a long pause. I feared talking had exhausted her when she began again.

"One day I sang for the famous Yvette Gilbert." She must have seen my raised eyebrows, for she nodded her head. "Yes, *Liebling*, your Eva is that old. As old as Yvette Gilbert was when I sang for her. I was much in awe. Who could ever forget those posters of her by Toulouse Lautrec? Who could ever forget that face? When I finished singing, she remained silent; then suddenly she said, 'I would like you to say for me, I can't go with you, and say it ten different ways.' I could only manage seven. I know I disappointed her, but again, I learned a great lesson. There are many different ways of singing the same thing. One must always keep searching for other channels—keep moving on. There is a favourite saying of mine that goes, 'The rain doesn't fall for its own sake. You yourself are created for others and not for yourself.' Now that I find myself with a sickly body, I realize, I must not only teach you how to sing, but how to dig for more wealth in your soul, how to live with meaning."

The moment was suddenly broken by the sound of the bells summoning us back for the next act. I collected what was left of our picnic and put it into the basket as Eva slowly got to her feet.

"I'll take these things to the car and meet you back in the theatre," I said, folding her chair.

Through the rest of the opera, I found it difficult to concentrate. My frequent thoughts of soon losing this great and wise human being kept imposing themselves on the drama at hand, dampening my enjoyment of a most perfect evening.

3

Dashed Hopes in Bayreuth, Germany

T he letter penned en-route to Bayreuth was written on heavy hotel notepaper, making it easier to read.

July 1, 1952
Dominion Day
Baden-Baden, Germany
(A place for pleasure)

Hi,
    So far so good! I'm still alive, though a little the worse for wear.
    It was great to hear your voices over the phone the night before I left for the continent and to be able to tell you firsthand about Glyndebourne. Mom, you really must go sometime.
    By the way, did I mention how sweet brother Rob coerced me into taking one of his friends as far as Basel, Switzerland? He introduced him to me at his cocktail party as, "Sis, this is the man I told you about that would like a ride as far as Basel. I said you'd be delighted, as you wanted someone to share the driving."
    Since this was the first I'd heard about it, I was a little more than taken aback. In fact, I was too dumbfounded to object. "Thanks, Sis," he said, and that was that. So here I was stuck spending three nights and two days in the company of someone who had absolutely no sense of humour and zilch charm.
    As a driving companion, his rating was pretty damn low. When I was behind the wheel, his foot would press down on an imaginary brake on the passenger side while gripping the sides of his seat, his knuckles bone-white and his body as tight as a drum. He would then mutter through clenched teeth, "Do you have to drive so fast? It makes me nervous!" For my part, his slow driving made me edgy and quarrelsome. His average was a steady thirty miles per—and he wanted to stop in each town to look at the "quaint churches and monuments," while I was anxious to get to my destination on time. I had given myself four days to get to Bayreuth, with two nights and a day in Paris. Usova's instructions were that I was to meet her in Bayreuth, July 2. "If you do not appear on time, Lana will worry. She will think you've been gobbled up," she warned when she phoned her instructions from New York before she left.

We finally got to Paris about 7 PM, having left London at 6.30 AM. The trouble started when we began looking for a hotel. The first two we stopped at were full. The next one had one double room only.

"We'll take it," says my companion.

"No way," says I, emphatically.

"It'll be cheaper," says he, as the lady behind the desk gives him a knowing wink. (God bless these French and their quest for romance).

"You can have it," I said over my shoulder on my way out the door.

So by eight o'clock we'd found another hotel up the street with two single rooms. My friend pouted all through the evening meal. When I said "Goodnight" to him, I told him I would be leaving first thing in the morning, day after tomorrow, and would see him then if he still wanted a ride. I really shouldn't complain too much for so far he's paid for the gas, which, incidentally, is very expensive over here.

Spent the day in Paris with Aunt Suzanne and she was in fine fettle. We began by buying out the perfume shops (slight exaggeration, but at the time it felt like it) and then went on to department stores, where I bought three beautiful scarves, (which I needed like a hole in the head) for next to nothing, to add to my collection. Of course, after every store we went into we simply had to stop at a sidewalk cafe for a cup of coffee and a croissant.

I took the car everywhere in Paris. It is a little gem and so far is running beautifully. It's a real challenge driving through one-way streets with Aunt Suzanne as guide, though. Most of the time she directed me up the streets the wrong way.

"Ooh la la," she'd exclaim, holding onto her large hat while we headed toward the oncoming traffic. "Everysing ees so deeferent now een my Paree!" By the way, she sends her love.

That night I went to bed early for I felt a cold coming on, the only thing I managed to get free of charge in Paris. The next day the cold was with me in spades—and by the time we got to Langes, France, which was the next stop, I felt like dying. Langes is a fascinating walled town, full of charm and Cezannish-looking people. I would have adored exploring it, but I left that to my travelling companion. Instead, I crawled into bed (I can't ever remember feeling so miserable) and died. There was no argument from my friend about taking single rooms!

My cold must have been a condensed twenty-four hour job, for when I woke up in the morning, I felt human again (a few sniffles, that's all) and then, thank God, Basel Switzerland, when I finally got rid of my escort, after lunch. By that time we had formed a sort of armed truce. His parting words were, "It's too bad we have to say goodbye when we're finally getting used to each other. Say hi to your brother when you see him next."

So here I am at 2 AM sitting in my hotel room writing to you, exhausted but ready for the next adventure. I decided to stay here in Baden-Baden because the name sounded familiar, but I couldn't remember whether one came here for a 'bath' or a 'cure.' It turns out neither. You come here for pleasure, and by the time I got here, I sure needed some.

Having felt and acted like a dish of sauerkraut when in the company of my travelling companion, it was a pleasant change indeed to have the boy behind the hotel desk beg me to stay for several days. He'd have me speaking perfect German by the time I left, he said. He gave me a free pass to the casino and told me to come back after midnight, when he was off duty and we could have a drink together. (He's all of nineteen, but at this moment, even a kid looks good). A much needed lift was supplied at the casino, where I was picked up by a Turk (in a discreet way, mind you), and by the end of the evening, he had me convinced I must have been a princess in some former life—a real talent these Middle-Eastern men have!

Tomorrow I'll be in Bayreuth. I can hardly wait to be subjected to more of Usova's torture.

Love to all,
Jess

P.S. Would you save my letters for, so far, I haven't had a moment to write in my diary, and I suspect that's the way it's going to be most of the summer—that is, if I continue writing these long epistles home?

When I finished reading the letter, my mind instantly floated back to that morning in Baden-Baden when I awoke early. I remember everything was shrouded in gloom. There were low, angry-looking clouds looming menacingly in the sky. There was intermittent heavy rain throughout most of that day, making driving hazardous. I had difficulty following the road signs and twice became hopelessly lost, adding immeasurably to my frustration. To keep my spirits up, I breathed and I sang. I was aware of skirting scores of towns and villages, but the countryside remained a blur while I pressed on. By the time I reached Nürnberg and the autobahn to Bayreuth, it was four o'clock in the afternoon. I had less than an hour's drive ahead. I could feel my heart quickening with excitement at the thought of beginning in earnest my intensive studies. Until now, my sessions with Usova had been little more than a prelude.

Entering the city, it soon became obvious that Bayreuth was the home of the Wagnerian Festival. Every other street bore the name of a member of the composer's family or of one of his operatic characters.

I purchased a map and had no trouble finding the house on Hollanderstrasse where I was to live for the next week. Because Bayreuth is a *kleine Stadt*, the street was but a short distance from the Festival Theatre. Both sides of it were flanked with sizable white, or cream-coloured plastered houses with red tile roofs. Each looked like it had been built from the same square plan and each had its well-tended garden. When I parked the car, I suddenly I realized how tired I was!

The rain had gradually diminished to a foggy drizzle. Entering the waist-high wrought iron gate at the side of the house, I noticed two little metal plaques. One read Schmidt, the other *Vorsicht Hund* (Beware of dog). Within seconds, I was at the door marked Schmidt, ringing the bell. It opened, and I was greeted by a kindly, pleasant-faced woman with grey hair neatly tucked into a bun at the nape of her neck. "Frau Schmidt?" I asked.

She nodded and motioned for me to come in. In the darkness of the hall, I could vaguely see another figure standing closely behind her, a carbon copy of the original; the same face and hairdo, only the hair was a sandy colour, the figure a little taller and less full. Frau Schmidt closed the door behind me, and we stood silently looking at each other. She seemed uneasy and turned back to the figure behind her as if for moral support. Under a dark, heavily-carved side table, I noticed a rather unattractive, well-fed medium-sized dog of dubious pedigree. He lay motionless except for his eyes, which opened with great effort. They focused on me for a moment and dropped shut again. I guessed this must be the *Vorsicht Hund,* I was to be, 'beware of.'

The two women were obviously waiting for me to speak first.

"Ist Madame Usova hier?" I asked hesitantly.

They shook their heads in unison and each looked to the other to speak. Finally the older woman said slowly, pronouncing each word with careful deliberation, *"Madame Usova ist in Rome und ist sehr krank. Sie wird nicht nach Bayreuth kommen."*

It was as if this sweet little old lady had suddenly taken her fist and plunged it into my solar plexus. The thought of Madame Usova not coming to Bayreuth because she was seriously ill in Rome made me crumble like a stone wall detonated by explosives. My whole life seemed to burst into meaningless fragments. What if she should die? I had already begun to believe that she alone was my path to success. I sank into the nearest chair. My eyes welled up with uncontrollable tears, and I began to sob. I felt alone in a vacuum of disappointment and exhaustion, and I had no way of communicating. I let the tears and sobs flow as I had neither the will nor the strength to stop them.

Slowly I became aware of a gentle hand on my shoulder and two frightened and confused faces close to my own. The intensity of my outburst was reflected in their eyes, and I was overcome with shame to have given them cause for such concern.

My fears over Madame Usova's welfare finally brought me to my senses and, with a tear and mascara-stained face, I looked up inquiringly to Frau Schmidt, who was standing over me with a box of tissues.

"Wie krank ist Sie?—Was ist es?"—and finally in a desperate outburst in English, "How sick is Madame Usova? What's wrong with her?"

The two women looked at each other. They shook their heads and shrugged their shoulders. They said something to each other in German, and finally the younger woman put her hand under her left breast and said, *"Herz."*

With gestures, my limited German, and the patience and kindness of both women, in time I was able to understand that Richard Alexander had been in Bayreuth. He had left for Rome that morning to be with Usova. Neither of the women knew when Usova had had her heart attack or how serious it was, although they suspected the worst as Richard had left to be with her.

Throughout that evening the two women, Frau Schmidt and her daughter Ilsa, fussed over me like mother hens. They put before me a light supper, which I pushed around on the plate in a vain attempt to eat something to please them. My attic room couldn't have been more comfortable and spacious. All their kindnesses, however, failed to relieve my aching head and drained spirit.

That first night in Bayreuth was the longest and most troubled I can remember. Would Madame Usova survive? If so, would she be able to teach this summer? Would she ever teach again? Eva wouldn't be in Salzburg for another week. Where would I go and what would I do in the meantime? These questions kept spinning over and over in my tired head. I must have finally drifted off to sleep, for the last thing I remember was that it was dark and when I awoke at seven o'clock, the sun was shining brightly. I hoped this was a good omen.

During breakfast, my mind continuously wrestled with my problem of what to do next. I seemed incapable of making any concrete decisions when the phone rang.

"Es ist für Sie," Ilsa said.

It was Madame Usova in Rome. "Darlink, are you sad without your Lana?" The voice sounded as strong and oily as ever.

"Yes, of course, but how are you?" I asked, earnestly.

"Darlink, last week the lions in my chest began to roar. In a few days, the doctor says they will become pussy cats again and Lana will meet you in Salzburg on July 8. Little one, have you a pen to write down my address?" She must have assumed I had, for she continued without a pause.

I clumsily fished around the top of the desk by the telephone, knocking things helter-skelter. Ilsa could see that I was looking for something to write on and produced a pen and a piece of paper out of the air.

"Can you repeat that? I missed it."

With a touch of impatience in her voice, she repeated the address slowly, spelling it out letter by letter. "You have that? Now you will make good use of your time in Bayreuth. I will call Wieland Wagner to arrange for you to attend all rehearsals. You will learn what some day will be expected of you. Richard will be back in Bayreuth in a few days and will take care of you." Then, again in her oily voice, "You do still love your Lana, don't you, and will forgive her for letting you down so?"

It was a question which obviously required no answer, for, before I could speak, she had hung up.

I spent most of the next four days in the Festival Theatre. True to her word, Madame had arranged that all the usually locked doors be magically opened for me.

A few hours after Usova's phone call, I presented myself at the stage door of the Festival Theatre and was handed a complete schedule of rehearsals for the week. A cordial, pasty-faced young man led me through a labyrinth of corridors and into the small and unassuming lobby in the front of the theatre. There wasn't an ornament of any kind in sight, unless one could call white-globed lights on simple wrought-iron brackets, ornaments. It was Wagner's wish that the theatre be built without any superfluous decoration and that the interior be purely functional. That is, the whole theatre was designed solely with regard to its artistic purpose and requirements.

My companion motioned for me to be quiet as there was a rehearsal of *Das Rheingold* in progress. It had just begun. When the young man opened the large wooden door, I was immediately enveloped in blackness. He nudged me forward, down a steeply descending aisle, and guided me into a rear row of the theatre. Bending down, I could feel the hard wooden seats strung close together like a bench. I began to feel my way along, crab fashion, until I was pushed to a sitting position by my guide.

"When is the opening?" I whispered to the young man in halting German, feeling sure it was imminent by the finished appearance of the performance on stage.

"In three weeks," he whispered, indicating silence with his forefinger to his lips.

I learned later that, after weeks of staging rehearsals with piano, there is almost a month of rehearsals of the complete work with orchestra, then costumes, makeup, and lighting, and finally dress rehearsals, which are virtually performances. In Canada and the United States, because of union demands and extremely high costs of production, an opera company feels lucky if it can afford more than one orchestra rehearsal and one dress rehearsal. I have heard of a poor tenor at the Met in New York City having to go on stage without knowing who he was supposed to make love to that evening.

My eyes gradually grew accustomed to the dim light, and I could see my guide had disappeared somewhere into the darkness. I was alone, with the exception of a group of figures huddled together around a lighted desk in the centre of the theatre. I became completely absorbed in the opera. I had never seen *Das Rheingold;* the first opera of Wagner's *Ring*, and thus was unprepared for the drama which was unfolding before my eyes. I had a vague idea of the story of *Die Ring des Niebelungen* as told by the comedienne Anna Russell, on a favourite recording. Also, once in New York City, while at Columbia University, I'd been able to wangle a score desk reserved for students. It was at the Metropolitan Opera for a performance of *Die Walküre*—the second of the four operas making up *The Ring*.

Starting with the best is often a good way to begin. Having few pre-conceived ideas of how Wagner should be performed, I was now convinced that what I was seeing was what the composer must have had in mind. During the week, I saw the four operas of *The Ring*, all masterfully designed and directed in a simplistic fashion by Wieland Wagner, grandson of Richard. The concept was one of infinite space. The action in the operas took place in the never-never land of abstract space. It was magical.

In the first scene of *Das Rheingold,* the Rhein maidens are playfully swimming about on the bottom of the Rhein river, a challenge for any designer or director. In the brilliant hands of Wieland Wagner, from the proscenium arch to the floor of the stage there was an illusion of water created by fluctuating aquamarine lighting behind a scrim. The floor was shaped like the top of a sphere in which the sylph-like Rhein maidens, with their finned tails and long seaweed hair, capriciously rolled over and around the sphere, appearing and disappearing as they sang. The whole concept was breathtakingly effective in its simplicity.

When the lights came on at the end of the scene, I remained sitting, hoping not to be noticed by the small group in the middle. The deeply-raked auditorium was in the shape of an amphitheatre, with seating, rows of wooden, cane-back benches. The orchestra pit was completely hidden, three-quarters of it being under the stage, and the remaining quarter obscured behind a shell-like structure. The broad auditorium was flanked by wooden-pillared buttresses which continued onto the stage, creating the effect of a double proscenium arch. The beams of the comparatively low wooden ceiling spread out in a fan-like fashion reminiscent of an awning. The ceiling was painted a warm cream with aqua green and brown accents. The wooden pillars continued along the back of the theatre as well, supporting a row of narrow boxes with a balcony in between. Throughout the auditorium, there was the same simple global lighting I had noticed in the front lobby. Visibly missing but not wanting was the usual grand crystal chandelier of the period.

The building was designed from within, the most important pre-requisite being the equipment and the stage. All the structural features contributed toward the unique acoustics. Wagner's thick orchestration at no time overpowered the singer. Small wonder he wanted his works performed only in Bayreuth. The whole auditorium was like an oversized stringed instrument. It was like sitting inside a cello.

For days the sound of *The Ring* echoed through my ears. When there was no rehearsal to attend, I would sit with Frau Schmidt and Ilsa in their peaceful little garden, enjoying the smell of roses and sun-drenched strawberries. I would take every opportunity to engage them in conversation, which wasn't too difficult. Although I knew I could never master the language in two months, I did hope that by the end of the summer, I could at least understand and be understood sufficiently to communicate on demand.

In the evenings, I would walk in the woods behind the *Festspielhaus* until sundown, my ears treated to a symphony of bird sounds I could not identify, and my eyes to the sight of dappled sunlight dancing through the tall trees. When I tired of the woods, I would sit on a bench and gaze at the rolling fields, decked in their mantle of various shades of green made vibrant by the setting sun. Through my nose would waft the sweet scent of freshly cut hay. Nature is surely the greatest healer of a troubled spirit. By the time I left Bayreuth, the torment of that first night had dissolved into a vague cloudy memory, and I was refreshed and raring to go.

Friday afternoon, while sitting in the now familiar blackened auditorium of the theatre, engrossed in the first act of *Siegfried*—the third opera of *The Ring*—I felt a wet peck on my cheek. Siegfried, on stage, was in the midst of slaying a dragon, a monstrous fire-spewing, man-eating creature the size of a dinosaur, which lumbered out of a cavernous pit.

"Having fun?" asked the deep, resonant voice close to my ear. It was Richard Alexander.

He motioned for me to follow him. When we reached the lobby, he said, "Come on, I'll take you for a ride. You've been cooped up in that black pit long enough."

Walking toward the gleaming white sports-model Porsche parked illegally in front of the theatre, I had a chance to study his face. I could see what Madame meant when she said he was born with the right face; he didn't have to make one. That slight sneer was natural to him, and the wide face was full of space where the sound could resonate. The sinuses both above and below the eyes were large, healthy bulges. The wide nasal passages leading to the well-flared nostrils invited resonance. The generous, thick-lipped mouth and sizable jaw supported by a massive column of a neck, combined to guarantee a magnificent sound.

Richard demonstrated the adroitness of his new toy on the autobahn at well over a hundred miles an hour, and my heart was constantly in my throat. It wasn't until we slowed down in front of Frau Schmidt's house that I dared ask him how Madame Usova was.

"Was her heart attack serious? Has she had heart problems before?" I asked with deep concern.

His casual response surprised me.

"I don't think it's her heart at all. I think it's her gall bladder. Every time she'd O.D. on chocolate, she'd have a 'heart attack.' Of course, she does have high blood pressure, but if she'd give up chocolate she'd probably outlive both of us." Then he added, "I'll pick you up for dinner at eight o'clock," and the subject of Madame's health was closed.

Until I left on Monday morning, Richard dutifully wined and dined me, attending to my every wish. His world-wide acclaim seemed not to have adversely affected him. He was an amusing and thoughtful companion, willing and anxious at all times to help in whatever way he could. At no time did he make me feel the somewhat gauche and inexperienced student I was.

"You must be sure to come back to Bayreuth next month when *Parsifal* is on. It's a magnificent production. There are only five performances, so let me know in good time, and I'll get you a ticket," he offered when he dropped me off at Hollanderstrasse, Sunday evening after dinner.

When I began to thank him for his many kindnesses, he cut me short. "Say, has anyone ever taught you how to say prunes properly?" he asked with a grin.

"No," I said in all innocence.

"Try it," he commanded.

He planted a resounding kiss on my puckered, prune-shaped lips and with a, "See you in Salzburg," he was gone in his low-slung Porsche, like a bullet shot from a rifle.

The temperature had been building over the past few days, and by the time I left Bayreuth at ten the next morning, it was hot and steamy. The picture of Frau Schmidt and Ilsa leaning out their front, second-storey window, with wide smiles on their faces, energetically waving goodbye and calling, *"Haben sie eine sehr gute Fahrt,"* would remain with me forever.

The *Fahrt* to Salzburg was by autobahn all the way. The countryside was ablaze with sunshine and, after many weeks of rain, the undulating fields were cloaked in dazzling colours. The distant villages and quaint churches capped by tall, black witches' hats, passed by in quick succession. Speed, like many things, is relative. On the autobahn, there was no speed limit. While I felt I was travelling at a good clip, my little Hillman would shudder in protest as the Mercedes and Porsches flew past at speeds which should have been left to the race track. I sped past forests of straight and strong pine standing tall in their regimented formation, like the army of the Third Reich; past fields upon fields of trellised hops. My first glimpse of the Alps in the distance came soon after Munich. For some time, I followed the mountains on my right, reaching the Austrian border just outside Salzburg around two o'clock in the afternoon.

Throughout the four-hour drive, I tried not to think of Madame and the lions in her chest for fear she would still be ill in Rome.

4

Continual Confrontation with Usova in Salzburg

July 11, 1952
Salzburg, Austria

Dearest Mom,

Salzburg is fantastic. I feel as if I'd never left the place. I arrived Monday (this now being Friday), and each day has been packed full of exciting new things.

Madame Usova was already here when I arrived. My first glimpse of her was in her studio, reclining on a chaise longue, resplendent in a taffeta housecoat and surrounded by her anxious pupils. I was sure she must be having another heart attack, but I needn't have worried for all was back to normal (that is, as normal as it gets) the next day. I have plunged headlong into work and how wonderful to be "back in the saddle again." I spend most of my time listening and singing. I still find Usova's temperament difficult to deal with, though!

Yesterday I ran into friends I knew from New York days, Jack and Trish Tattle. Jack has a job coaching at the Festspielhaus. *He plays mostly for the famous Richard Alexander, Usova's star pupil, whom I met again in Bayreuth. In fact, he looked after me the last couple of days I was there. It was wonderful.*

Forgive this scribble but I just don't seem to be in the mood to write, however, remembering your last words to me before I left—"Don't forget to write, and often"—I guess a bad scribble is better than no scribble at all. Talking about that, I have yet to receive a letter from home!

My love to all,
Jess

When I finished reading this letter, my mind instantly drifted back to the city of Mozart's birth. Images of Salzburg's narrow cobblestone streets with their wrought-iron signs, floated toward me like a blizzard of dots. I saw clearly the spacious squares with their sculptured fountains. I saw the rococo architecture and the Salzach River winding through a city dominated by its castle five hundred meters high on top of the Mönchsberg.

Driving through the tunnel under the Mönchsberg, there was a moment when cool, damp air drifted through the open windows of the car affording a brief respite from the steamy quaint narrow streets of the old town. I remember being suddenly girdled with a delicious feeling of belonging. The two years since my last visit melted like butter in a hot pan.

Finding Madame's studio should be easy, for I had studied my well-weathered map at the German-Austrian border a few miles outside Salzburg.

Crossing the Salzach River at the Staatsbrücke, I turned right onto Steingasse. Within a few hundred yards, I was at the entrance to Arenbergstrasse. The little Hillman climbed the steep, narrow, one-way street running along the foot of the Kapuziner Mountain with ease. Though surrounded by large homes with beautifully-groomed gardens, the number Madame had given me was, by contrast, a most unprepossessing building. It appeared to grow out of the cobbled sidewalk at the side of the road. Because of its close proximity to the street, there were windows on the top floor only, giving it the appearance of a prison. The outside was covered in a faded pink rough plaster. Even from across the road, I could see the flaking white trim around the windows was in need of attention.

I crawled stiffly out of the car. I could hear a violin grinding out repeated phrases of double-stopping. I listened carefully for sounds of singing, thinking they might guide me to Madame's door, but there were none.

Standing in front of the unpainted double doors aged to a dark grey-brown, I wondered which of the four buttons I should push. Only one of them had a name on it, and it wasn't Usova. I peered through one of the diamond-shaped windows and could dimly see stone steps leading up to the second floor. They were protected from the elements by the balcony above. I tried the door; it was locked. While I was wondering what to do next, the latch snapped. The door opened, and a young girl emerged with a bloated Dachshund at the end of a long lead. We exchanged "*Grüss Gotts*," and she walked down the street, leaving the door unlatched. I hurriedly slipped in. Mounting the stone steps, I noticed an overgrown garden to my right. When I reached the top, I found a covered landing running around both sides of the building. Directly in front of me were double doors with a pair of wooden shoes beside them. I was certain this couldn't be Madame's door, as it was hard to imagine her clomping around in clogs. Following the upper walkway around to the back of the house, I came upon more stone steps leading to the third floor. At the top, I was confronted by another set of double doors. I rang the doorbell, my racing heart doing flip-flops under my sweat-soaked tank-top. Though the drive from Bayreuth was only four hours, it had been a hot one, with the sun pouring in on the driver's side and an open window the only air-conditioning. It was *Ray Darling,* whom I had met at Usova's studio in New York, who opened the door.

"Welcome," he said, smiling and opening it wider. Then, with an expansive sweep of his arm, he motioned for me to come in. "You are just in time for the final act of *La Traviata.* The curtain's already up, so hurry and take your place among the rest of us extras."

He led me through a small entrance hall, down a long corridor with closed doors on either side, and into a large, sky-lit studio. Directly underneath the skylight, on a plush, rose-coloured chaise longue, reclined Madame Usova, propped up by numerous cushions in various shades of pink. She was flanked by four concerned-looking young women who were fussing over her, patting her cheeks and stroking her arms as if trying to bring her back to life. I recognized Ray's wife, who was holding Usova's hand and at the same time fanning her with a sheet of music. Madame's long, cream-coloured taffeta housecoat and flame-coloured hair completed the picture. Sunlight poured in the skylight, making her white face appear ghost-like. Ray was right; what I was witnessing closely resembled Violetta's death scene in *Traviata.*

My first reaction was one of fear. I was sure Madame was in the midst of another heart attack. Suddenly Ray joined the tableau by slipping behind the couch out of Usova's line of vision. With an expression of acute grief on his face, he heaved a deep sigh as the back of his hand went to his forehead.

Before I could stop it, a slight smile escaped my lips. Unfortunately it failed to escape Madame Usova's half-closed eyes. Instantly sparks flew from them and her face turned a blotchy red. She drew herself up on one elbow, pushing the young women rudely away with her free arm. The same outstretched arm completed a full circle, ending with a shaking forefinger pointing at my head.

"When I am gone and dead, you will r-realize, Mademoiselle St. James," She paused and I braced myself for what was to come, for I knew when she called me by my last name she had reached the end of her patience. "You will r-realize," she repeated, "that I am to singing what Christ was to r-religion." Her *R*'s sounded like hail-stones on a tin roof as she spat out her last words.

For seconds her finger remained pointed, her slitted, green-lidded eyes still spewing sparks. Then her finger relaxed and, with another sweep of her arm, she dismissed "the cast".

"Leave me, all of you. Lana's heart is calm now. Go … go." Her temper faded as quickly as it had flared. With the same finger that moments before had been pointed between my eyes, she beckoned me to come closer. "Come, darlink, give Lana a kiss and tell her how you are."

I became aware again of my sweat-soaked tank top, clinging to my body. "I think I'd better take a shower before I go near anyone," I said, not moving.

"*Du Lieber Gott*, you English and your infatuation with water," and then the familiar oil came back into her voice while she introduced her famous guests. One was Richard Alexander's current girlfriend, who would be singing the Queen of the Night in the festival's production of Mozart's *The Magic Flute*. The young woman standing next to her would be singing the role of Pamina in the same production. The other famous guest, Maria, who by this time was at my side, was a student of Usova's from Nürnberg with whom I would later share a room.

It didn't take long for me to find out that many of the artists performing in the Salzburg Festival flew in and out of Usova's studio like bees in a hive.

After the introductions were completed, Madame assured us that the lions in her chest had gone to sleep and we shouldn't worry about her. She asked Richard's girlfriend to show me where I would be living, for she had lived there the year before. Madame ended by telling me to be sure to be at her doorstep at ten o'clock the next morning to begin my torture, and we all left the studio together. No one spoke of Usova's outburst. Perhaps the others thought it natural that they should be in the presence of one who believed herself to be the singers' messiah. Perhaps that was why they were there! For that matter, perhaps that was why I was there!

The only good thing about my accommodation turned out to be its close proximity to Usova's studio. Though it had, according to my landlady, served as a home-away-from-home for many a famous personage, such as Lilli Lehman, Lotte Lehman, and Elizabeth Schumann, the room was small, dark, and oppressive. The oversized and heavily carved wooden furniture took up most of the space. It was obvious the bed had served her clientele for many years, for every night it groaned and creaked in protest with the least movement of my body. It was a gross exaggeration to think that anyone, famous or not, could have slept in that bed unless they were used to sleeping on the floor. The small window had no chance to shed light because of its heavy, dark green velour curtains. Judging from the price my landlady was charging for the room, I was paying for the honour and not the comfort. I found, however, that my German improved rapidly, for she was not one to be satisfied with mere questions; she expected answers as well. She was fascinated by Madame Usova and wanted to know who went in and out of her studio and what they said and did. After a week of this, I decided the honour wasn't worth the expense and I would have to ask Madame if she knew of a cheaper place for me to stay, for I was fast running out of money.

When I arrived the next morning for my lesson, I gave Usova the pirated recording I had so carefully guarded during my travels. She looked at the label.

"Darlink, what is this? The Don Cossack's for me?" It wasn't hard to note the disdain in her voice.

"No, no. Look at the other side. Do you have a record player? You must hear it."

"Later. Now we must work."

"No, now!" I unfortunately insisted, thinking she'd be thrilled with my gift.

She went over to the far corner of the room, taking the record from its cover, reading the label as she walked. "Usov? I don't understand!" She put it on the small record player, which was tucked back in the corner of the room. The minute the aria began and she heard her own voice, the blotchy red crept over her face, and I knew I was again in for it.

"Where did you get this?" she said slowly, her voice icy cold as she lifted the needle arm from the record.

I told her the whole story.

"They have stolen Lana's voice, and I have never received a penny for this." She glared at me as though I was the guilty party. "You gave me this to make Lana unhappy?"

If it had been anyone but Usova, I would have thrown up my hands in resignation and despair, for no matter how hard I tried to please this uncompromising woman, I seemed destined to fail.

In spite of the inauspicious beginning, my lesson went well. Madame said she was pleased with my progress while planting a wet kiss on my mouth. Even so, I left wrapped in a thick blanket of depression. I found myself wondering if I would ever be able to survive her complex and mercurial personality. I could only hope that she would prove to be, as she claimed, the saviour of my voice and not the destroyer of my soul.

At this moment, I felt my soul very much in jeopardy.

It was a lovely day, and I began to wander down Arenbergstrasse towards the Staatsbrücke and the old town. I had no thought of where I was going or what I would do next. I had as yet nowhere to practice, and I shuddered at the thought of going back to my *Gasthof* to be subjected to my landlady's constant onslaught of questions. I reached the bridge and was about to cross over when I heard my name being called. I turned and saw two people excitedly waving in my direction.

Jack Tattle had been a coach in the opera department during my Columbia days in New York and Trish a fellow voice student. They had married shortly before coming to Salzburg and were on what they called a working honeymoon. Jack had been engaged by the festival to accompany some of the singers, one being Richard Alexander. They lived on Rainerstrasse, across from Mirabell Gardens. The powers that be at the Festspielhaus had found them a room in an apartment owned by Frau and Herr Kurtz.

After a generous lunch of *Schnitzel* and *Kartoffensalat* at a nearby restaurant, Trish and Jack took me to meet the Kurtzes. I was instantly struck by their handsomeness. Frau Kurtz had on a rose-coloured *Dirndl* with a deep burgundy linen bodice and Herr Kurtz, grey *Lederhosen*. They couldn't have looked more Austrian. Their eyes shone with friendliness and *Gemütlichkeit*. Though we exchanged little more than *"Grüss Gott"* at that first meeting, I knew we had connected. The Kurtzes' apartment soon became a much-needed haven from the continued storms of Madame's studio. I spent most evenings there indulging in long, intense philosophical discussions in German, brought about by Jack's compulsion to learn the language. He thought it mandatory that all opera coaches and conductors speak the three operatic languages: German, Italian, and French. My lack of inhibitions helped me to hold up my end of the conversation when it came to speaking. If I didn't know a word, I made it up and waited for the laugh. It surprised me how seldom I got one. To correctly understand the language was another thing. I would often guess and completely misinterpret what was said. This frequently got me into trouble during my stay in Salzburg that summer.

At my daily lessons, Usova would make me repeat the same phrase of four or five notes over and over. Before I could utter the second note, she'd exclaim, "No, no, darlink *Lieber Gott*—you're like a teenager. You hear but you don't listen. Relax—your jaw is tense. Look in the mirror—you see? Drop your chin—now drop your shoulders and take that frown from your English face." She would shake my shoulders back and forth, and then with a clenched fist, push hard against my stomach. "You are not using your diaphragm. Now breathe and push against my fist. No, no, no, no, don't suck in the air. You must make room for the air to flow in, as in opening a door to a room. The air should not be drawn in but should fill the space automatically as you expand your ribs. By now you should know this."

"I do, Madame Usova, but old habits are hard to break." As usual I was on the defensive.

"It is Lana, and in my studio you leave your old habits outside the door with the wooden shoes. You still do not love Lana; you do not trust her."

"I do, I do," I would protest, "but I have to know why I do things."

"No, little one, you do not have to know why." Then the red would begin to creep up her neck and the steel appear in her voice. Each word became a word unto itself. "You ... do ... it ... because ... I ... say ... so. That should be enough. Is there a God? Did Jesus Christ exist? A good Christian does not question these things; she falls to her knees and gives thanks."

And so my lessons continued each day with constant confrontation. I began to dread each breath I took. Gone, was the fun of just opening my mouth and letting the sound come out. Once I was allowed to sing a simple song, however, I was surprised how, in a few weeks, my voice had grown like a precious plant, nurtured by Lana's daily dose of potent elixir, despite our head-on collisions. For the time being, her attempts to strangle my spirit seemed to have no adverse effect on my vocal cords.

Eva finally arrived three days late. She had spent eight days in the hospital in Basel having injections and tests, costing her a small fortune. She said the pain had disappeared, but I noted that her morale was low. She said that I could practice at her place every day if I wished. She could then keep a close watch on my progress.

My days quickly fell into a pattern. Mornings were spent with Madame. Lesson first, followed by listening to others submit to her "victimizing" until noon. Afternoons were spent with Eva, practicing and listening to her wise counselling while I burdened her with my problems. She became my bridge over troubled waters, but she gave me little sympathy.

"If Lana Usova insists that you kiss her on the mouth and tell her you love her, then so be it. If she insists that you put your money on the piano before each lesson, then do it. My dear, be clever! She is giving you what you need. Is it not fair exchange for you to give her what she needs?"

At the end of my first week, I moved to Schloss Augen, close to Eva. It was arranged by Madame that I would share my room with Maria, her student from Nürnberg. Maria was singing in the Bayreuth Festival and would be in Salzburg only occasionally, consequently, most of the time I would have the room to myself.

Schloss, like chateau, can mean either a castle or a country mansion. In the case of Schloss Augen, it was very much a country mansion. It was but a ten-minute drive from the centre of Salzburg, however, the surrounding fields and the mountains in the distance gave it a feeling of country. The laneway leading to the Schloss was lined with huge old chestnut trees that made a green arch overhead in which the sun danced through the leaves. This gave the surface of the road an appearance of fine golden brocade. Immediately before driving through the rococo archway leading to the courtyard of the Schloss, was a little old baroque church with a black slate turret roof. Its stone walls dated back to Mozart's day. The Schloss was tucked in behind it. It was not grand as Schlosses go, but more intimate and friendly. It was still owned by the family who built it in the eighteenth century. The present *Graf* (count), his wife, and his mother, lived in the main building. The stables across the road had been recently renovated into a *Gasthof* with about twenty rooms.

Entering the small, unassuming entrance hall, I saw a man in *Lederhosen* behind a desk. He resembled the English actor James Mason. He spoke to me in German, and his voice had that same soft, velvet quality. After registering me, he shyly came out from behind the desk and muttered something in German which I took to mean, "I'll show you to your room." I learned later that he was the Graf, who was the receptionist, the bookkeeper, and general factotum. His wife looked after the rooms and prepared the breakfast. Because I appeared to be the only guest, the work load was not as heavy as it would seem at first glance. The Graf led me up the wide, wooden circular staircase and along the narrow hallway of the second floor. My room was small and basic. No frills. It had the sweet smell of new wood. On a little table in front of a large window, which overlooked a meadow, was a vase of daisies. This took away from the room's starkness. It was a great improvement over my last accommodation, with its over-stuffed dark furniture. I sat down on one of the beds. It was new and soft. Yes, I would be happy here.

Breakfast was brought to me in my room the next morning at eight o'clock because the Schloss had no dining room. When I left for my lesson about an hour later, there was a young woman behind the desk. I took her to be the Graf's wife.

"*Der Schlüssel bitte, Fräulein,*" she said, holding out her hand.

"*Ja, ja!*" I answered, shaking her hand while safely tucking the large key into my handbag. When I came back that evening, the breakfast tray was still in my room and the bed not made. Because the breakfast trays began to stack up during the next three days, when Usova asked me how I liked my new place, I told her I thought it charming, but I was running out of places to put the trays under my unmade bed. As was her wont, Madame's temper instantly flared, and she went into action. When the poor, unsuspecting person at the other end of the phone answered, he or she was treated with a barrage of complaints and threats, which made me sorry I had said a word.

That evening, my roommate Maria, arrived. Before she could get past the front desk the Graf confronted her and insisted she immediately call Madame

Usova to explain. Apparently there was only one key to my room. Each morning when I left, I was asked *for* my key. Each time, I nodded and said with a sweet smile "*Ja, ja,*" and left, with the key securely in my purse. As usual I had misunderstood; I thought they were asking me if I *had* my key. When I arrived for my lesson the next day, Madame was not amused.

"You do this to me on purpose? You put me in a terrible situation. You make Lana lose her temper at those poor people. No, it is not funny; it is embarrassing. I will have to put a sign on your back, *Bevor sie mit dem Mädchen sprechen, rufen Sie bitte Madame Usova an.*" (Before speaking to this young woman, please telephone Madame Usova).

When I returned to the Schloss that afternoon, the Graf was behind the reception desk as usual. I was feeling so ashamed that I thought of ducking out of sight and returning to my room later. He looked up and caught my eye. I offered him a weak smile and began scratching about like a hen in chaff, searching for any word in German that would convey my feelings of guilt and stupidity. I saw Maria coming down the stairs toward us.

"Maria, help," I called. I asked her to explain to the Graf how I had misunderstood when they asked me to leave my key. When she told him, the Graf began to laugh. He laughed so hard the tears rolled down his cheeks. From then on, we were friends and, whenever I passed his desk, his face lit up with a radiant smile.

5

Eva Arrives

Salzburg
July 18, 1952

Dearest Folks,

I say, are you still there? I feel as if I'm carrying on a one-way conversation, for not a murmur has there been from the direction of Canada since I left home.

Eva finally arrived last Monday. It's a great comfort to have her here. She counsels me on how to study with Usova and survive. It takes more than vocal talent, believe me.

I've seen Irma a few times since I've been here. The first time was when Madame managed to sneak me into a dress rehearsal of The Marriage of Figaro. Irma was singing Susanna. We went backstage to see her after the rehearsal. She didn't know I was studying with Usova, and she was surprised when I told her I'd followed her advice. Honestly, how grateful I am to her for that "hot tip." I've had two weeks of daily lessons now, and I can hardly recognize my own vocal cords. It's simply a miracle to me what Madame's accomplished overnight, so to speak (though it hasn't been easy on either of us).

I tried my "wings in song" last Sunday night when the family my friends the Tattles are living with, took us to a little Wein Garten. There was a piano and friend Jack began to play, his wife began to sing, then I began to sing—and Mom, you would have been proud. It sounded and felt so good. We sang until the wee hours as the locals kept begging for more. The evening was one I shall never forget, and it couldn't have happened anywhere but in Salzburg. My, how I love this place!

We've had a great deal of rain and it's been quite cool, so I've spent a lot of time in my slacks. My wardrobe, by the way, has been perfect. Everyone says I must have trunks of clothing, as they never see me in the same thing twice. The possibilities of two basic outfits and lots of trimmings are endless; I'm perceived to be quite well-dressed. Even you (I think) might approve.

Please—just one letter before I get back to Canada! I feel isolated not knowing what's happening at home.

My love to all,
Jess

P.S. I've run out of money. Everything is so much more expensive this year. I will have to call on my "letter of credit." Hope I have enough in the bank to cover it!!!!

The evening at the *Wein Garten* shines through in vivid colours. I remember, after a movie, we went with the Kurtzes to their favourite tavern for wine. Fritz, the owner, greeted us as if we were family, and his fat face crumpled into smiling folds when he led us to the far corner of the crowded, dimly lit room. I could hear muffled sounds of a violin and a piano over the din of the alcohol-induced conversation. We had barely ordered our wine when a tenor sitting at one of the tables in the centre of the tavern joined the two musicians who had been fighting a losing battle trying to be heard over the continuous clamour. They were struggling with Puccini's *La Bohème*.

Gradually, a hush came over the place as the strong tenor voice enveloped the room. He was singing Rodolfo's first act aria in a way that demanded to be heard. When he finished, there was a noisy round of applause. Trish noticed that the musicians were still playing, and she was right there with them. They had continued into Mimi's aria, "*Si, mi chiamano Mimi.*" Her clear, brilliant soprano voice floated into the ears of her audience, soon silencing them. For almost half an hour, we were treated to arias and duets from *La Bohème*, the two voices blending from opposite corners of the room, creating a stereo effect. Everyone sat in rapt attention. When the singing stopped and the musicians stood up to leave, those usually dignified Austrians showed their approval by rhythmically tapping the table with whatever cutlery was close at hand, demanding more. When they realized there wasn't going to be any, for the moment at least, they resumed their noisy chatter.

With a smile that could charm the legs off a chair, Frau Kurtz turned to me, "*Jetzt sie ist dran.*" (Now it's your turn.)

I was grateful the musicians had left, for there was no way I was about to try my wings as yet. There had been many moons and many gruelling sessions with Usova since I last sang in public. I knew I could no longer sing in the former way and was frightened that my as-yet-insecure new technique would let me down. After all, I had sung little more than scales since studying with Usova. I shook my head. "The musicians have gone. Besides, if they return, they probably can't play the stuff I can sing anyhow."

"But I can," said Jack, getting up from his chair. "Come on, you can't get off that easily." And he grabbed my hand, pulling me through the crowded tables toward the piano in the opposite corner of the room. His left hand began the chords of the four rhythmic bars of introduction to the 'Habanera' from *Carmen*. Before I knew it, I was off!

Maybe it was the two glasses of wine I'd had during *Bohème*, but everything felt good and, what was more important, I was relaxed and having fun. Jack masterfully led me through three arias, playing the *Carmen* score from memory. By this time the tenor and Trish had joined us at the piano, and we sang through all the duets and trios we could think of that we all knew. We sang until after midnight, and the tables remained full.

Fritz offered us a bottle of champagne and said that if we came back again, drinks would be on the house. The best thing about the evening for me, however, was to know that some of my biggest vocal problems were gone; all this in but a few weeks. Usova must indeed be a "messiah." The Tattles were amazed, too, at how much bigger and richer my voice had grown. Jack's comment was, "Whatever you're doing, kid, keep it up, 'cause it sure works."

We repeated the exercise frequently during the next few weeks, but it was never the same. Trish and I both sang, but it was always arranged beforehand what we would sing. Gone was the spontaneity of the moment. Our phantom tenor never appeared again, and with him went some of the magic of that first night. But each time I sang, the sound was more controlled, more even. I kept thinking of Madame's words, "Darlink, you do not open your mouth to sing, for that requires a muscle. You only have to drop your jaw and, darlink, when you go up the scale, you think down. When you go down, you think you're going up; then you will have an even sound throughout." Her sometimes confusing instructions certainly appeared to work.

For a while, things seemed much better at my lessons. I was trying hard to accept Usova's possessiveness without being swallowed up by it. However, I can't pretend my lessons took place without frequent setbacks. It soon got back to Madame that I had been performing free of charge in a "dive." Jack had mentioned to Richard that he had heard me sing one evening in a wine cellar and had been amazed at the improvement. When Richard passed this information on to Usova, she erupted, and I got the full force of the aftershock at my next lesson.

"It is so cheap; you prostitute yourself. You are not ready to be heard by anyone. Someone important may have been in that place and heard you sing. You will audition for him later and he knows you are my pupil. No, I will not have it.

You sing in your wine cellar and you no longer belong to Lana. Never forget, you all are my emissaries and, as such, you do me honour at all times!"

So, once again, I had to pick myself up and slowly crawl back into her good graces.

By mid-July, I had completely run out of money. Everything was much more expensive than it had been two years earlier. Though I had tried to be frugal, having to always eat my meals in restaurants as well as plant a wad of schillings on top of the piano at the end of each lesson had gobbled up my traveller's cheques at an alarming rate. The American Express office was in the Mozart Platz, close to the Festspielhaus. It had come to my rescue two years before when I was broke.

I left my car at Usova's and decided to walk and take advantage of the perfect day. Besides, it was impossible to find a parking spot anywhere near the Mozart Platz. The bright, warm sun on my shoulders felt like a soothing massage after a week of wet, miserable weather.

When I entered the Mozart Platz, the memory of the first time I had stood on this very spot and watched the American flag being lowered at sundown, crept into my psyche like sand sifting slowly through a sieve. It was 1948, three years after World War II, and Salzburg was still occupied by the Americans. I had been attending the festival with my mother. Watching with us were groups of bitter and grim-faced Austrians. How quickly it has all changed. Now, four years later, the platz is awash with tourists and prosperous-looking locals.

Ambling back to my car via the Sigmund Haffner Gasse with my fresh traveller's cheques tucked safely in my purse, I noticed a gathering of people ahead. Approaching, I heard the sound of a glorious coloratura voice singing bell-like high notes as easily as picking grapes off a vine. I stopped to listen with the rest of the large group collected under the second-storey window. I thought, "I know that voice; who else can sing the Queen of the Night from Mozart's *Magic Flute* like that but Trish?" Then I remembered she had said that Richard Alexander had arranged an audition for her with the director of the festival.

When the singing finished, the Austrians around me burst into applause; a great tribute from people who were used to the best!

The next morning, when I arrived at Usova's studio for my lesson, Richard was there and I asked him if he had heard how Trish's audition had gone. He told me that the maestro had been impressed. He had immediately offered her eight *Magic Flutes* that next season, two in Nürnberg, two in Dusseldorf, and four in Munich.

"Do you know what that girl said? She said, 'Oh I don't think I want to leave my husband for that long,'" and Richard mimicked Trish's coy voice. He went on to say that the maestro's response was a steely, "Why then, Madame, are you wasting my time? Do you want me to tell you what a pretty voice you have? Go home, my dear, and raise children." And he stormed out of the room.

While Richard was speaking, I listened in disbelief. Why would God give anyone such a beautiful instrument if she wasn't prepared to serve Him to the fullest? Such an offer comes only once in a young career. How I envied her. If I was ever offered such a plum when my time was ripe, I would fall on my knees daily and give thanks, husband or no. "And Jack said nothing?" I asked.

"No, he just smiled and looked smug," Richard said. "I'm sure if he was offered the job of conducting her, it would have been a different story."

In 1952, tickets for performances at the Salzburg Festival were at a premium. Even more difficult to obtain was a ticket to a dress rehearsal. These were only issued to locals or VIPs at a nominal price. Due to Usova's ingenuity and my cooperation, I was able to get into two of these rehearsals for free.

My roommate, Maria, had a week off from her performances in Bayreuth. We both wanted to see *Marriage of Figaro*, as Irma Mensinger was singing Susanna. We asked Madame Usova how we might get tickets.

"Darlinks, Lana will find a way to get you in."

When we arrived at the Festspielhaus shortly before two in the afternoon, Madame was waiting for us. She led us to the stage door at the side of the theatre and directed us to "stay," as though we were her pet dogs. She returned to the front entrance of the theatre, leaving us in the company of an officious-looking attendant. Moments later, she appeared at the stage door and excused herself to the guard with a charming smile. She pushed past him and resolutely marched over to us. Circling us like a wolf with its prey, she muttered out of the side of her mouth, "One of you follow me." Maria, being in the more strategic spot, fell in close behind her, and the two of them disappeared back through the stage door. The attendant never gave them a backward glance. I stood waiting for some time, not daring to move from the spot on which I'd been ordered to "stay" for fear I might miss out on my promised reward. Eventually, I heard a distant hiss from the front of the theatre. I ran up to join Usova, and she abruptly turned her back to me, but not before she had slipped something into my pocket. I saw her edge her way past the people standing in line to go into the theatre. She smiled sweetly to the man taking the tickets and, with a demure little wave, she said, "Hello, it's me again." She was then swallowed up by the milling crowd.

I felt in my pocket. It was a ticket. She had taken Maria around the back of the stage and out into the orchestra seats and left her to fend for herself. On her way to the front of the theatre Usova had been very careful to find out which seat was hers, so she no longer needed her ticket.

Once inside, I spotted Maria half-hidden behind a pillar. I joined her, and the two of us slunk around, trying to avoid the ever-watchful eyes of the ushers who were buzzing around like hornets. Soon, a red curly mop whizzed by under my nose, and I heard that hissing noise again. "Keep moving, you silly children." The red head quickly disappeared, only to reappear at the other side of the theatre, this time beckoning for one of us to join her; she had found an empty seat. I nudged Maria to go ahead, and I looked around to see if there wasn't something I could hide behind to make my five-foot-ten inches less conspicuous. Before I knew it, Usova was again at my side. She took hold of the upper part of my sleeve and pulled me down to her level. "When one speaks the international language," she whispered in her strong Russian accent while taking a hundred schilling note out of her purse, "it is so simple." She walked over to an usher, discreetly put the note into his hand, said something to him, and pointed in my direction. The lights began to dim as Usova took her seat on an aisle near the stage. The usher came over to me and led me to an empty seat at the side of the hall as the overture began.

When the *Probe* was finished, Usova collected Maria and me to take us backstage to see Irma.

"What are you doing here? I thought you were singing *Carmen* somewhere in the States?" Irma's eyebrows lifted in surprise, and she gave me a great hug.

"It's orders from above," I said with a glance in the direction of Madame, who was busy doing her royal rounds.

I saw Irma often after that. We spent many afternoons together over at Eva's, who held court most days around tea time if she was well enough, for I sadly watched her health gradually dissipate throughout the summer.

On one of the afternoons at Eva's, I took Irma aside. I wanted to know how she was dealing with Usova's overpowering personality. Maybe she could give me a few pointers on how to cope. She laughed her wonderful infectious laugh when I broached the subject.

"She puts on her finest kid gloves with me. She still hasn't convinced me I need her, and she knows it. I've only had a few lessons with her; enough to put me on her wall of fame." Irma laughed again. "For me, it's like going to the doctor for a checkup. I only go when I think I need it."

Obviously our situations were different. Her answers shed no light on how to find the right tack with Usova. I tried a more direct approach. "I seem to annoy her no matter how hard I try to avoid locking horns. Just when I think I've discovered a way to please her, I get slugged again."

Irma immediately became serious, as if she felt responsible for my well-being. "You have to understand her possessiveness. Until she's sure of your loyalty, you won't have her trust. *Complete trust* is an important part of a teacher-student relationship. If you don't have this, then you're in the wrong hands. What works for one person doesn't necessarily work for everybody. The teacher has to be tuned in to the needs of her students, and the student has to be willing to be moulded without questioning." She took hold of both my shoulders and gently shook them, the full concentration of her gaze penetrating my eyes. "Give it your best shot. Let your voice speak for you. If, after a few months, it's not working, then you'd better move on—and quickly."

"But she wants to take over my whole life," I protested.

"Face it, girl. At this moment, it is your whole life—or at least it should be."

"What are you two talking about so seriously? I thought you came to see me." The sound of Eva's voice ended our discussion, never to be resumed.

Later, weighing carefully what Irma had said, I knew peace lay in my hands only. I had to completely surrender to this higher authority or learn to exist with constant turbulence. My voice had spoken. It could tell I was in the right camp.

The next dress rehearsal was *The Magic Flute*, four days later. Maria was able to get a ticket from a colleague in exchange for a ticket to Bayreuth. As before, I was posted near the stage door, waiting for Madame to emerge from somewhere. This time, she appeared from the front of the theatre minutes before the curtain was to go up. She strode past me, past the guard, and through the stage door as fast as her little legs could carry her, and I trailed in her wake like a large cruiser being towed by a little tugboat. The only way one could get to the orchestra seats was to go behind the stage set and through a door on the opposite side of the stage. However, the set was placed so close to the back wall that we had to cross the stage itself. The picture of us trying to weave our way in and out of the intricate set, desperately searching for an exit, as the overture began, is still a vivid one. Thick foliage covered the stage. There were trees everywhere. Each time we'd head for a hole in the thicket, we'd run smack into another tree. The tenor was in the wings, like a race horse ready to take off. The dragon was already in its place, spouting flames. The three ladies, their spears raised, were behind a tree at the back, ready to plunge them into the dragon's heart. I looked at Madame's face when she turned sideways to try to manoeuvre around the dragon. It was the colour of her hair.

"Oh my God," I thought. "All we need now is for the lions to start roaring in her chest. Unless we can find a way out soon, this will surely be the first and last time I shall ever set foot on a stage in Salzburg." At last Usova disappeared through a hole in the entangled leaves, and I followed closely behind. We dashed across the wings and out the door into the theatre as the overture finished.

Once inside the theatre, my battle began in earnest. It was packed, and I had to find somewhere to sit before an usher found me. Madame had gone to take her seat, and I was on my own. The curtain went up, and I was still wandering about trying to spot a vacant seat. It passed through my mind to look for an usher to speak to in the *international language*, but this would require the kind of chutzpah that I lacked. I spotted an empty seat on an aisle at the back. No sooner had I sunk comfortably into it when it was claimed by a latecomer. I never did find a seat to call my own. I went through the entire long opera worrying about where I would sit next, or where I could hide to keep out of sight of the ushers. No performance was worth this! I decided I'd had enough of Usova's ingenuity.

One evening, Eva took me to a concert in the beautiful concert chamber of the Residenz Palace. The world-renowned Elizabeth Schwarzkopf was singing.

When I drove up to Eva's *villa*, she was already outside. The rose afterglow of the setting sun lit up her beautiful face, changing its grey pallor into a healthy radiance. In her special Austrian *Dirndl*, with its rich brocade bodice, she looked truly splendid. Yet I couldn't help but notice, when she leaned down to get into the car, that the bodice, which two years before had struggled to cover her ample girth, now hung loose. I tried to sweep my concerns into a shadowy corner and with forced cheerfulness, told her she must be feeling much better, for she looked terrific.

The hall was small and intimate, and Madame Schwarzkopf was resplendent in a tomato red filmy dress that complemented her blond hair. Her performance was outstanding, and the audience went wild. I came to my lesson the next day overflowing with praises for this extraordinary diva. I raved about her beauty, her voice, her artistry.

"Are you quite finished?" Usova said with scorn. Then, in a patronizing tone, she added, "Darlink, a river cannot rise higher than its source. She has a little voice, a little talent, and she has no idea how to use either."

So much for poor Madame Schwarzkopf, who had just been pulverized into a sack of fine powder! I learned then, if you didn't study with Svetlana Usova, you were nobody.

Usova was aware of Eva's existence. She knew, too, that I frequently took her famous pupils to visit at tea time.

Irma had a concert coming up and I took Eva. We were joined by two of Usova's pupils; Ray's wife and Richard's girlfriend. We went back after the concert to congratulate Irma. Suddenly Madame appeared. I was about to introduce her to Eva when I saw that she was staring at her with one of those penetrating, unblinking, cold stares. There was an embarrassing pause when Usova rudely turned her back on Eva and went over to embrace Irma without saying a word.

How dare she snub this great lady like that?! I could feel the colour rising in my cheeks. Eva put her hand on my arm. "It's not worth getting upset. What difference does it make? We need no introduction. We know each other well through you."

My next lesson was a disaster. I was greeted by a cold silence the minute I entered the studio. I felt as if I had stepped into a walk-in freezer. Madame's back was toward me. Without bothering to turn around, she started slowly, her voice like steel. The evenness of her words was intensified by her heavy Russian accent, making her lisp more noticeable. "You cannot serve two masters at the same time. You still do not belong to Lana. You do not love Lana. How can I give of myself if you will not give yourself to me? You will believe in me without question, or you will go your own way. Oh yes, you have improved because you have talent. But Mademoiselle St. James, you have still a long road to travel. If you keep fighting Lana, she will be a cripple before you reach the enchanted city. You believe in me," she repeated. "You are mine totally, or Lana is finished with you."

I knew it would be foolhardy to explain my special relationship with Eva, for Usova could never understand it. Besides, I suspected what really triggered her anger was seeing not only me but her other students in what she considered to be the enemy camp. It must have piqued her as well to see the warm and tender greeting Irma gave Eva. I remained silent, not knowing what to say, trying to think how to defuse her.

"Well, what do you say?" She turned and leveled those piercing eyes at me. I was still convinced that, if ever I was to have a serious career, Usova was the only one to show me the way. I would once more have to manoeuvre carefully through this treacherous channel full of mines if I wanted to reach the open sea in one piece.

"Lana, you must know I believe in you or I wouldn't have followed you to Salzburg." This wasn't going to be easy. I have never found crawling easy. "Madame Stein is a dear friend and not my master. She's very ill, and I help her whenever I can," I lied, knowing full well it was Eva who was helping me. Usova remained silent, her eyes still searching my face for more. I continued crawling, trying to worm my way back into her good graces. "I am truly grateful for what you have already done for me."

"Darlink, I don't want your gratitude," she snorted. "I want more, much more. I want your devotion, your love."

I took a deep breath, thought of Eva's wise counselling and, with a practiced smile used exclusively for this particular recipient, murmured softly, "You have it."

For the time being she seemed satisfied and no more was said, but the remainder of the lesson was no easier than its beginning. The minute Usova hit a chord on the piano and I prepared to utter my first pear-shaped tone, my face distorted to open up the cavities, she growled, "Get that sound out of your throat. You have not opened all the pathways of your face so that the sound can resonate in the caves." Then she stood up and, with her thumb and forefinger, pushed my cheeks up with such force that the bones under them trembled. "There should be nothing between the top of your head and your diaphragm but space, wide open space, and a steady flow of controlled air. Up—up, in the mask." Again she pushed my already tender cheekbones, only harder this time. "Out of the throat," she commanded. For the rest of the lesson, I was mercilessly pummelled and pushed in the ribs and stomach until my release an hour later. There was no "Darlink" that day.

Outside was cold and wet. The black clouds had sunk over the surrounding mountains like a shroud. Even the castle, high on its dolomite rock, had gone into hiding behind a thick blanket of mist. As I drove toward the old city, the world outside my little Hillman car was a mass of varying shades of grey broken only by the black umbrellas of those who had ventured out into the soggy rain in search of food. I was so distraught that, when I found my car taking me up the wrong way on a one-way street, I decided it would be safer to park the car and get out and walk. I wandered aimlessly for over an hour, unaware that the rain had filtered through my lightweight jacket, making it cling to my skin like an overly tight sweater. My whole being was bathed in a deep depression. Would I ever be able to find a way to work peacefully with this woman, whose knowledge and omniscience I greatly respected but whose possessiveness, jealousy, and smallness of spirit I found difficult to accept? This question kept ringing through my head. I had searched out Svetlana Usova to nurture my voice and not my soul. If I could only stop judging her and learn to accept; learn to dangle my resistance gracefully in order to veer away from the constant confrontations.

I had reached the Müllnersteg and was about to cross the river. I must have walked at least a mile from my car when I realized I was shivering uncontrollably and turned back. By the time I got to the Schloss, I was soaked through from head to foot and chilled to the bone. I could think only of jumping into a hot bath.

Once in my room, I stripped off my wet clothes, wrapped myself in my warm dressing gown, and headed for the common bathroom at the end of the hall. I turned on the light and went over to the long, old fashioned tub to turn on the taps. Halfway up on the inside of the tub, I noticed a daddy-longlegs. It was motionless. I was about to take my slipper and squash it when it dropped to the bottom of the tub. Immediately it began to climb up again. I became fascinated watching it struggle to reach the top of the tub. It would place each of its legs tentatively, moving one at a time to make sure it adhered to the tub first before trying the next step, its antennae outstretched scrutinizing the surface to find the safest and most secure route. I saw it painstakingly reach the spot halfway up where it had fallen from before. It stopped, its antennae twitching and pecking at the surface to find the best way to proceed. It remained there for some time before the legs slowly and cautiously began to move forward. It had gone no more than a few steps when its legs slipped from the tub. For seconds, it adhered to the side of the tub with a front leg, the others extended downward, ready for the fall. It let go and dropped to the bottom again. I watched, hypnotized, as the daddy-longlegs repeated the climb, patiently and determinedly time after time, always falling to the bottom from the same spot. Minutes passed before I finally reached for the taps to wash the poor creature down the drain and out of its misery, but something held me back. Was it because I identified with this unfortunate creature? How like my struggle with Usova. I began to wonder why she hadn't turned on the taps and flushed me away or squashed me under the spike heel of her shoe.

I went back to my room to fetch my glass. I returned to the bathroom, scooped the daddy-longlegs into the glass, covering it with the palm of my hand so the creature couldn't escape. I ran down the stairs and outside into the cold wet grass. I tipped the glass and tried to shake my poor captive free, but the spider clung to the side, preferring the safety of its confines to the possible dangers of the unknown. I bent down and carefully placed the glass on the ground; I'd let the poor creature find its own way out and retrieve the glass in the morning.

Moments later, I was relaxing in hot water, soaking up its delicious warmth. My mind, if not totally at peace, was at least more settled. I resolved again that, no matter what, I would persevere in my struggles with Usova.

One day my lesson was in mid-afternoon instead of the usual ten o'clock in the morning. I had come straight from lunch with the Kurtzes at a smoky restaurant and had indulged in a rare treat of a cigarette with my coffee. Madame greeted me with her usual wet kiss, and I heard a sniffing sound close to my ear. I glanced at her face and saw that her wide nostrils and cheeks were quivering up and down.

"Darlink, you've been smokink," she accused.

I guiltily nodded. "Yes, I do occasionally have the odd cigarette."

"Little one," she drawled, "Why do you think I kiss you on the lips? Do you think I enjoy it? No, darlink, people in my studio do not smoke. It is no good for the voice. I say no more." A pause and then, "Now, let me see if I will be proud of you today."

6

Disastrous Love Affair—Severed Relations with Usova

*Salzburg
August 25, 1952*

Dearest Mom,

Now it's my turn to feel guilty, for it's over a month since my last letter. Time has sped by so quickly it makes my head spin.

It was great to get a letter from home (finally) and to hear that you are cozily settled in your new house. No wonder you didn't write. The move sounds exhausting. I hope you've both recovered by now.

The weather has been changeable, which, as you may remember, in Salzburg means one day sunshine, four days wet, miserable weather. I've had another rotten cold due to the fact that I never seem to manage to dry off. It didn't help that I've had trouble sleeping these last few days, I suspect caused by my continuous battles with Usova.

Eva left last Sunday, and I really miss her wise counselling. She wasn't at all well. She had to have more X-ray treatments in Vienna as the cancer had broken out in her shoulder. She was very tired from always having so many people around her sapping her strength. Everyone seems to want to get as much as they can from her, feeling they might not see her again. Eva being Eva, however, is marvellous through it all. I can't help but wonder how much more she can take. Thank God I will be going back on the same boat with her in case I can be of help.

We sail from Le Havre September seventh, arriving Quebec the thirteenth—I think. Anyhow, it's the SS Atlantic, the same ship Eva came over on. It's the Home Line. Remember, the Hillman comes back with me as originally agreed. I'll drive Eva as far as Montreal, where she'll spend time with her brother, and I'll drive home alone.

Frankly, I'm ready to go home. I've had enough of Usova's possessiveness. I'm afraid if I remain in her "clutches" any longer, she will kill my love of singing. I have gained much from my studies with her, but enough is enough!!

I guess this will be my last letter home. I'll be spending a few days in Paris with Aunt Suzanne, then—
See you soon.

Can hardly wait.
Yours, Jess

Reading this, my final letter from Salzburg, I began scraping images from the deepest recesses of memory. It wasn't what I wrote but what I didn't write that festered through the layers of obscuring dust. I remember those last few days in Salzburg shattered my life, or so it seemed at the time. Their events almost crushed my spirit, almost broke my heart, and came close to ending my singing career before it began.

The difference between a warm friendship and an affair of the heart can be nothing more than a touch of the hand or a shared glance. Ever since my stupidity over the key at the Schloss, the Graf had paid me special attention. He would stop me on the stairs to shyly ask me a question of no consequence, simply to engage me in conversation. I would answer in German as well as I could, always hoping I'd understood the question correctly.

One day I found a red rose in my room instead of the usual daisies. I knew it was meant for me, for Maria hadn't been at the Schloss for weeks, and I was sure it wasn't the Graf's wife who had left it. There was a change, too, in the way the Graf looked at me. I would have taken all this in stride, even been flattered by the attention, had my heart not reciprocated with an extra beat every time I saw him. The last thing I wanted at this point in my career was an affair of the heart, particularly with a married man. As long as I took care to avoid any compromising situation, I thought I could handle it.

A week before I was to leave Salzburg, my lesson began with the usual wet kiss and then, the oil. "Darlink, we have only a few more days together in Salzburg. Tomorrow will be a beautiful day. The sun will shine, and we will have a picnic." She always spoke in the absolute. What she decreed would be. Even the weather had to bend to her will.

"You will ask the Graf and Gräfin. They will drive with you, and I will go with Ray and Mona in their car. We will go to the Grossglockner."

The Grossglockner is the highest mountain in the Austrian Alps, and it is at least one hundred miles from Salzburg, with much of the road through mountainous terrain. It would take a good three hours each way; an adventurous and ambitious outing for a picnic.

"Must we ask the Graf and his wife? I'm sure they won't be able to come. Who would look after things at the Schloss?" I dared not tell her I felt the stirrings of a mutual attraction that I wished to avoid encouraging.

"Why do you have to always argue with me? It is so tiresome. Just do as I say and be a good girl." In her usual fashion, she diminished me to the status of a difficult child.

When I arrived back at the Schloss, I discovered not only that Lana had already asked the Graf, but she had asked his wife to prepare the picnic as well. So that was the reason she wanted them to come along. I had to hand it to her; she always thought of everything!

Usova of course was right. The next day was bright sunshine. The streets glistened from the rain of the day before. At ten o'clock sharp, the phone rang at the front desk. Lana told the Gräfin they would be there in fifteen minutes, and we were to follow Ray's car.

I drove to the front of the Schloss and waited. Sure enough, Ray's car appeared through the archway at the designated time. He drove into the courtyard as the Graf came out the front door of the Schloss—alone. He was carrying a huge basket of food with wine bottles sticking out of each end. *"Grüss Got,"* he said to everyone as he loaded the basket into the trunk of my car. Without another word, he opened the door on the passenger's side and sat down beside me. We sat in silence, waiting for his wife to appear. Closing the car door, he called back to Ray, *"Weiter fahren."* (Drive on.)

"Isn't your wife joining us?" I asked in my halting German.

"Nein, she has to remain at the Schloss to take care of things. She said she's sorry she can't come and hopes we enjoy the picnic." At least, I assumed that's what he said, but it didn't matter, for the sound of his soft velvety voice washed over me like a caress. I was sure he must have noticed the mounting colour in my face when I felt the sudden rush of blood. I knew I was cornered.

"Follow me, kid. I'll take it easy around the curves, I promise." Ray's sandy, curly head appeared from the open window of his car when he sped by us, leaving a trail of dust behind him.

We drove along the sun-dappled laneway arched with its old chestnut trees. The Graf remained silent. Unease lay under the surface like quicksand. I concentrated hard on keeping Ray's car in sight. We turned left onto the main thoroughfare and out of the town, following the road to Zell am See. Finally, the Graf broke the silence. "I have a first name. My friends call me Karl."

"Yes, I know." There was another long silence while I kept my eyes glued to the back of Ray's car.

"Would it be so difficult to call me Karl?" Again, that gentle soothing voice I found so disturbing.

"No, of course not," I assured him, still not able to speak his name.

We followed the Saalach River through the Saalach Valley, which forms a gap in the northern limestone Alps. Most of the way, we were flanked on both sides of the road by steep, rocky cliffs. The road was excellent and surprisingly free of traffic for August. Soon after leaving Salzburg, we were at the German border. Fifteen minutes later, we were back in Austria.

For at least half an hour, neither of us spoke. When he began again, his voice wrapped itself around me like a soft cashmere shawl. I was surprised to hear him struggle with English. I had never before heard him utter one word of the language. "I will tell you a story. What do you say in your English? ... I must explain my situation. I will try with my small English, for I want to make sure you understand all I say to you; no guessing." He smiled his lovely, warm smile and then just as suddenly, he became serious again. "It's too important, you understand."

Telling his story, he switched back and forth from English to German, weaving a web of pathos while he spoke. I became increasingly moved with each word. Occasionally glancing sideways, I thought how sad and lonely he looked. My former apprehension gradually turned to distress.

"During the war, things were very hard for us. I was, what do you say—excused from military service because I must take care of *meine Mutter*. The Gestapo took over the Schloss, and we must live in the stables. *Meine Mutter* had a close friend. She was eine *Jüdin* (a Jew). Her husband, a Catholic, was killed at war with Leningrad. They had a daughter. The friend of *meine Mutter* was sent to concentration camp in Poland. *Meine Mutter* promised to take care of the teenage daughter. She lived with us in the stables, but because she was half *Jüdin* the Nazis gave us trouble. I married her, thinking they would then leave her alone. We have never lived as *Mann und Frau*, but like *Schwester und Bruder*. We live separate. We do not love, but we are trapped because we are Catholic. Verstehen sie? Do you understand why I tell you this?"

I honestly wasn't sure. Where did I fit in; was this some kind of proposition? My heart was pounding. I found it difficult to breathe.

It was at this point I saw Ray's car veer off to the side of the road into a lookout area. I guessed it was to take a photo of the river rushing through a picturesque, rocky cleft, or to have a good stretch for we had been driving for over an hour.

"This is taking much longer than I thought it would," Lana said. "We should stop at Zell am See and picnic there. If there's time after lunch, we will continue on." Lana was obviously having second thoughts about the Grossglockner.

In five minutes, we were again on our way. We passed a village with a chapel built into a rock. We entered the mouth of a ravine where we could see the snow-capped mountains in the distance. I was only vaguely aware of my surroundings. The atmosphere inside the Hillman was charged with tension as the Graf kept inching closer and closer, until his thigh touched mine. I froze, not knowing what to do. A part of me wanted to respond by timidly returning the pressure with my leg. The rest said, "Beware, this isn't in your plans." My heart again began to pound. I rolled down my window to get some air.

Closer to Zell am See, the traffic became heavier. I tried to focus all my concentration on Ray's car ahead, which I kept losing sight of on the increasingly curvy road. Several times, he had to pull over to wait for me. I began taking in great gulps of fresh mountain air when I felt the heat from the Graf's leg flow into mine. Everything seemed suspended in a vacuum. We drove by cliffs with their stripes of reddish iron glowing vividly in the bright sunlight. In the opposite direction, the snows of the high mountains could be seen through the valley formed by Lake Zeller. We reached Zell am See by skirting the higher shore. The surrounding countryside with its snow-capped mountains was mirrored in the waters of the lake. In the bright sunshine, the effect was magical.

When we reached the centre of the town, Ray pulled over. Madame had decided we would drive two kilometres beyond Zell am See and take the cable car to the Schmittonhohe to picnic at its summit. We parked our cars beside each other in the cable car parking lot. Ray left to purchase tickets while Karl went to the back of my car to take the picnic basket out of the trunk. I followed. I reached in to see if there was something I could carry to make the basket lighter, when he gently took my hand and lifted it to his lips. He gave me such a look of tenderness that it sent a charge of electricity all through my body. From then on, all my resistance evaporated, gathered up by the gentle warm breeze blowing around us. He held my fingers to his lips for what seemed a delicious eternity. When he let go of my hand, I glanced over his shoulder. From her perch beside Ray's car, I saw Lana's eyes shooting sparks in our direction. She had obviously taken in everything. From that moment on, her eyes seldom left us.

The ten-minute cable car ride seemed to take forever. In the cramped quarters of the cabin, Usova pushed her way between me and Karl to make sure we were well-separated. When we reached the summit we were treated to a glorious panorama of the surrounding mountain ranges. There was a clear view in the distance of the Grossglockner in all its majesty. Because it was now one o'clock in the afternoon, I knew that this was as close as I would get to it—at least today.

There was no one else in sight; we had the mountain to ourselves. We selected a grassy slope near the summit. Karl spread a large, dark green blanket over the grass and unloaded the basket. There was every kind of German sausage, cheese, fruit, and *kuchen* one could imagine, breads of all kinds, plus four bottles of wine. The Gräfin had outdone herself.

Because Madame was busy making sure everything and everyone was where she wanted them to be, I was able to study Karl in detail without having to worry about being watched. Though his hair was peppered with grey and slightly receding around the temples, life as yet had not printed its cruel map upon his boyish face; I thought him somewhere in his early forties. He was not handsome in the usual sense; his eyes were a little too close together, his nose a little too small, his mouth a little too generous. However, all together it was an attractive, sensitive face, enhanced by his captivating smile. In his dark green Tyrolean jacket and *Lederhosen,* he looked every inch what he was: a country squire.

By three o'clock, we had consumed most of the food, and Lana announced she thought we'd better start back if we wanted to get to Salzburg before dark. From the way she had glued herself to Karl, I wasn't surprised when she said she would drive back with us. "The little one might get lost," she said. Was she trying to protect me from the approaches of Karl, or did she want his attentions for herself?

Ray and and his wife decided to continue on to the Grossglockner, another hour's drive. Because they were leaving for New York in a few days, they thought they might not get another chance to see one of the most spectacular views in Austria.

On our way back to Salzburg, Lana insisted on sitting in the back seat with Karl. Understanding only the occasional word, I found their continuous chatter and frequent bursts of laughter most disconcerting. I wanted to know what she was up to. I didn't trust her for a moment.

When I dropped Usova off around six o'clock, Karl, after kissing her on both cheeks, climbed into the front seat beside me.

"I'll expect you at ten tomorrow morning," Lana called over her shoulder while she opened the gate. Then she stopped, turned, and, as an afterthought, added, "Make sure you have a good night's sleep. We have only a few lessons left, and when we are finished, I want to be proud of you." With that, the gate clicked shut, and she was gone. Her last words sounded more like a threat than a casual statement.

Karl and I drove back to the Schloss in silence. Better I say nothing than something I might regret.

When I arrived at the front door to let him out, he again took my hand, his moist, soft lips brushing my fingers. "May I come to you later?" he whispered softly, his intense gaze stripping away all resistance. I looked into his eyes with equal longing and put his hand on my breast so he could feel my pounding heart. My "yes" seemed to come from some far-off place and was barely audible.

For over three hours, I waited in my room. I had put some of the leftover food from the picnic in my purse. I nibbled at it, not knowing what I ate. My whole body was alive with anticipation and desire. I had never before experienced such intense emotion.

Finally I heard his footsteps. There was no knock. The door slowly opened. He entered, and our bodies, as though drawn together by a huge magnet, melted into one.

When I awoke, it was daylight. Karl had gone. I ran my fingers over the spot where he had lain, and it was still warm. I looked at the clock beside my bed. Eight o'clock. I'd better get moving. My lesson was at ten.

Driving to my lesson that morning through the same streets I had driven daily for the better part of two months, I was aware how different everything appeared. It all looked clearer, sharper. I noticed how the overhead leaves on the trees in the courtyard made coins of sunlight on my car. Going down the laneway, I marvelled at the intricate pattern the shadows of the chestnut trees made on the pavement ahead. It was as if before, everything had been shrouded in a light fog.

It is said love is like a flame, visible for all to see. I wondered whether Usova would notice my new inner light. After her obvious disapproval the day before, I was sure she would be watching my every move with those penetrating eyes. She'd probably lecture me on the sins of the flesh and their detrimental effects on the voice. On the other hand, I could be met with a deep freeze.

In both cases I was wrong. After the wet kiss, everything progressed as usual; no mention of the day before. Maybe I had imagined her eyes following Karl and me everywhere.

Lana guided me up and down the full range of my voice, stretching it to its fullest. The sound poured out of my throat with such ease and freedom, I felt I could do anything with it; sing anything. The sound was richer, fuller, too. She must have noticed the difference but, if she did, she said nothing. Even the "I am so proud of you," never came.

For the next two nights at about the same time, Karl appeared at my door and silently let himself in. Each night, when he expertly navigated me through the delicate channels of lovemaking, my body became more alive with each gentle caress. Each night when he declared his undying love, I became more convinced I had found my destiny. I would be willing to forego everything, even singing if I must, to be with him always.

My next lesson was my last. Usova began her attack the minute I entered her studio. She was facing the piano with her back to me. The tone of her voice was menacing. "I hope you are not taking this man seriously."

I was not prepared for her greeting. I remained speechless, not knowing what to say. Was her network of informants already at work? Maria was still in Bayreuth, so I knew she couldn't have said anything.

"You are a foolish child. This man is married with three children," she said in her steely voice, turning to face me.

I smiled, knowing full well she was lying. If Karl had children, they would have been fathered by the Holy Ghost. She must have noticed my smile, for she continued with a vengeance. "He is a well-known philanderer and not worthy of your attention. He is a dull, stupid man who knows only his own vanity." While she continued with her slandering, tearing to shreds the man I had fallen deeply in love with, my hatred for her welled up, almost choking me. I lashed out, feeling sure from her performance during the picnic a few days before that jealousy was sprouting like a bean shoot in the darkness of her heart.

"That he's in love with me seems to upset you. You can't possess everyone you meet. It's all your fault, you know. You wanted to ask the Graf and I begged you not to." My voice was shaking with uncontrollable fury.

"Careful," she cautioned. "Lana will not tolerate rudeness."

"I'm glad you asked him," I spat out, ignoring her warning. "I love this man and I don't give a damn what you say, and I don't give a damn if I never sing another note." The last sentence disgorged from my throat with the force of a geyser.

She came close to me, and there was about her a frightening calm. Her eyes were slits of green. Her words came out slowly and evenly with no sign of emotion. Her strong Russian accent with its slight lisp made her words somehow more ominous. "I had a visitor shortly before you came. She asked me to warn you. She is worried you will get hurt. She told me it was not the first time her husband had played on the emotions of an inexperienced young girl. His children mean everything to him. His constant affairs mean nothing; they are but passing amusements, so beware, my dear Mademoiselle St. James."

So that was it! His wife was afraid she'd lose him. "She's lying," I shot back. "They have no children. She's making all this up. It's been a marriage of convenience. He's never loved her."

Lana burst into a hollow, mirthless laugh, shaking her head slowly in disbelief. "Oh, my poor dear child; can you really be so gullible—so *leichtgläubig?* You should be kept under lock and key until you grow up," she scoffed. Her condescending tone was more than I could take. The storm within me began to rumble and roar, reaching a crescendo of rage. I slowly and deliberately went over to the same couch which, two months earlier, had held her tragic reclining figure. I picked up my music case and walked out of the studio and down the hallway for the last time.

"You leave now," she shouted, "and we never meet again. I am finished with you; you are ..." I closed the door behind me, not knowing what her final words were.

Tears of rage welled up in my eyes as I drove down Arenbergstrasse. Spinning around in my head, like dead leaves in a whirlwind, were the harsh words Usova had spoken. Was she telling the truth? Did Karl have a family? Was he leading me on? I quickly put these questions from my mind. He couldn't have lied to me. He couldn't have spoken those words of love which poured from his lips unless he meant them. I would disperse my doubts in the winds of fact; the sooner I confronted Karl, the better.

Driving to the Schloss, I found myself heading up Reitgutweg toward Eva's villa. Even though I knew she had left a few days earlier, I stopped at the first house on the lane. I couldn't go back to the Schloss until I had pulled myself together. I went behind the house to sit in the delightful garden, with its view of the mountains. I sat watching a large leaf float on the surface of the brook, which ran along the side of the property. I watched as it found its way under a little bridge and disappeared out of sight. Turning my head I could see the steeple of the church beside the Schloss. It was only a few minutes' drive from Eva's, but I wasn't ready yet. I sat there for at least half an hour, hoping her spirit with its wise counsel would wash over me, would tell me what to do next. I struggled to keep the malignant doubt from creeping back into my mind. If Karl had children, where had they been these last two months? Why had I not seen them? Maybe they weren't his. I was desperately grabbing at straws. No, that didn't make sense. If there were children, they would be his; but why? Why would he lie? If they were so important to him, why would he deny their existence?

The fact was, I didn't want to know the truth because I was afraid of it. How could my future happiness be snatched from me so quickly? What would Eva say if she were here? "Silly girl," she'd say. "Go, find out the truth. Don't waste your time agonizing over what might be." I stood up, calm at last. I would tell Karl of his wife's visit to Usova and ask him for the truth.

I drove through the courtyard and parked my car in its usual spot behind the stables. Entering the Gasthof, I noticed the Gräfin was behind the front desk. I quickly retreated, hoping she hadn't seen me, and began to walk around the grounds in search of Karl. In the garden behind the Schloss, I noticed some people playing *boules*. Looking closer, I saw it was Karl with three children, ages somewhere around seven, nine, and eleven. So it was true; these must be his children. I tentatively approached, not knowing what to do or say. It was then he noticed me.

"Is there something I can do for you?" He looked at me coldly, as though he'd never seen me before, as though I was intruding on their game. Gone was the velvet softness in his voice.

"Are these your children?" I asked, trying to sound as casual, as if I was asking for a room in the Schloss. "Where have you hidden them all summer?" My voice began to quiver, and I could feel my jaw tighten.

"They've been with their *Grossmutter am* Wolfgangsee." (Grandmother at Wolfgangsee) There was impatience in his voice.

"*Komm, Papa, du bist an der Reihe* (It's your turn, Papa)," said the older girl.

"*Entschuldigen sie* (Excuse me)," he said with a click of his heels and a slight bow. He bent down to pick up *a boule*, dismissing me as though I had been an annoying buzz of a deerfly in his ear.

I turned away so he couldn't see the tears in my eyes. Anger once more consumed my body. I wanted to lash out and strike him—to hurt him as he had hurt me. I felt somehow soiled, but mostly I felt betrayed, my heart squeezed and wrung dry like an old rag. I walked quickly past the front desk and up the stairs of the stables. I didn't stop to notice whether the Gräfin was still at her post. I threw my suitcase onto the still unmade bed, which only hours before had heard ardent promises of everlasting love.

How quickly love can turn to hate. I hated him for taking advantage, for robbing me of my innocence, for crushing my oh-so-tender heart. Trust, from now on, would always be replaced by doubt. I put enough schillings to cover the week's rent on the little table beside the bed, not wanting to confront the Gräfin at the desk, and left.

Following the Salzach River on to Linzer Bundes Strasse, I wasn't sure what to do next. I was like a rudderless boat turned loose in a turbulent sea, struggling to stay afloat. I only knew I had to get as far away as I could from this man who had so callously played upon my emotions. I longed to go home, for there was nothing now to keep me in Salzburg. I was finished with Usova, or rather, she with me. Unfortunately, I had promised a student of Eva's I would drive her as far as Paris. At the moment, she was in Italy and couldn't be reached. She would be back in Salzburg in a few days to pick up her things. I would have to remain somewhere until then.

My car seemed to be driving itself. I had no idea where it was taking me, nor did I care. At the outskirts of Salzburg, I noticed a road sign: "Fuschlsee twenty kilometers." Fuschlsee was a place I knew well. I had frequently swum in the lake on hot sultry days with the Tattles, Ray, and his wife. There was a Schloss built into the mountain cliff overlooking the west end of the lake. It had recently been turned into a hotel. The owners never seemed to mind if we swam off their dock as long as we had lunch in their restaurant first. It was a beautiful setting with paths through the woods surrounding the long narrow lake. We used to idle away many a pleasant afternoon walking around the grounds. Maybe they could put me up for the remainder of my stay. I drove down the picturesque, winding, wooded lane and parked near the front entrance to the Schloss. Getting out of the car, I saw that threatening clouds were gathering overhead. The air, too, felt like a storm was brewing. There was nobody in sight, no cars parked anywhere, all seemed deserted. Approaching the large front doors, I noticed a sign, *Heute Betriebsruhe*. No wonder there was no one around; the hotel was closed. Disappointed, I began wandering aimlessly down to the lake and through the woods. I must have walked over a kilometre when the gathering storm finally burst, discharging sheets of water.

By the time I got back to the car, I was dripping from head to foot. I took my suitcase from the trunk, got into the car, and, with difficulty, changed into the warmest clothes I could find. By now, darkness had closed in, and I was tired, cold, and hungry. I hadn't eaten since breakfast. The events of the day had begun to take their toll. Miserable in both body and spirit, like a wounded animal, all I wanted to do was crawl away and hide. I curled up in the back seat of my little Hillman and began to sob.

I must have drifted off to sleep, for when I awoke, the first thin thread of scarlet had split the night on the eastern horizon. Soon a crimson streak of sunlight shone on the tower of the Schloss, making it glow as if on fire. I must have dozed once more, for the next time I awoke, it was bright sunshine. I tried to move my body and found it ached from head to foot from the cramped position it had been forced to endure all night. My head and throat throbbed; I felt terrible. The singers' scourge, another cold! Gradually, my thoughts gathered into focus. I remembered I had promised the Tattles I would take them to the station that morning. They were leaving for Munich on the ten o'clock train, and it was now eight.

I arrived at Rainerstrasse around nine o'clock. Frau Kurtz took one look at me and exclaimed in horror, "*Du siest sehr krank aus. Die Sache gefällt mir nicht* (You are sick. I don't like the way you look).

I must have looked as sick as I felt. When she discovered I had left Schloss Augen, she insisted I take the Tattles' place and move in with her and her husband so she could take care of me.

After driving the Tattles to the station, I went back to Rainerstrasse and crashed. Frau Kurtz was as good as her word. For four days, she nursed me back to health.

Before I left Salzburg, my one concern was, should I apologize to Usova? Naturally she had been correct in all she said; I had been stupid and naïve, but did she have to be so cruel and unfeeling? "No," I thought. "I have had enough of Svetlana Usova. Now is the time to sever the chain; to break free and fly with my own wings."

7

New York—Back in Usova's Clutches

My relationship with Svetlana Usova did not end that summer in Salzburg, for she had spun her web of dependency well. I had been totally caught up in her tight threads of silk, believing that only she had the keys to open those locked doors I would soon have to face. After all, she knew everyone connected with the world of opera. I felt, too, that only she could nurture my voice to its greatest potential.

I was about to place the "Summer—1952" letters back into the shoebox when I noticed there were more letters. The top one was in Usova's large, bold handwriting.

New York City
September 7, 1952

Dearest little one,
   Why have I not heard from you? The Saison *begins, and all my teaching places are fast filling up. If you don't call your Lana, soon she will have no room for you.*
   No—I do not tell the truth. There will always be room for my little one.
   Richard will be in New York end of September to begin rehearsals for Boris at the Met. You will be here then, for you should learn the role of the Polish princess, Marina, the most important female role in Boris Godunov. *Richard will arrange for you to be at all the rehearsals. I will teach you Marina in Russian so one day you will sing the role with my Richard.*
   At the same time, I will arrange an audition with the director of the City Center Opera Company. I want him to know you exist.
   Wolfgang will be in Hollywood for a six-week coaching course and then he goes to University of Colorado. He will not be back until the end of November, so you will stay here with me, and we will work, work, work. I will use my forceps to pull you from the darkness of the womb into the world of enlightenment.

I wait impatiently to hear from my little one. Until then, let me embrace you with all my heart.

Your,
Lana

This letter was waiting for me when I returned home from Europe. Recalling the events of the prior month, I found it hard to believe what I was reading. It took years for me to accept that the tumultuous explosions of lava which continuously flowed from Usova's studio were included in the price of each lesson. They were but an extension of her mercurial personality.

I made up my mind that if I was to crawl back to Svetlana Usova's studio, it would be on my own terms. Engagements were beginning to open up in Toronto. I now had several minor roles under my belt: Third Spirit in *The Magic Flute*, Rosette in *Manon*, and Marthe in *Faust*. This winter there would be three performances of Menotti's *The Old Maid and the Thief* in which I had the lead role of Miss Todd.

Our fledgling opera company had recently broken from the National Academy of Music and had now taken on the grand title of the National Opera Company of Canada. It was about to try on larger wings, and I knew they had their eyes on me for bigger and better roles.

The first thing I had to do was decline the invitation to stay with Usova. While studying at Columbia University, I had lived outside New York City in Westchester with my teacher, and it had been a disaster. I was cloistered like a nun, cooking and keeping house for her in exchange for free lessons. My every move was monitored, and I was constantly chastised if caught trying to sneak a few moments of freedom. With Usova, it would be even worse.

I must have thought a phone call would be dangerous and full of confrontation, for on the back of her letter was scribbled my carefully worded answer; I obviously had no desire to stir the fragile pot or light a fire and make it boil.

September 15, 1952

Dear Lana:

I was surprised and relieved to receive your letter of September 7 when I arrived in Toronto yesterday. After our last lesson in Salzburg, I was sure we were finished with each other forever.

New York would be impossible until October. I have two performances of Faust *booked for end of September and, beginning in November, I will be rehearsing Menotti's* The Old Maid and the Thief. *The director of our newly formed opera company here has given me the role of Miss Todd, a big leap up the scale from Marthe in* Faust. *Naturally I jumped at the chance. As soon as I know my*

schedule of rehearsals, I'll let you know when I can get away and for how long. While in New York, I will stay with my friend Joyce as before, but many thanks for the offer of a bed. Some day I may take you up on it.
   I look forward with much anticipation to being again in your "clutches."

Until then, I am
Your "little one"

Eventually, I was able to arrange to be in New York from October 15–29. To find a place I could afford for those two weeks wasn't going to be easy. Joyce had let her apartment go, for she was no longer studying in New York. She said I should try the Women's Arts Club on Central Park West, where she frequently stayed. "It's cheap, and you can get your own meals. It'll do for a couple of weeks if you can stand the other things that go with it."

I asked her what she meant by the other things. All she offered in explanation was, "You'll find out." Because I was desperate, I accepted the challenge.

My memory has fogged over as to what happened next. I looked again in the shoebox to see if there wasn't a specific letter which would help me piece together more of the rich Russian fabric that had encircled me.

The next letter was penned by me to my parents, who, I now remember, were vacationing in Europe.

October 5, 1952
Toronto

Dearest Ones,
   I shall quickly try to bring you up to date before I go to New York tomorrow for more "enlightenment" (Usova's word, not mine). Madame and I seem to have patched things up, but I'm not sure how!
   The performances of Faust *in Windsor and St. Thomas last week were, shall we say, interesting!*
   In Windsor, the performance went off without too many serious mishaps, except when Faust was about to seduce Margarite, he took off up the ladder with such fervour, by the time he reached the poor girl's window, he'd gained so much momentum he couldn't stop. Instead of embracing her through the window, he embraced the whole backdrop. It came crashing down in a mass of confusion before they could bring down the curtain. In the wings, the director began yelling, "Bravo, Bravo! It's the first time I've seen a tenor show any goddamned temperament!" The poor stagehand, whose carefully set up scenery had just been beaten to a pulp, looked up at me and said, "Jesus, does he always get carried away like that?" I informed him that it was really quite a pleasant surprise to all of us.
   St. Thomas was another kettle of fish. The performance was in a Church. Believe me, it was quite something to be chasing the devil all over a church!

> *I must close now, for I have much to do before I leave for New York at the end of this week.*
>
> Miss you.
Yours, Jess

I remember we arrived in St. Thomas around six in the evening, unwashed, with no place to either warm our voices up or clean up. We were totally unprepared for what greeted us. The stage was little larger than a conductor's podium. There were no sets, few props, and no lighting except for the occasional dim bulb doing its best to throw its ten watts far enough for people in the back pews to make out what was going on.

When we saw the setup, we all sat down and roared with laughter—all except Max Fremstad, the director. He also roared, "This is no joke. You are professionals, and this show will go on." And on it went.

We had barely time for a partial run-through first to check entrances and exits, which all had to be changed. Someone had put two six-inch high wooden boxes, one on top of the other, at the side of the little platform stage to function as steps to the floor below. Unfortunately, by accident or on purpose, the smaller one was placed on the bottom. While chasing Mephistopheles around the choir loft, onto the platform, and down to the front pews beneath, I had to step on the boxes. The top one tipped, and I went flying, landing on all fours at the foot of the grand piano.

"I think you'd better try that again," said Fremstad, attempting to keep his volatile temper in check.

"It wobbles. It isn't safe," I protested.

"Just do it again, and this time don't be so clumsy," he commanded, chewing on his unlit cigar to soothe his frayed nerves.

I tried it once more with the same result, only this time I demanded someone investigate the problem because I wasn't adding more bruises to my already battered body. The boxes were switched and firmly attached to the floor.

Throughout the performance Fremstad hid behind one of the six screens, directing traffic, sweat pouring from his face. My first entrance was out of the minister's office. I ran through the front pews and in and out of the choir loft (where later the lovers committed their indiscretion). When I got to the platform, subconsciously, the earlier run-through must have penetrated deep, for before I knew it, I had taken a flying leap over the boxes, missing them completely. I didn't stop running until I was back to the safety of the office.

There was a review of the performance, with a few lines underlined in red ink, clipped to my letter. The underlined read:

Perhaps a concert version would have been just as acceptable, but it would have done away with the smooth comedy and athleticism of Jessica St. James in the small role of Marthe, and the audience would have been a great loser.

I remember, I left for New York two days after the performance of *Faust* in St. Thomas. I arrived at Grand Central Station around 10:00 PM, having boarded the train early in the morning. I hailed a cab with a high-pitched whistle, using thumb and forefinger, a useful tool acquired from boarding school days. The taxi came to a screeching stop. When the driver put his head out the window, all I could see was hair. I tried to imagine the face beneath all the brush, but I could find no point of reference except the tip of the nose. Chin, face, forehead were all covered with dark brown wiry hair.

"Holy shit, where'd ya learn to do that?" he asked.

My whistle technique never failed!

I bent down to pick up my suitcase and open the cab door, but the driver was beside me in a flash. He had the rough shaggy look of someone's pet Newfoundland dog. "Here, give me it. Anyone who can look classy and whistle like that, lady, ah's yer slave!" He picked up my heavy case as if it were weightless. Despite his obvious strength, I was surprised how gently and carefully he maneouvred my suitcase into the front seat. "Where to, your majesty?" he asked with a bow, opening the cab door for me.

Central Park West and sixty-fourth Street, I told him as I stepped into the cab. No sooner had I uttered these words when I had one of my sudden fits of coughing left over from the Salzburg cold a month and a half before.

The cabbie leaned across the front seat and pulled a small tin box from the glove compartment. "Here, try one of these. It'll moisten the throat and kill the tickle."

"Thanks," I gasped, ready to try anything. The minute the little black ball hit my throat, I felt as if I'd swallowed a lighted match. I though it might kill me before it had a chance to cure the tickle.

Like most New York cabbies, mine needed no encouragement. Verbiage started to flow like water in a fast moving stream. It began with the inescapable question, "Where-ya-from?" in all one word.

I took my time answering, frightened it would again bring on the cough, but the medication had worked its magic, the tickle had been replaced by fire. "Toronto, Canada," I whispered painfully.

"My mom's from Canada. Three Rivers, Quebec."

Soon began the account of his life. I noticed the taxi had slowed to a crawl. I suspected he wanted to make sure he had time to complete the saga before losing his captive audience. At this time of night, with little traffic, the drive to Central Park West should take ten minutes at the most. Happy to remain silent, I sat back and let him talk.

At age six, his mother decided he should be a concert pianist. For ten years, he struggled, but the practicing she demanded of him eventually cured him of any ambition along those lines. In his late teens, because of his size and strength, he was sure he was destined to be a wrestler, but he found it wasn't mentally stimulating enough. After finishing high school, he enrolled in the Art Students League to become an artist. This took more time and effort than he was willing to give; besides, he discovered he couldn't draw, and he didn't like starving. Friends talked him into driving a taxi because it was an easy way to make money. This gave him time to follow his real passion, opera. "I am now in the process of learning *efficient costal-epigastrium breath control*," he said grandly, stressing each word. He paused, obviously waiting for me to ask him what it meant. I said nothing. Then his expansive shoulders rose as he took a large breath and began a resonant even hum which lasted for over a minute.

"Now, try that again, only this time keep your shoulders down when you take your breath." I said, sounding like Usova without the Russian accent.

He pulled over to the curb and stopped the taxi. Our eyes met through the rear-view mirror. "Don't tell me you're a singer too?"

"Hope to be someday."

"Well-wa-da-ya-know!" He took another deep breath and this time let out a loud tenor sound that could have shattered glass. He had burst into a free rendition of the flower aria from *Carmen*. It was a rough, loud, untrained voice, but I could tell it had potential. When he finished, not to be outdone, I joined him in the duet which follows the aria. It ended in unrestrained laughter from both combatants.

"Lady, you sure have a gem in your throat."

The laughter had brought on another bout of coughing. "The only gem in my throat is in the shape of a frog," I croaked.

In true New York fashion, the few dark forms floating by our taxi never turned an enquiring glance in our direction. It was as if hearing opera shouted from a parked cab on Madison Avenue was a common occurrence.

When my cough subsided, the competition continued. It went from bad to worse. We launched into a dual rendition of the spiritual "Old Man River," ending in a heated argument as to whether the final note was a low *E* or *F*. He decided the only way to solve it was to find a piano; he had a friend who had a bar on nearby Lexington Avenue.

Arriving in front of a red, flashing florescent sign reading "BAR," he pulled the taxi over and got out with amazing agility for such a large man. He strode into the bar like a battleship in full throttle. Stumbling behind in the wake, I couldn't help but notice a slight list to the left. It wasn't a limp, just a lean, as if the ballast had shifted.

He strutted through the half-empty, smoky bar to the back. He confronted the unsuspecting instrument and, standing, pounded the E key below middle C.

"You see, it's an F," I purred.

He sat on the bench, swung his legs around to face the keys, and, with grand bravura, swept into the introduction to the long, second act duet from Saint-Saens' *Sampson and Delilah*. I was astonished he knew the music from memory.

"Come on, let's have some fun," he said.

When he began to sing, he looked like an animated bear trying to shake flies from its nose. *"En ces lieux, malgré moi, m' ont ramené mes pas,"* he began in credible French, his powerful tenor voice immediately demanding silence in the bar. I joined in, *"C'est toi, c'est toi, mon bien aimé."*

His piano accompaniment was sparse but adequate as we hammed our way through the long duet. We soon emptied the bar. Our vocal gymnastics had left us with a definite thirst. Two free drinks later and many blocks further, I was let out at my destination. The usual ten minute drive from Grand Central Station took over an hour.

"This is it," said my hairy friend.

I'd have to take his word for it, for I could see no number anywhere. He had stopped in front of what appeared to be a dark alley with a faint light at the end of it. I leaned over the back of the front seat. "What do I owe you?" The meter read forty dollars; he'd forgotten to turn it off while we were in the bar.

"Nothing," he said. "I should be paying you. It's not every day I have the chance to sing with a future Madame Flagstad."

Getting out of the taxi, he went around to the passenger side, took out my suitcase and started down the alley. I followed. We had gone about fifty feet when we came to French doors. Above them was a big arched window. The only light came from the vestibule inside. Over the entrance was a large smoked-glass half globe, fanning out over the potted Japanese junipers on either side. The effect was one of a fashionable apartment building. Joyce never ceased to amaze me; always crying poor, but always managing to find a quality place to live.

My companion took my suitcase inside and dropped it in front of the elevators opposite the entrance. He took my hand and planted a hairy kiss on its back, looked ardently into my eyes, and whispered, "Till we meet again." He let go of my hand and in seconds was out the French door. "See ya at the Met," he called over his shoulder as he disappeared down the alley.

It never occurred to me to ask his name, nor he mine; somehow it didn't seem to matter. It was just one of those special moments.

I stood for a time to get my bearings. There was a sign on the elevator to the right, "Out of order." By the indicators above the elevators, the one to the left was for the odd floors, the one to the right, the even. This meant I would have to walk up four floors to the Women's Arts Club, apartment number forty-eight.

The small lobby was simple but clean. There was an ordinary light fixture hanging overhead. There were matching wall sconces on the two side walls and along the narrow stairs on either side of the elevators. To the left, by the entrance, was a plain wooden desk with a gooseneck lamp on it. There wasn't room for much else in the lobby. I took a deep breath and began to climb the stairway to the right, dragging my suitcase, wishing I'd opted for a smaller one.

To live at the Women's Arts Club is to be one of twenty girls tossed together like a mixed salad into two adjoining apartments, sharing two bathrooms, a large kitchen with pots, pans, cutlery and dishes, and the landlord, Mr. Hicks, a bestubbled LOM—*lecherous old man.*

By the time I arrived in front of the door of the apartment, it was almost midnight. I was so exhausted I could hardly raise my hand to ring the bell. I was still trying to catch my breath when the door slowly opened a few inches, until the chain lock snapped tight. A staring, watery eye set in folds of what looked like uncooked pastry peered out from the crack in the door.

"You the girl from Canada? What kept ya?" The voice was low and rumbled like a gravel truck unloading.

"I'm very sorry, my train was late," I lied.

He lifted the chain off its hook and opened the door wide enough for me to squeeze through. He never offered to help me with my suitcase; I had to turn and drag it in myself.

My hopes, which had been raised by the attractive entrance below, were soon dashed when I entered the apartment. The air was heavy, as if exhaled many times; the hall dark and cheerless. The walls, ceiling, and rug were a dingy grey. In the dim light of the hallway, I was able to see the untidy form of Mr. Hicks more clearly. The most unnerving parts of his face were his pale, beady, staring blue eyes. In between them were folds of perpendicular skin, forming a deep scowl. The high forehead with its rivers of crinkly flesh was topped with wisps of white, feathery hair. The entire pale face appeared covered in layers of hanging tissue—under his eyes, jowls, and neck. Together, with the thin pursed lips, the effect was reminiscent of the hind end of a chicken in the wind. There was at least a week's growth of stubble on his chin. From the top of his head to his slippered feet, it looked like neither Mr. Hicks nor his clothes had seen water for months.

"You smell of gin," he growled as he shuffled down the corridor to the back of the apartment. I followed close behind. "We don't allow drinkin' in the Arts Club," he continued.

I remained silent. Mr. Hicks didn't appear to be the type who'd understand a few harmless drinks with a taxi driver.

He stopped at the end of the hall. The door on the right was open. When he switched on the light, I could see, with the aid of a single bulb in the ceiling, the room was small and oppressive. The walls and furniture were all covered in the same grey paint as the rest of the apartment and were well-chipped from years of hard use. "There are no locks on the doors. We're all friends here. We got nothin' to hide."

I later discovered he meant this literally, for Mr. Hicks' main pleasure in life was to walk into a girl's room unannounced, any time of the day or night. Getting dressed was a real art. If you couldn't find a sentinel to post outside your door, you had to make sure your clothes were put within easy reach at night so that in the morning, you could emerge from under the blanket fully clothed.

After Mr. Hicks excused himself and shuffled back down the hall, I took careful inventory of what was to be my home for the next two weeks. A mixture of stale cigarette smoke and years of foul breath hung heavily in the small space. I crossed over to open the window to see if I couldn't find a little sweeter air. Exhaust fumes floated in on a hazy cloud. A large parking lot lay below and in it was parked a menacing-looking garbage disposal belonging to the hotel next door. I was no sooner asleep when I was wakened by the crunching sound of grinding cans and bottles outside my window. It felt as if the walls of my grey cocoon were crumbling: the hungry garbage disposal had begun to masticate. I soon found out its appetite was titanic; it ate constantly throughout every night. Combined with the loud rumble of the subway underneath the building, it made a symphony of sounds not unlike many contemporary compositions.

Everyone was known to Mr. Hicks as "girl." I was told I had been paid an unheard-of compliment by being addressed as, "Hey, you Canadian girl." The club's only saving grace was that, as well as housing its twenty girls and Mr.

Hicks, the W.A.C. had an upright piano which no one used. I would have a place to practice.

It hadn't taken long to discover what Joyce had meant when she said, "If you can stand the other things." After my first few days there, I wasn't at all sure I could survive two weeks of Mr. Hicks, much less the nightly cacophony of sounds.

With the memory of my taxi ride from the train station the night before still fresh, I mounted the steps of Madame's brownstone on West Seventy-Second Street, full of confidence in my eventual success as an opera diva. My cabby had been a great boost to my ego.

There was no *Ray Darling* in the vestibule when I opened the outer door. There were no sounds of torture coming from behind the double doors of the studio when I rang the bell. Before I took my finger off the button, the door opened, and I was greeted with a wide, toothy smile as Madame pulled my face down to meet hers.

"Darlink," she said and gave me her usual wet kiss. This time, it was firmer and longer with more pressure, her lips fuller and softer. I instantly recoiled. She sensed my displeasure and took my face in both her hands. She looked into my eyes with affection I had never seen before. "Darlink, what must I do to gain your trust?" No answer was necessary for she quickly went on. "We will begin afresh. You will not question my authority, and Lana will be a little more tolerant. Now, let us see what you have forgotten." She implied that it would be more significant than what I remembered. With her arm about my waist, she led me to face the enemy—the mirror over the mantle.

While she walked to the piano, I looked at the reflection in the mirror of the now familiar studio. It was as impersonal and uninviting as ever. Only Usova's "wall of fame" and the photos on the piano gave a feeling the room harboured the living, not the dead. The faded blue couch in the corner looked more dejected than ever, the Oriental rug more threadbare. No paintings enhanced her beige walls. No pieces of sculpture adorned her tables. For what she charged her victims, I thought she could probably afford any masterpiece she chose.

"All great art died with Leonardo da Vinci and returned to life with Jackson Pollock," she announced one day with her usual authority. No wonder her walls were bare. Nothing had been created worthy of her consideration.

Sitting at the piano, Usova sounded out the usual series of scales. Fighting my reflection in the mirror, I began. I tried to concentrate on the sound to make sure that each note was properly placed in the cavities of my face, that I had the proper sneer when breathing in, that my jaw was without tension, my face free of a frown, my tongue flat. Before I knew it, my eyes closed to shut out the image before me.

"Open your eyes: Look at what your face is doing," came the sharp command.

"If I look at myself, I can't concentrate on the placement of the voice. I find it distracting. I don't see tension. I see tired eyes and smudged eye shadow." But she was not amused.

"You will learn to both see and feel. If your face looks like a corkscrew, you will sound like one." Then a deep sigh. "Why do you always argue?"

Nothing had changed. Usova and I were obviously destined to create dissonances, not harmonies.

I arrived back at the Arts Club around 7:00 PM after a quick, cheap dinner at an automat close to Madame's. She had given me a score of *Boris Godunov*; I was to look over the role of Marina in preparation for the next day's lesson.

There was no chair or desk in my room; the bed was the only source of relative comfort. I quickly got undressed and into my nightgown, leaning against the door in case Mr. Hicks should pick that moment to pay me a visit. No sooner had I propped myself comfortably in bed with the score open on my lap than Mr. Hicks appeared, his disheveled form framed in the door opening.

"You, girl, I have to search your room. The girl before you just phoned. She lost her gold earrings and she thinks she left them in the drawer of the table beside your bed."

Before I could grab my dressing gown he was all over me, reaching across me to open the drawer on the other side of the bed. As he lay on top of me, I could feel the hardness between his legs grinding into my groin. *Boris Godunov* fell to the floor beside the bed while I struggled to free myself from under his heavy, sweat-ridden body. Panic set in. At such times of terror, conscious thought disappears and survival instincts take charge, at least they did that night. Without realizing what I was doing, I went into my gorilla act.

As a young girl of fourteen at boarding school, I had visited a fellow student for the weekend. On the Saturday night, there were two extra couples for dinner, friends of her mother and father. For amusement after dinner, the father's two men friends began chasing us two girls around the house. One particularly fat and unattractive friend chased me into a bedroom and closed the door behind him. I was cornered behind the bed. Frightened, not knowing what to expect, I froze. When he came inching toward me with a menacing look, I went into my gorilla act. I bent over and ruffled my hair. Then, with my fingers scratching at my arm pits, I put my tongue between my lower teeth and lip and began to snort loudly as I lumbered toward him. His eyes widened in disbelief. He bolted for the door and sped away as fast as he could. He was careful to avoid me the rest of the evening, thinking I'd gone mad.

With the success of that evening leaping into my subconscious, I put my tongue in the appropriate position and loudly began to snort into Mr. Hicks' ear, which was close to my face. Most of my movements were limited because of his sprawling body covering mine, but with effort, I managed to free my hands and arms. I began to furiously ruffle my hair, snorting louder than ever. The reaction was instantaneous. The drawer fell from his hand, landing on top of poor *Boris Godunov.*

"Shit, girl. Whaddya think yer doin'?"

I should have asked him the same thing, but I only kept snorting, rubbing my nose all over the side of his bestubbled face. He tried frantically to get up, but his age and girth prevented him. I put my hands on his shoulders to assist and pushed with all my might, still snorting, my lower lip protruding over my tongue. Finally, he managed to get to his feet and stumble to the door. I thought to follow him and give him the full benefit of my creation, but I could see it wasn't necessary; he was already out the door. From then on, I had no trouble with Mr. Hicks. The fact was, I never saw him again.

A few days later, I was sitting at the table in the kitchen with another inmate, having breakfast. We were making conversation when she suddenly paused. "Say, have you had the earring treatment yet?" I began to laugh. "I see you have. How'd you make out?"

"We had a little *gorilla warfare.* I haven't seen him since, so I guess I won." I got up and gave her a demonstration. We were immediate friends. My notoriety spread quickly and, from then on, I was a celebrity. The rest of my stay at the club was almost enjoyable.

For two weeks, Usova worked with me daily, placing each note of the role of Marina carefully into my voice. The Russian language was strange to me and the consonants difficult to execute convincingly, particularly the '*L*', but as long as the vowels were placed well forward I was surprised how singable the language was.

The rehearsals for *Boris* were long over by the time I arrived in New York, and there was only one more performance of the opera at the Met. The run had been completely sold out, but Usova was quick to point out that, because of the goodness of Richard's heart and his clout, he was able to get me a ticket for my last evening in the city. I was relieved, too, that the promised audition for City Center Opera wouldn't take place because the maestro was out of town. I knew I wasn't ready to audition for anyone. Though my voice was improving with each lesson, I had yet to master the transition between the three registers. There should be a smooth ride all the way; that is, one must mix the chest tones with those of the middle register so that no discernable break occurs. The same applies when approaching the top register. The head tones were still a problem.

"Support, support," Usova would command. "Your diaphragm is tense; that is why you are having trouble. Lighten up the lower part of your voice; mix those chest tones with the middle register; think down when reaching for that high note.... Oh, my little one, you still have so much to learn."

I longed for the time when I could open my mouth and just sing, knowing the voice would respond; that I could play on it as I would an oboe or cello, concentrating on the music. However, as long as the voice was responding favourably to Svetlana's Svengalian treatment, no matter that she played me up and down like a yoyo, the toll on my ego was unimportant. I had to be patient.

8

Toronto—Meeting the Future Husband

Once back in Toronto, there were daily rehearsals for the upcoming performance of Menotti's *The Old Maid and the Thief.* I was surprised how easily my voice worked its way into the score. Any doubt that had again seeped into my consciousness as to whether I was in the right hands, quickly vanished. Obviously Usova knew what she was doing, for each time I came home from a concentrated dose of her sometimes bitter medicine, I sang more freely and easily.

Miss Todd was the perfect role for me at that particular stage in my development. It lay comfortably in the middle register, with few high notes. It was a one-act opera of no more than an hour in length. There was enough vocal challenge to satisfy my creative instincts, but at no time was I worried about straining my voice. Every note in the score was a perfect fit, and I was free to concentrate on forming a believable character. The opera was a bit of froth. I could have fun creating an eccentric old maid without having to dig deeply into her psychological problems.

The story was about a middle-aged maiden lady, Miss Todd, who becomes so convinced that a chance male visitor loves her that she enters into a career of petty crime in order to hold onto him. The piece was written for radio in 1939 and was made up of fourteen short scenes linked by the remarks of a commentator. This was ingeniously delivered by our stage director, Max Fremstad. The production was a romp from beginning to end for all four of us. There were two old maids, one young maid, and the thief.

In the beginning of the opera, Miss Todd is serving tea to her friend, Miss Pinkerton. Opening night, when I began to pour tea into the nearest cup, I noticed what I believed to be a dead mouse in it. I dared not switch cups, for the audience would notice, so I went on pouring and watched with fascination as the poor creature floated to the surface. "Here is your tea … how many lumps … lemon or cream?" I sang.

"Cream, if you please," Miss Pinkerton answered.

I poured some cream over what I now realized was a clever facsimile and handed her the cup, then poured a cup for myself. Miss Pinkerton picked hers up, her mouth poised to take a dainty sip.

"Isn't the weather awful?" I sang, looking up, waiting for her reply of "awful." She had frozen with the cup halfway to her lips. Her free hand had gone to her mouth to muffle a scream. With an expression of horror on her face, she took in a great gulp of air but her "awful" never came. Eventually I sang it for her, and her next three lines as well, hoping I was making some sort of sense as I went along.

There was another pause before I was again to sing, "Isn't the weather awful?" I waited as long as I dared, hoping Miss Pinkerton would pull herself together.

The conductor, who had no idea what was happening on stage, with a frenzied look nodded his head and, pointing his left forefinger at me, mouthed the words, "Isn't the weather awful?"

Finally, Miss Pinkerton composed herself and followed my "awful" with one of her own. We then continued on track until the end of the opera. The cup, with its floating captive, was put aside and Miss Pinkerton went without tea. I learned afterward that the director had placed the fake mouse there to test our mettle, a dangerous thing to do at the best of times, but doubly so when we were far from seasoned performers. It was the first of many pranks he pulled on us throughout my tenure with the company. His explanation was always, "No matter what happens, the show must go on."

Having yet to be burned by unjust and hurtful reviews, I eagerly searched out the morning papers at dawn to see what the sages thought of our performance. The only less-than-good review I scored was when one reviewer accused me of applying my makeup with a trowel. The others were definitely collectables. One said, "Miss St. James was the personification of spinsterly vigilance and properly sagged at the seams: and that I sang very well and my diction was the best in the show." Another, "Miss St. James' theatrical artistry and brilliant sense of the comic made my performance memorable."

My head spun with these adulations. At the first opportunity, I sent the reviews, air mail, to Usova and impatiently waited for her "pat on the head." If I had been temporarily puffed up by this flattery, I was soon deflated. A short note arrived a few days later.

December 5, 1952.

Darling little one,
  Don't preen yourself over paltry crumbs. How naïve you are! These learned people know nothing. If before the opera they have had a good meal in charming company, then you are the beneficiary. If they suffer indigestion, then you will surely feel the knife. These reviews mean nothing. When you receive your first unkind and agonizing one, you will remember Lana's wise counselling. You only must work harder.

Lana

How expertly she was able to puncture my fragile ego. She never missed an opportunity to cut me back to size and try to shape me into the mould she had carved.

I remember with the clarity of immediacy that what happened next completely changed the direction of my fast-flowing river.

The newly formed board of directors of the opera company had just hired an artistic director from Italy. The president of the board was giving a party at his house to welcome the new director. I was among eight company members invited. I was never comfortable on these formal occasions where I knew no one, but I felt it would be politically wise to make the effort to meet my future boss socially before working with him.

It was a large mansion in Forest Hill, one of the posh neighbourhoods in the centre of the city. The eight of us decided to go together in the same car, for at least we could entertain each other. We squeezed ourselves into a dilapidated four-door sedan.

The house looked intimidating as we drove up to the grand entrance. A liveried man came over to us to park the car, and I detected a slight rolling back of his eyes and a sharp exhalation of breath when he got behind the wheel. Entering the house, I could hear the sound of a ping-pong ball coming from the floor below. I knew that at least two of my compatriots were hot-shot ping-pong players, and I had cut my teeth on the game. Perhaps the evening wouldn't turn out to be as bad as I had previously thought.

Shedding our coats, we took one glance at the grandly dressed people in the large foyer, looked at each other, and headed for the stairs, following the sound of the ping-pong ball as children would follow the sound of the pipe of the Pied Piper. There were two men who looked to be in their late forties giving the ball a good run for its money. They were the only ones in the large game room. We watched, full of admiration, until the game ended. The man with the sparse head of hair immediately came over to us.

"And you must be our talented artists!" He called each of us by name before introducing himself. "I'm your host, and it's time you met Maestro Arturo Moretti," he said, indicating his opponent with a nod of his head.

Maestro Moretti had a swarthy complexion which accentuated his striking mass of silver hair. He had a twinkle in his deep brown eyes which his glasses couldn't hide. As one by one we were introduced, his face lit up in a charismatic smile, displaying perfect teeth. His lean, athletic body had the look of a young man's. When I extended my hand in greeting, instead of taking it, he put his ping-pong bat in it.

"Come on, let's give it a go." I could hear a distinct English accent instead of the Italian one I had expected.

He took his host's bat and headed for the other end of the table. While taking my place opposite him, I could feel a disturbing increase in my heart beat. I gave him back as much as he dealt, and a fierce battle ensued. The ball travelled back and forth across the net at breakneck speed, and I was aware of a strong magnetic charge accompanying it. I did everything I could think of to put him off his game short of stripping, but to no avail. His concentration and determination was unflinching. When his eyes weren't on the ball, I could feel their penetrating gaze sending electric sparks through every fibre of my body.

None of us managed to get upstairs for refreshments. We played until the young hours of the morning. The games were wonderfully competitive; we all played the same way—that is, with loud enthusiasm. It wasn't long before many of the guests from upstairs crowded into the recreation room to watch and cheer.

Throughout the evening, when not absorbed in the game, I found my eyes, against their will, being pulled in the direction of our new maestro. I watched while he captivated the guests with his quick wit and natural charm.

When the party broke up and we all were leaving, Maestro Moretti appeared at my side to help me into my coat. "May I take you home?" he asked softly.

Unwanted colour began creeping up my neck, flooding my face. Feelings that had first been awakened by the Graf last summer in Salzburg began to envelope me, putting me instantly on guard. Assuming he was married, I said off-handedly, "Thanks, but I'm with friends."

In the car on the way home, someone said, "Our new maestro is quite something. Too bad he's married, eh, Jessica?" I feigned indifference, but disquiet began to eat away at my insides, and I knew that something important had happened to me that evening.

Soon rehearsals began for the company's upcoming performances at the Royal Alexandra Theatre. Again, the role I was dealt had sufficient meat and potatoes to whet the appetite but was not too rich to cause indigestion. The Secretary in Menotti's opera, *The Consul*, was an important role but not vocally taxing. I had seen this opera in New York when it was first produced on Broadway. It was an instant hit, even with the non-opera-going audiences. Menotti wrote both the music and libretto; he took a contemporary theme and made it into a powerful drama. *The Consul* deals with bureaucracy in its most destructive form. When I saw it, I was so overwhelmed that it haunted me for weeks. It was as if I had been put through a threshing machine. I was churned up, spun around, and finally spit out, a complete wreck. I wasn't sure I ever wanted to see it again.

In brief, the plot centres on the Sorel family—John, his wife Magda, his baby, and his mother—living in a dictatorship outside their native country. John is hunted by the secret police as a freedom fighter, and when the opera opens, he has been shot and wounded by the police. He flees his home to get across the border into another country, leaving his wife, Magda, to get papers for the rest of the family so they can join him. She spends weeks at her country's consulate, trying to see the consul, but no one ever manages to see him. The others in the waiting room seeking help sit for weeks, months, sometimes years, filling out papers at the bidding of the unrelenting secretary. The action moves swiftly, piling up tragedy upon tragedy for the Sorels. The opera is cleverly crafted, with each of the characters so well defined that they leap off the page.

At the beginning, I wasn't sure I could play the role of the secretary convincingly and not become emotionally involved. I learned when you are a cog in the wheel, you turn with it; you don't see the overall impact of the drama, you are only aware of your own little space. At no time did the tragedy surrounding me touch me. Even when all six desperate people in the waiting room of the consulate continually face death for either themselves or a member of their family and are suffocating under the accumulation of papers to be signed; even when Magda, in desperation, breaks down and sings her heart-rending Papers Aria to the secretary, I still managed to remain indifferent while the whole theatre was afloat in tears.

Still, the role had its challenges. The secretary is on stage throughout two of the three acts. Although not always singing, she must remain busy, getting on with whatever a competent secretary has to get on with. The sound of the typewriter was an important part of the action in the consulate scenes. It had to be heard over the orchestra even before the curtain rose. Having never learned to type, I had to practice to bring my fingers up to what was considered a believable speed, touching the keys at random. Many times I would get going so fast the keys would jam. This caused no end of problems for our conductor during the dress rehearsal, for frequently he had to stop the orchestra while I extricated the mess.

"You'd better go home and learn to type before opening night; this is costing us time and money," he ultimately said in disgust.

Fremstad did a brilliant job of both casting and directing. We were a homogenous group of thirteen, all loving the roles we were portraying and determined they would be as powerful and gut-wrenching as the composer meant them to be. There was one exception, which turned out to be a bit of a trial. Most of us were well-acquainted, having frequently worked together over the past two years. One woman, playing a minor role in the consulate scene, was a newcomer from Europe, a stranger to us all. In looks and type, she was perfect, but unfortunately she didn't sing well and seldom knew her music. She had the arrogance of the old world wrapped around her like a shawl and felt it her duty to give us free lessons in singing.

One evening during an orchestra rehearsal, I overheard her say to our leading lady, "Your tongue, it wobbles up and down when you sing. That's why your sound has a wobble. You must learn to keep your tongue flat." She proceeded to demonstrate with such a strident sound, it was as if dental floss was being pulled through the ears.

One time, while waiting in the wings to go on stage, she turned to the girl standing next to her and, in a loud voice for all to hear, said, "I hope you don't mind my telling you this, but if you'd use more support, your singing wouldn't be flat all the time." All of us sooner or later had the benefit of her expert tutelage. If she'd been able to practice what she preached, we might have accepted her advice with more grace.

We had a problem, too, with our maestro's circular beat, which we found disconcertingly hard to follow, never quite sure which part of the circle was the up beat and which was the down. Opening night during an ensemble number, I looked into the pit to see him frantically flipping pages of the score back and forth; he had lost his place. Ignoring him, the orchestra played on. On stage, we did the same. The critics seemed not to notice, for we all got raves and the show received five stars.

"*The Consul* shouldn't be missed. I saw it a few months ago in New York City, and this production tops it," one reviewer wrote.

From the beginning of staging rehearsals for *The Consul,* which took place in the large rehearsal hall in the basement of the academy, Maestro Moretti often put in an appearance; sometimes brief, sometimes for over an hour, silently watching.

When Fremstad was working on the first act which I wasn't in, the maestro would sit at my side, sharing my score. It made me uncomfortable, but because he was the director of the company, I could do nothing about it. And to be honest, I wasn't sure I wanted to. He seldom spoke except to say, "May I?" and "Thank you," yet his mere presence upset me. I was aware of that same electric current I had felt when we first met.

A week before the performance, rehearsals moved to the Royal Alexandra Theatre, and I no longer needed the score. Maestro Moretti would still search me out and sit by my side in the darkened theatre. One rehearsal he finally spoke. He leaned disquietingly close and whispered, "Tell me, are you frightened of me?" There was a wicked smile on his face.

I remained silent, for to admit "yes" would reveal how naïve I really was. A few moments later, he spoke again, this time as if addressing the seat in front of him. "I'll try a different approach. I notice you wear a ring on your third finger, left hand. Does this mean you're spoken for?" He said it as though commenting on the weather.

I was so unnerved by his question that I said the first thing that came into my head. "I notice you're always alone. Did you leave your wife behind in Italy?" The minute I said it, I wished I could collect the words and shove them back down my throat.

"My wife died two years ago," he said quietly.

If there had been a hole within a few feet of me, I would surely have crawled into it. I could only stammer, "Oh, I am so sorry."

He sensed my embarrassment and took my hand and squeezed it. "It's all right." He paused. "Now, I'd like an answer to my question."

I was still trying to collect myself after my stupid blunder, and I didn't know what to say. I could hear my heart pounding. I knew the telltale rush of blood to my face must be standing out like a beacon. He leaned close again. "Well?" he said, prodding for a reply.

I tried to be offhand to disguise my confusion. I pulled my hand from his. "Oh, you mean this ring. I only put it on this finger when I have to remember something." We both laughed.

Thus began a courtship that ended in marriage six months later.

After the opening night performance of *The Consul*, the cast was lined up on stage behind the closed curtain to meet the dignitaries who had attended the opera. There was the Governor General, the Lieutenant Governor, the Mayor. Even the General Director of the Metropolitan Opera in New York City was among the honoured guests. In the distance, I saw Maestro Moretti speaking with my mother, who had come from London to attend opening night. When she came up to me afterward to give me a hug, she exclaimed with delight, "Even Maestro Moretti thought you were wonderful."

I wondered if I should tell her he probably wasn't referring to my performance. No, I'd tell her later when the time was right.

9

Usova's Attempted Seduction in New York

In early May, a letter arrived from Usova.

New York City
May 4, 1953

Darling little one,
Yesterday I had lunch with the director of the City Center Opera. I told him about you, and he would like to hear you. I have set up an audition for Monday, May 20. You will stay with me so that I can properly prepare you. In the meantime, you will revisit Amneris' aria, Act IV from Aida, *"L'aborrita rival a me sfuggia," all Carmen's arias, and Orpheo's* "Che farò" *I will want them letter perfect from memory. I will expect you Friday, May 17, some time in the afternoon. Wolfgang will be away, so I will have someone else accompany you.*
Do not let me down, little one. It is very important at this point in your career that you step out of your little pond and swim in the oceans of the world. We are ready!
I embrace you with all my heart,

Yours, Lana

What to do? Three days stay with Usova I could manage, but was I truly ready for these large oceans she spoke of? Self-doubt began to swallow me up like quicksand. I was to be married in June and there were preparations to be made. Would there be time?

"Of course you must audition for City Centre. You must take every opportunity you can from now on to further your career. Sing for anyone who will listen," my future husband said with such conviction that my self-doubt evaporated.

My friend Joyce, who had been studying all year with Eva in Toronto, still got frequent injections of vocal technique from her diva in New York. As she now had a car of her own, I persuaded her to have another transfusion at the same time I was to have my audition so we could drive to New York together.

For me to arrive at Usova's mid-afternoon of May 17, we would have to leave the day before. Highway 90, the New York expressway, had yet to be built, and the old Highway 20 went through all the towns and cities of upper New York State.

Early Thursday morning, May 16, the phone rang. It was Joyce. "I'm just about to leave. See ya shortly."

She was as good as her word. My apartment was on the main floor of an old semi-detached house in a quiet street downtown. I was gulping the last bit of breakfast when I heard a deafening explosion followed by wheezing, sputtering, and squeals. I looked out the window; Joyce had arrived. I had thought when she said she had a new car it meant a *new car*. When I saw the old wreck parked in front, it was obvious that what she meant was a new car *to her*. Looking at it, I was doubtful it would reach the outskirts of Toronto, much less navigate the six hundred-some miles to New York. The front bumper was at a precarious angle, the front fender looked like it was made of corrugated cardboard, and there were generous sections of rust in the lower regions. Its pedigree was obscure, obviously neither thoroughbred nor North American. It was small, like a European car. It would be difficult to find a garage with the right spare parts if it should fall apart. With Joyce, it was always certain to be an adventure.

Luckily my street had a small incline, for we had to push the thing down the hill to get it going. I was relieved to arrive safely at the border two hours later, having had to stop for oil, coolant, and a fill up on the way. By eight o'clock that evening we were tired and thought it a good idea to stop for the night so we could get an early morning start. We were several miles beyond Schenectady when we saw scruffy-looking cabins at the side of the road. They were ablaze with lights, and overhead was a large flashing bright red sign, "Connley's Cabins." Behind the desk was a middle-aged person of dubious propensity. "Welcome to Connley's contraceptive cabins," he lisped cheerily. "So far you have the place to yourselves."

We looked at each other, not sure what to do next. Obviously we both had the same thought—there was no way we'd be sexually violated by this proprietor. "We'll take it," we said in unison.

In spite of the cabin smelling of stale cigar smoke, the bed springs sounding like Joyce's car coming to a noisy stop, and the mattresses full of what felt like rocks, the sheets were clean with nothing crawling under them. We slept well and were up at the crack of dawn, as planned.

I was relieved to hear the car start without a hitch. When Joyce yanked the gear into first, I sat prepared for the usual sudden jolt. There was a loud grinding sound! The whole gear shaft had come out of its box on the floor and was dangling free in Joyce's hand, as the engine came to an abrupt halt.

It took two hours before the Automobile Association could reach us and tow us to a garage in Albany that was capable of servicing our exotic automobile. I phoned Usova to tell her I would be late.

"No, darling, you will not be late. Lana has to go out at seven. You will take a taxi from wherever you are now and be here by six," and she hung up.

Joyce managed to drop me off at Seventy-Second Street by seven that evening before heading off to the Women's Arts Club, where she was courageously staying.

"Give my best to Mr. Hicks. See you Monday afternoon," I called as she drove off. I wondered if I'd ever see her and her car again.

Madame took her time answering my ring. When the door finally opened, I saw she had shed her usual uniform of a taffeta housecoat for a smart-looking bronze silk pant suit the colour of her hair. Floating over it was a long sheer duster of what looked like spun toffee which cut her oversized figure in half. She had a paddy green taffeta scarf matching her large emerald earrings and the eye shadow on her prominent eyelids.

"Hurry and change, little one, we must leave in fifteen minutes. One of my children is singing in *Fledermaus* at the Met; I promised I would be there for her. We mustn't be late." It was obvious she was struggling to control the annoyance in her voice.

What could I change into; I had nothing that wouldn't pale beside her grand ensemble. I had brought only a small overnight case. Thank God I had at the last minute thrown in my simple black dress and a couple of scarves.

Our seats were, of course, in one of the more prominent boxes in the house. It was the Gala Closing of the Met season. The program included Act I of *Madam Butterfly* and Act III of *La Bohème*, both by Puccini, and Act II of Strauss's *Die Fledermaus*. Since Usova's "child" was singing Rosalinda in *Fledermaus*, Madame disappeared backstage during the second intermission to give the girl courage, reappearing in time to be noticed as the curtain went up. I had never seen *Die Fledermaus,* so I had no idea what to expect. The part of Prince Orlofsky was sung by Rise Stevens, a role I would later take on. Orlofsky is one of the many trouser roles generally sung by a mezzo-soprano. Stevens was rightfully thought to be one of the greatest exponents of this role. This statuesque woman played the role of the eccentric Russian prince to perfection with believable elegance. Usova's pupil was charming and sang beautifully as Rosalinda, but Orlofsky dominated the scene.

I was dragged backstage afterward while Usova did her thing. She knew everyone and, as in Salzburg, she switched effortlessly back and forth between Italian, German, French, Spanish, and English, each language sounding like Russian. We were all crowded together on the stage and, from my perch behind the grand circular staircase in Prince Orlofsky's palace, I watched with admiration as she circulated with ease through the white ties and beautiful gowns.

I wasn't the least surprised when, in the taxi on the way back to the apartment, Usova began to lash out at the inadequacies of Prince Orlofsky's performance. After all, Miss Stevens had never come to Usova for help.

When I first arrived at Madame's apartment earlier in the evening, I'd had no time to look around before quickly changing. I knew the studio well but I had only glimpsed the rest of the apartment through the arch where I had first seen the impressive figure of Richard Alexander. My designated bedroom was Usova's absent husband's. It was dark and impersonal, the furniture looking as though it had been purchased from a recycling store on Second Avenue. Even though the room was generous in size, it appeared crowded with the massive dark furniture. On the beige wall behind the oversized desk was Wolfgang's *Hall of Fame*, photos of him with the famous singers he had accompanied. The photos were less formal than Usova's in the studio, for the artists were standing beside the piano, their attention focused on the music and not on showing a generous mouthful of teeth for the camera. They were all inscribed with effusive phrases ending with, "Gratefully yours."

A large armoire and a dresser took up most of the other three walls, with a double bed squeezed in between. En suite was a small, old fashioned bathroom with a pedestal basin, a toilet with an overhead tank and chain, and a small shower stall. I found myself wondering how many years both Madame and her husband had lived here. Some day I must ask her!

I was exhausted from the long drive down and the stimulating evening with no sustenance. The bed looked particularly inviting, and I crashed, remembering nothing until I woke to the sounds of a soprano voice navigating the hemisphere. I drifted off again until a baritone took over. I looked at my watch. Ten o'clock. I was to work with Usova at eleven, and I was starving from my fast of the day before; I would have to move quickly. The only things I could find to eat in the old-fashioned, dimly lit kitchen were a few bagels on the counter under a glass cover and some juice in the fridge. The kitchen was immaculate and looked as if it was seldom used for cooking. The stove looked ancient and untouched. I bolted down my meager fare and emerged from out of the archway on the stroke of eleven when the singing stopped.

After a few warm-up scales, we began the "torture," ending with Amneris's aria. The sound flowed freely. I had expected the long, tiring drive and late night to have taken their toll on my voice, but the diaphragm kicked in immediately. The throat of a singer is always the first place to show fatigue. If one is tired and the lower pelvic muscles are not working properly, the support of the diaphragm goes, the throat tightens, and the sound becomes strained.

"Well, *finally*, this is singing," Madame said. As usual, her praise was well-disguised. We had worked hard for two hours, and my voice wasn't the least bit tired. It felt great!

"I have two lessons you should hear this afternoon. You will walk a little, rest a little, and tonight we will go to City Center to hear my child in Rossini's *La Cenerentola*, a role you should learn." As is her wont, I was programmed like a mechanical doll.

Sunday morning, Usova drilled me technically for an hour. After a light lunch of a bagel and coffee, we worked with the accompanist. My hard preparatory work back in Toronto paid off. I never had to think what came next; words and phrases flowed automatically. I was able to put myself unreservedly into her expert hands. I never questioned her meaning or authority, and she gave freely of her irrefutable knowledge and concentration. Under her intense scrutiny, my voice opened like a vibrant rose. Even the sometimes troublesome upper register responded to her gentle cajoling. I became alive with an almost sensual pleasure; my body and voice were one. At that moment, I had no doubt that my sole purpose in life was to sing, with Usova as my mentor. When we finished Amneris's aria, there was silence. From where she stood behind the piano, she dismissed the accompanist, telling him to meet me in front of Studio 3, on the eighth floor in the back of Carnegie Hall at ten o'clock next morning, and to be sure not to be late.

She waited until he had left then slowly walked over to me. She took both my hands and, with tears in her eyes, she began gently, "You see what can happen when you don't question your Lana. Darlink, I am so proud of you." And this time, I knew she meant it. Still holding my hands, she went on in her usual authoritative way. "I will again be going to Salzburg to be with my festival children. I will expect you to be there with me so I can prepare you for what will surely come your way next season. If you sing the audition tomorrow as you have just sung I'm sure you will captivate the director."

I had never thought beyond this weekend! "Oh, Lana, I … I wanted to tell you but … but I was afraid. I didn't know how you would take it." The words came out, tumbling all over each other. "In July I plan ... that is ... I'm to be married. He's ..." I got no further.

She dropped my hands as if they were two dead crows. Her eyes were slits of bright green ink and from them spewed the frightening sparks I knew so well. I had again ignited a bomb. "*Basta!*" Enough. Her voice had the ring of steel. She turned and, without another word, her body rigid with anger, she went through the archway into the back of the apartment. I heard her bedroom door slam shut.

I sat on the piano bench, unsure what to do next. If I went for a walk as she had suggested, how would I get back into the apartment without confronting her? I wasn't sure how long it would take the fire under the boiling pot to quiet down. It was only minutes before I heard her bedroom door open, and she appeared in the archway. "Here is a key. You may need it." Her words sounded flat and indifferent. She put the key on the table beside her and retreated into the darkness behind.

For the next few hours, I walked north on Riverside Drive, occasionally stopping to watch children playing in the park that runs between Riverside and the Hudson River. It was a beautiful afternoon. The sun was making ribbons of diamonds dancing on the river. The park was ablaze with clumps of tulips in full bloom. When I became tired, there were benches where I could sit and watch the large boats and barges drift slowly down the river. By the time I reached Riverside Church, my watch said six o'clock. Close by was International House, where I had lived for two years. They had a cafeteria where I could get something to eat.

All this time my thoughts were whirling around in my head like an eddying river that never goes anywhere, and I would always end up back at square one, how to deal with this difficult woman? The wonderful intensity of my lesson had so inspired me that I was again determined to make our troubled relationship work, for I knew I needed her. I had to become a stone which the turbulent waters would easily wash over without wearing it down. I went back to the apartment, determined anew to find a way around her overwhelming possessiveness and still maintain control over my own life.

I let myself into the apartment, but Madame was nowhere to be seen. I went to the back and saw her bedroom door was open and knew she must be out. I was relieved not to have to face her; I wasn't ready for another confrontation. On the other hand, I knew sooner or later I'd have to try to convince her that my upcoming marriage would be an asset not a detriment to my career.

I went to my room and slowly undressed. I took my music out of my briefcase and got into bed. It would be a good idea to run through all of it again in preparation for the next morning's audition. By ten that night, Madame still hadn't returned. I switched off the light.

Suddenly I awoke from a deep sleep to find Usova staring down at me. She stood silently by the bed, not moving. In her white négligé over her short, stout body, her white face devoid of makeup and her red hair hanging loose over her shoulders, she appeared to be a supernatural apparition. With my sleep-filled eyes, I gazed at her in horror.

"You are very beautiful in your sleep." Her deep Russian voice was soft and gentle, like the sound of a cello. She sat down on my bed and leaned over me, her large, heavy breasts pressing down on my chest. I could hardly breath. When her long hair fell on my face she brushed it aside and gently stroked my cheek. Her face was so close to mine I could feel the warmth of her breath on my mouth. "I love you, little one. You must believe I want only the best for you."

Instinctively, I raised my hand to put space between us. She sat back and took hold of it, raising it to her lips, pressing them into my palm. I pulled my hand free, recoiling in fear and terror.

"Yes, Lana, but surely you …" I began to protest, trying to disguise the intense revulsion I was feeling.

She put a finger to my lips. "No—not another word until I am finished." Then, with cajoling words, in an effort to seduce me, she went on. "When you walked into my studio a year ago a frightened and innocent child knowing nothing of the art of singing or even the world about you, I felt fate had sent you to me. You sang monstrously, but there was about you an excitement that bewitched me."

I lay staring at her, not knowing what to do or say. I could only gape in disbelief.

"Yes, my dearest little one, you bewitched me. That first week, when I saw how well you worked and how quickly you improved, I saw in you the career that could have been mine if fate had dealt me better cards. I decided right then I would make of you the star I should have been had my health and my little peasant body been different." She looked hard into my eyes. "To do this, I need your help."

By now I was sitting up, more frightened than ever, not knowing where this was leading. She took both my hands, emphasizing each word with a squeeze. "You must be willing to work, work, work, and make many sacrifices. You will give yourself totally to Lana and trust her. When you sing poorly, I feel as badly as if it were my own voice. When you sing as you did this afternoon, it sends a thrill of pleasure and excitement all through me." Again she leaned over me, her face close to mine, her words gentle and tender, pouring from her like honey from a pot, coating each word in her heavy Russian accent. "It may have been your voice this afternoon, but it was my soul that spoke." She softly kissed my cheek, caressing my ear with her wooing words. "Darlink, you must forget this man. For now, there is no time for him. There will be many others to take his place. This is a small sacrifice you must make."

Her dismissal of Arturo as inconsequential, someone easily replaced by another, quickly changed my feeling of fear to that of anger and repugnance. "I assure you," I said angrily, "he's not just any man. He is a brilliant ..."

She cut me off again and said in a patronizing tone, "My dear child, when one thinks one is in love, no man is just any man." Impatience was beginning to show in her voice. "You will delay this marriage for a few years. Sleep with him if you must, but your soul will remain with me." She paused and, after a deep sigh, continued, "I have always given myself completely to you, and I expect the same in return. For my sake—no, for both our sakes, you must wait and come with me to Salzburg."

"Lana, please ... please," I pleaded. "Will you listen to me just once?" I was becoming desperate. I must weave my way carefully through this field of land mines, for any wrong word could trigger an explosion. "You can't own me as if I were some prize possession. You have to give me space to breathe. I am eternally grateful to you for what you have done for me, but ..."

"I have told you many times," she snapped before I could finish, "I don't want your gratitude, I want your love." The contempt in her voice was chilling.

I took a deep breath to try to calm myself. For the first time, I believed I knew the source of her possessiveness. "I can never give you the kind of love you want," I said evenly and firmly. When I defied her before, it had been in anger and bitterness; this time I was calm and in complete command of my emotions.

"Then there is nothing more to be said." Her voice had the hollowness of resignation. Her body appeared hunched into itself as she stood to leave. Her usual proud carriage looked rumpled with sadness and disappointment. Without turning around, she walked from the room, her words devoid of expression, trailed her like a shroud. "You have hurt me for the last time."

The taste of victory was bittersweet. I sat in the darkened room as the tears began to stream from my eyes. My feelings at that moment were like a cloth made of finely woven guilt and pity. I wanted to call Usova back and take her in my arms to comfort her as a mother would a child. I understood now how much I cared for this difficult and extraordinary woman, feelings that had grown out of respect for her knowledge and ability as a teacher. I knew I had badly hurt her;

however, the sacrifice she asked of me was unrealistic and unnecessary. My future husband was as anxious for me to further my career as Usova was and thoroughly approved of my choice of mentor. It had never occurred to me that she wanted more than friendship; it now made any further relationship with her impossible. She would always try to conquer me. I would now have to struggle on without her and use, to the best of my ability, what she had already taught me. I would have to float free and hope the prevailing wind blew me in the right direction.

I spent a sleepless night juggling between what had taken place and what was soon to take place. The thought of my impending audition had begun to unravel my already fragile nerves. At the best of times, I found the pressure of auditioning gruelling; it always nurtured my garden of negative thoughts like a spring rain. I tossed and turned for what seemed hours. Finally at seven o'clock, I gave up all hope of sleep. I dressed, packed, dropped the key of the apartment on the table where Madame had put it the day before, and left. I was relieved to notice her door was still closed.

It was another beautiful day, the sun's rays generating warmth over the cool pavement. With suitcase in hand, I walked east on Seventy-Second Street to Fifth Avenue, down Fifth to Fifty-Seventh Street, breathing deeply, trying to untangle the knots in my stomach. I wasn't hungry, but I knew I should eat something or I wouldn't be able to sustain energy through the pressure of the audition.

The Russian Tea Room was next to Carnegie Hall; I hoped by nine o'clock it would be open. Thankfully it was! A cup of tea might help settle my stomach. The warm liquid felt good sliding down my constricted throat. I sat at a small table at the back of the empty tea room, close to the ladies' room in case my gyrating innards should suddenly rebel. To eat was out of the question. Self-doubt was running rampant through my nervous system. The thought of going into this audition without first singing a few scales to see if the voice was still there was like getting out of bed to run an Olympic race without first doing stretches. Perhaps the washroom would sufficiently blot out my vocalizing so as not to disturb the few patrons who had drifted in.

No sooner had I let loose with a few high notes than there was a knock on the door. "Do you need help?" I could see there was no other way; I would have to go into the audition cold.

I left the Tea Room and began to walk slowly around to the back entrance of Carnegie Hall on Fifty-Sixth Street. I still had fifteen minutes to kill. The accompanist was already sitting on a chair in the hallway in front of Studio 3 by the time I arrived. Soon I began to pace back and forth, champing at the bit like a racehorse before the crown derby.

"For God's sake, sit down. You're making me nervous," he muttered. It was a quarter past ten, and the director had yet to appear.

"Another five minutes, and I'm leaving." No sooner had I said this than the elevator door opened and the maestro stepped out. He was short for a man, but then anyone shorter than I, was short, as far as I was concerned. He had a thick head of grey hair that fell exactly where it should. His face was long, with a beautiful, chiseled profile. He looked serious and formidable, someone to be reckoned with.

"Sorry to have kept you waiting. I have only a few minutes. I have to be at a rehearsal next door at eleven o'clock." His tone was abrupt and unfriendly. He turned to the accompanist, who was standing with his hand extended expecting a hand shake. "I won't need you. I prefer to accompany the singers myself."

He took a key from his pocket, unlocked the door, leaving the poor man's hand in mid-air, and went into the studio. I hesitated, thinking I should thank the accompanist and say goodbye. I was about to ask how much I owed him when an impatient command came from within the studio. "Hurry up. I told you I haven't much time."

With little encouragement, I would have gladly followed the accompanist out of the building. The altercation with Usova the previous night had so upset me, I could think of little else. The director seemed to have the patience and understanding of a prison guard. There would be little chance of captivating this *gauleiter*. I braced myself as though ready to face the electric chair and entered his studio, head held high, faking confidence.

"How many roles do you know?" he asked. I was about to list off the eight *one-liners* I had done, but something told me this was not what he meant. He wanted to know the major ones, the important ones.

"I have performed Miss Todd in *The Old Maid and the Thief* and The Secretary in *The Consul*."

He gave a loud snort of disdain, clearly dismissing their importance.

"I know most of Gluck's *Orpheo*, all of *Carmen,* and the fourth act aria of Amneris in *Aida.*"

"The other three acts are just as important too, you know." was his brusque reply. "Well, come, let's see what you've got." He sounded weary and bored. I put my music on the piano in front of him as he sat down. He took a cigarette from a packet that had been left on the piano from the day before. "Hmmm—*CarmenAidaOrpheo,*" he muttered, running them all together. Have you sung yet today?" He took a lighter from the breast pocket of his jacket and lit his cigarette.

"No, I had no place to warm up."

He took a long deep drag on the cigarette. "I see. Well, in that case we'd better begin with *Orpheo*." He sounded resigned to a fate worse than death while the smoke drifted out of his mouth in small puffs with each word. He put the cigarette back between his lips. He left it dangling there and began the introduction to the aria. The smoke floated upward in a straight stream past his nose, past his hair, and into my open throat as I took a deep breath to begin. Aggravated by the smoke, my throat felt dry and congealed, with a lump the size of an egg lodged in it. My diaphragm became a limp dead fish rendered inert by my frayed nerves. When the *"Che faro"* escaped from my smoke-coated throat, the support from down under refused to cooperate; the sound belonged to someone else; it could have gravelled a road. I was grateful when he stopped me after the first few phrases. He took the cigarette from his lips and put it in an ashtray beside the packet, directly in front of where I was standing.

"Do I understand that you are a pupil of Svetlana Usova's?" I nodded. "Hard to believe," he said, raising his eyebrows and shaking his head. He sighed. "We'll try again."

I wanted to tell him it was no use; it wouldn't be any better next time. All I wanted to do was escape; go home, crawl into bed, and never sing another note. I watched as the smoke drifted up from the ashtray in a steady flow, covering my face with a heavy grey veil. I turned away before taking a large breath, hoping this time to be able to avoid most of it. He began the introduction to the aria again. This time the sound was still not my own, but at least it bore some resemblance to singing.

He let me finish the aria and then there was a long pause. He reached up and butted his cigarette in the ashtray, twisting it to a pulp as though making a statement. Another deep sigh escaped from his half-closed lips, making a hissing sound like air coming from an inner tube.

"Young woman, are you certain you want to pursue a career in opera?" He closed the cover over the keys and stood. "You are obviously so nervous that I have no way of knowing how well you sing." He collected my music and handed it to me. "I suggest you not sing another audition until you are better prepared," he said, opening the door and dismissing me.

I went back to the Russian Tea Room. The knots in my stomach had vanished, replaced by weakness and hunger. There was a pay telephone. After a man-sized breakfast, I phoned the Women's Arts Club to see if Joyce would be ready to leave immediately. She was!

Suitcase in hand, with a heavy heart, I began to walk north along Central Park West. My mind was a stew of inadequacy and despair. The experiences of the past two days had left me totally drained. I wasn't sure I ever wanted to sing again; I wanted only to get out of New York as fast as I could, back into the arms of my future husband to be comforted and loved.

10

The Wedding

Arriving home, I had no time to dwell on the fiasco of the last few days; soon I was to be married, and I had much to think about. When Arturo asked me how things had gone in New York, I casually tossed off the question as if it was of no consequence, "It's hard to tell." He never delved further; it was not his way. For my part, the sooner I put the whole painful business behind me, the better. From now on, it would be life without Usova—again.

At the end of May, the Metropolitan Opera Company was coming to Toronto for its annual tour. The company would be performing in Maple Leaf Gardens. Arturo was hired by the *Toronto Star* to write the reviews. The first opera scheduled was Puccini's *Tosca,* and Richard Alexander was singing Scarpia, a role for which he was famous. Because Scarpia is stabbed at the end of the second act, I wanted to go backstage to see Richard before the third act began in case he left early.

The minute we entered Maple Leaf Gardens, I sent a note backstage to the touring manager, whom I knew from opera school days, asking him if he could take us to see Richard during the second intermission. At the end of the first act, an usher told us to meet the manager at the stage door during next intermission; he would take us to Richard's dressing room. I hadn't seen Richard since last summer in Bayreuth. He greeted me as if I was family. When I introduced Arturo as my fiancé, he seemed unusually interested.

"Does Lana know you're engaged?" he asked. "Am I right to think she wouldn't exactly approve?"

I agreed she didn't, but I wondered how he knew. Had he gone through the same ordeal?

"By the way, did you know she'd had an operation?" he asked.

"No, when?" It had been less than two weeks since our altercation and she appeared healthy then. "Was it serious? How is she now?" I was surprised how concerned I was.

In Richard's usual way, he made light of it. A week before when he'd been staying with her, she had suddenly been stricken with acute abdominal pains and nausea and had been rushed to the hospital. The doctors X-rayed her and saw a large shadow. They weren't sure what it was and decided to operate. When they opened her up, they found an enlarged gall bladder and closed her up again without removing it.

"I suspect she OD'd on chocolate. A bad habit of hers," Richard said.

Richard had no sooner finished speaking than the tenor singing Cavaradossi, Jan Pearce, wandered in to say goodnight, knowing Richard would be leaving before the last act. When he saw Arturo he let out a ringing tenor greeting. "Maestro, what are you doing here?" He heartily embraced Arturo when suddenly, without warning, Mr. Pearce broke free, turned and bent over with a hand cupped over his left eye. "Damn it, my contact has slid up under my eyelid." Remaining bent with his head down, he flicked both lenses out with the thumbnail of his other hand. "Pain in the neck, these things but I'm blind without them." He straightened up. "There, that's better. Sorry! Now, where were we?"

Mr. Pearce spent the next ten minutes playing catch-up with Arturo, for they had worked together in Verona, Italy, two years before. At the same time, I played a game of hide and seek with Richard. I wanted to hide the fact that I had severed all further contact with Usova while Richard kept seeking information about Arturo; when and how we'd met. I said nothing about my last catastrophic visit to New York. It appeared Lana hadn't mentioned it to Richard either.

The bell signalling the end of intermission sounded, and the stage manager's head appeared through the open door telling us to hurry back to our seats. The third act was about to begin. "And Mr. Pearce, you're supposed to be on stage by now."

We said our hasty goodbyes and rushed back to our seats as the orchestra began tuning up. The conductor took his place on the podium and we waited. Five minutes went by and nothing happened. The conductor tapped his baton on the music stand and raised his arms to begin. After seconds, he lowered them again. We waited another five minutes. He again raised his arms and this time, with a down beat, signalled for the orchestra to begin.

The curtain slowly rose to reveal the flat rooftop of the Castle Sant'Angelo in the grey light of dawn. In the distance, we heard a soprano voice singing the shepherd's aria. The stage gradually brightened as Cavaradossi was led in by a soldier who guided him stage front, centre. With squinting eyes, Mr. Pearce stared out into the cavernous Maple Leaf Gardens, waiting for the prompter's cue. From then on, with the exception of shuffling his way with careful small steps to a table and chair where he sat to write his dying letter to Tosca, he stood with straining eyes, never taking them from the prompter's box. When he was finally led by a soldier and placed with his back against the wall of the castle to be shot, only then did he close his eyes and relinquish his stare.

When the curtain came down, there was a half-hearted clap from the full house. "How am I supposed to review that?" said Arturo, shaking his head.

We were later reprehended by the tour manager. The disastrous last act, according to him, was our fault. We had derailed Mr. Pearce's concentration and he couldn't remember what he had done with his contact lenses. They had looked everywhere, particularly in Richard's dressing room, and never found them.

"From now, on I travel with extra lenses," was Mr. Pearce's departing remark.

The next few weeks were a flurry of activity preparing for the wedding, which was to take place at my parents' home in London on July 12. Though Arturo and I would have rather slipped quietly away by ourselves, my mother insisted it had to be a grand affair. After all, I was her only daughter and this would be the first big event to take place in their newly-built home. It would not only be a wedding but a christening of the house as well. We compromised. There would be only eighty people in total—a few family friends, my parents, and close relatives. Arturo said he had no family. He insisted he arrived in Canada unencumbered by baggage.

As small as the wedding was to be, it would still need planning. I knew my mother would take care of food, flowers, and the photographer—the basics—but when music was mentioned, the very subject became mined with difficulties. My mother wanted a string quartet. My future husband wouldn't hear of it, for it would require making a selection from the ranks of his musician buddies. "Then what will announce the appearance of the bride?" my mother asked in exasperation. None of us wanted canned music.

The house had a large entrance hall with a sweeping circular staircase to the second floor. It was decided when I appeared on the landing above, my brother would ring the front doorbell announcing my arrival. My mother was far from happy with this arrangement and never would have agreed to it if she hadn't been in awe of Arturo. She had been a professional violinist in her younger days and respected his position in the music community.

My part in the planning of the wedding began with an appointment with the minister to discuss the service. He was from the same United Church where I had been christened. His first statement was, "Because your fiancé is Italian, I presume he is Catholic. This might be a problem."

"I don't know. I never asked," I confessed, feeling like an idiot. The minister's eyebrows rose in disbelief when I added that it didn't seem to matter. It was at that moment that I realized what little I knew about my future husband. I knew he'd been born in Italy, that he was a fine musician; that we shared our love of music, that his wife died three years earlier and that from the beginning, he projected an irrefutable chemistry that enslaved me. Those seemed to me to be the only things that counted.

Arturo had, in less than a year, begun to cause a ripple on the surface of the Canadian music scene. He was frequently engaged by the Canadian Broadcasting Company because of his extraordinary ability to sight read even the most complicated score. As well, the opera company had made great strides under his leadership. Not only was I very much in love with this fascinating man, I was also proud to become his wife.

A week before the wedding, a performance of *The Old Maid and the Thief* was scheduled. Arturo was to fill Fremstad's shoes supplying the running commentary. The newspaper reviewer the next day, appreciated the irony of the situation and wrote such things as: "it was difficult to picture the gaunt, grey-haired old maid who fluttered about the stage last evening as a winsome, blushing bride, but that's exactly what she will be in a few days," and: "Arturo Moretti, who did the commentary, described the hilarious antics of his old maid bride-to-be with great wit which added to the enjoyment of the production."

Finally the much-anticipated day of the wedding was upon us. The photographer arrived early. He sashayed in, followed by his young helper, who struggled with the copious equipment. He was the same photographer who had taken my baby pictures twenty-two years before. Mother decided there should be no candid shots during the ceremony; there would be posed pictures only. They would be taken immediately after the wedding, while the guests went below to the music room for refreshments.

The house was awash with Queen Ann's lace and day lilies. Since childhood, July had been my favourite month because of the roadside bounty it brought with it. Mother had sent my brother out into the countryside early in the morning with as many friends as he could ensnare to pick a carload of Queen Ann's lace. Day lilies were no problem; they grew in profusion in the ravine at the back of the house. By two o'clock, when the wedding was to begin, the house looked resplendent in its white and orange cloak.

As frequently happened, I wasn't ready on time. I had searched for flat shoes to match my champagne-coloured gown, for Arturo was slightly shorter than I. My mission being thwarted, I was forced to use fast-drying house paint, which I applied at the last minute, over my white flats. When I was sure the shoes were dry enough not to stain the carpets, I slowly walked to take my place at the top of the stairs.

Negative thoughts began to whirl through my mind. Doubts and fears were turning over like the pages of a heavy book. Was I really prepared to spend the rest of my life with a relative stranger, nineteen years my senior, no matter how much I loved him? Would I be able to live up to his expectations; be clever and witty enough to hold the interest of this brilliant, sophisticated man; be seductive enough to keep him from straying? With each step down the stairs, I clung harder to the banister, my legs feeling like soggy milk toast. I looked down to see my father on the bottom step looking debonair in his morning coat, winged collar, grey weskit, and striped trousers. His handsome, distinguished face shone with pride as he nodded his encouragement. My brother stood behind him, his lips in a Cheshire cat-like grin. Unbeknownst to me, Rob had decided his cuckoo clock would be more appropriate than the front doorbell to herald the arrival of the bride. When I was halfway down the stairs, the alarm went off.

CUCKOO! CUCKOO! CUCKOO!

The ripple of laughter coming from the drawing room forced me into an alternative reality of composure. When I reached the bottom step, my father took my arm. He had a wide smile on his face, and I could see he was fighting back the urge to laugh.

"It's not funny. I think I'm going to kill him," I hissed through my clenched teeth, pulling angrily on my father's arm while walking through the archway.

The sofas, tables, and chairs of the large room had been placed against the walls in order to accommodate the eighty folding chairs set in neat rows in the middle. My mother was not amused when Aunt Helen announced from the second row in her loud booming voice, "Hush, everyone. Quiet ... quiet. Here comes the bride."

I clicked into performance mode! With head held high and a forced smile on my face, I walked toward the front of the room on the arm of my father. The first person I saw was Arturo, his back to us. He was standing in front of the minister, the afternoon sun filtering through the picture window highlighting his massive mane of curly silver hair. After placing me beside my future husband, my father went to sit at my mother's side. Her aristocratic face had a scowl on it that would frighten a wild dog.

With a reassuring gaze, Arturo whispered, "I adore you." His words dispelled my lingering fears. I was sure my future happiness was secure in this man's hands.

The minister began, "We are gathered here today to join this man and this woman in holy …" I glanced sideways at my husband-to-be to give him a warm smile of endearment when I noticed a fly had landed on his broad forehead. I watched with fascination as it began to search his face for a succulent speck of nourishment. It went down his perfectly-shaped nose; hopped across to the glasses covering his heavy-lidded brown eyes; hopped onto his cheek bone and down the crevice formed by his frequent wide smile; went past the corner of his generous mouth and down his chin, ending by meandering all over his well-shaped jaw. Throughout the insect's travels, Arturo neither raised his hand to flick it off nor shook his head nor moved his facial muscles to frighten it into flight. He had schooled his features to betray nothing, giving the roaming fly free range.

The voice of the minister droned on, but his words were but vague sounds in my ears. Arturo's control filled me with awe as I watched, mesmerized. The fly, having taken its fill or been discouraged by lack of sustenance, finally flew off. I must have said, "I do," at the appropriate moment, for the next thing I knew, I was being kissed by my new husband and congratulated by my brother, the best man.

A stiff drink of scotch helped to fortify Arturo for the ensuing ordeal.

"Jessica dear, Maestro, this way please; time to be shot." The photographer giggled coquettishly at his little joke. "I've set up on the stairs. Now, Jessica dear, if you could stand on this bottom step, and Maestro, you go behind on the step above." The photographer wanted to make sure my being taller didn't spoil his artistic efforts. With a wicked grin on his face, Arturo took his place on the bottom step, while I stood on the next step up, towering over him.

"No, no, no," the poor man protested, shaking his head vigorously, stamping his foot. The next frame planned was with me sitting on a settee and Arturo behind, leaning affectionately over me. Reversing the instructions had the same effect. By the time we finished with the photographer, his nerves were in tatters. It was to his credit that he persevered and produced a premium product.

Many times over the past forty years I have taken the wedding album from its shelf and mused over the results, the colour still as fresh as the day the photos were taken. Arturo looked so sophisticated in his beautifully tailored white flannel suit, and so handsome without his dark-rimmed glasses. His sensuous lips were parted in a wide smile showing his perfect teeth, and his eyes twinkled with humour as he looked down at me from the second step. I looked so innocent, gazing lovingly up at him from the bottom step while leaning on the banister to diminish my five foot ten inches.

Returning from our month-long honeymoon touring the eastern townships, we began to have thoughts of moving from Arturo's rented one bedroom apartment near the academy. We wanted a larger nest, a house we could call our own. I had always loved the quaint historic district called Cabbagetown, a charmingly diverse neighbourhood in downtown Toronto, named for the cabbages that immigrants from Ireland and England once planted in little gardens in front of their houses. The decaying community had just begun to be noticed by the young and *with it* crowd, who were fast buying up the cheap real estate, spending big money refurbishing the much neglected homes. There was a place on Wellesley Street that had caught our eye. It was an 1880s Victorian row house that had recently been restored by an architect. He had put much thought and loving care into its facelift. The brick façade had been brought back to its original pink. He had left the rich-hued stained glass panel over the large front window and its diminutive replica over the impressive oak door. The place looked old, yet new. Luckily it was for sale at a price we could barely afford. We bought it and, in a matter of weeks, were happily installed in our new home with little more than a bed and a few tables and chairs. I spent most of the ensuing two months at auction sales buying up the biggest pieces of furniture I could find.

It was around this time that I learned from a pupil of Eva's that she was in the hospital and gravely ill. Joyce had told me while we were driving to New York last May that she was concerned, as Eva had frequently cut her lessons short because she had been in such pain. As soon as I could, I went to see her at Toronto General Hospital. She was in a hot, stuffy room with five other women. I was shocked when I saw her beautiful face sunken and lined with pain. She was the colour of stone, and her grey hair, usually in a neat bun at the nape of her neck, was hanging in loose strands, covering her pillow. She was asleep. I couldn't tell if it was Eva moaning or the woman in the bed next to her.

I had brought her a few daisies, knowing she loved them. Rather than disturbing her, I thought I should see if I could find a vase. When I returned, I looked for a place to put the flowers so she could see them. There was one large window which gave off little light because of the close proximity to the building next door. The sill was full of unattended, nearly dead plants, and flowers well past their bloom. The room was dark and depressing. I carried the one little chair on the opposite wall over, so I could sit beside Eva, and put the flowers on the movable table on her bed. I sat, wondering if I should disturb her. I gently whispered her name, but she didn't respond. Her arms lay by her sides above the blanket, and she was scarcely breathing, her face frequently grimacing with the pain that even sleep couldn't free her from. An occasional low moan escaped her lips as her head turned slowly from side to side, her beautiful long fingers clenching into a fist.

"Eva," I whispered again, "it's me, Jessica." There was still no response.

Looking at her, my mind drifted back to the first time we met. I had been studying in New York with Fritz Lehman, brother of Lotte Lehman, when he decided it was time for me to get my feet wet by giving a series of concerts in churches and school auditoriums in Ontario. Unbeknownst to me, my mother had invited Eva, through a mutual friend, to hear my Toronto concert. My parents were unsure if I had the talent to make a major career. Mother had heard of Eva's reputation as one of the foremost lieder singers and teachers in Canada; she wanted her opinion.

After the concert, my mother brought Eva back to meet me. I only had to look at her to know I wanted to study with this great lady if she'd have me.

"Yes, it's a raw talent, but definitely a talent," were her encouraging words to my mother.

From then on, there was never any question as to whether I should continue or not. Two months later, Eva took me on. She came into my unschooled head and lit a match.

Being ambitious and inexperienced, the first thing I wanted to study was Mahler's difficult song cycle, *Kindertotenlieder;* five songs about the death of children. Eva flatly refused. When I asked her why, her answer was, "Because they upset me too much." I later learned she had had a son who died at the age of twelve from tuberculosis brought on by malnutrition after World War I. She would never teach or sing the Mahler songs after that.

I was brought back suddenly to the present when Eva began to stir. She seemed to be trying to find a more comfortable position. She moaned, her face contorting with pain. I took her hand. It was cold and damp. She slowly opened her eyes and stared at me with no recognition. Finally, a faint smile came to her lips. "So you've finally come to see me." Her German-English accent was more pronounced than usual, her voice scarcely audible. It seemed to be coming from some far-off place.

"I brought you some daisies; I thought they might remind you of the field behind your villa in Salzburg. Forgive me for not coming sooner; I just got back from my honeymoon. We did the eastern provinces. It was fabulous. Arturo sends his love." I spoke quickly, trying to hide my guilt.

"*Liebchen,* I'm glad you came. I want you to have my Kokoschka sketch. It ..." Her words trailed off, sucked into the oppressive air.

"Eva, don't talk. I'll just sit here quietly."

Suddenly, with all the strength she could muster, her voice strained and determined, she blurted out, *"Nein, Ich werde nicht sterben—ich muss nicht sterben."* (No, I won't die. I must not die.) I felt her hand go limp in mine, as if her last words exhausted her. She remained still, hardly breathing.

"No, Eva, you can't die. We all need you." My voice broke as I fought back my tears.

Her eyes slowly opened, and she had that whimsical smile on her beautiful face which was so endearing to us all. She weakly took my hand again, her fingers trembling from the effort. "I'm tired. You go now, *Liebling....* Come see me again soon, won't you?" She let go of my hand and her eyes closed.

There was noisy chattering coming from visitors behind the curtain on the other side of Eva and behind me were sounds of loud moaning and mumbling. "Of course I will; I'll come again tomorrow. Eva, we've got to get you out of here and find you a private room."

She shook her head, "No, *Liebling,* it doesn't matter any ..." and her voice dwindled into a deep sigh.

I walked from her room, devoid of all emotion. I could neither cry nor feel. Even though for some time I had been aware I would soon lose this dearest friend and mentor, when finally confronted with it, the sense of loss was devastating.

She died the next day, finally out of her misery.

A month later a package arrived at my parents' home in London. It was insured and sent by special courier. It was the sketch of Eva by the famous Austrian expressionist painter, Oskar Kokoschka. Inside was a short note.

> *Liebling,*
> *I leave this, my most precious possession, in your hands.*
> *Enjoy it and guard it well.*
>
> Your,
> Eva

I was aware of the value in dollars of this famous painter's work. If Eva had sold the sketch, she would not have ended her life in poverty. Her long illness had siphoned off any savings she'd had. She no longer could teach, as her strength had gone. In her final months, she'd had to rely on the kindness of friends to survive. How very sad, this woman whose life had been lived bringing joy, inspiration, and learning to others through her exceptional talent, should end up penniless. Not a day goes by that I don't look at the Kokoschka sketch. Eva's left hand, which she always said was her only beauty, is stretched over her right breast, her shoulder bared by her unbuttoned dress. The artist had been known to be a collector of women. Had Eva been one of them?

11

Performance of Fledermaus in Toronto

The next letter in my shoebox was again in Usova's hand. I smiled as I read the large bold script. It was Madame at her devious, calculating best, consumed with self interest. Through Richard, she must have discovered my husband was in a position of importance musically. She immediately saw a new field to conquer handed to her on a large gold maple leaf. She could spread her tentacles of expertise across the border to encompass more of the unconverted. As a snake encircles its prey, she wove carefully in and out of each word.

December 15, 1953

My darling little one,
    I am sending you a wedding gift from my Russia. It's not much, but with it comes my affection and deepest love.
    Congratulations to Arturo. Tell him for me to treat you kindly but not to spare the rod. You will need a strong and understanding man at your side.

I couldn't help but laugh at this unmitigated hypocrisy, knowing full well how she felt about my marriage. I read on.

Your last visit disturbed me beyond description. Thoughts of it will not leave me until I put things straight.
    If you mistakenly thought that the love I wanted from you had anything to do with sharing a bed, let me hasten to assure you it did not. The love I want from you has to do with trust and affection only. As I have told you many times, I have no use for your gratitude or feelings of obligation.
    Your sudden announcement of marriage hit me like a truck traveling at full speed. I crumpled! I saw you throwing away a brilliant career, replacing it with a dull existence and sharing your future with a herd of wild pups. I felt I must gather together all the forces I could to save you from this fate. Never forget, God has bestowed on you special gifts. You are obliged to fulfill your debt to Him.

When I realized that nothing I could say would matter to you, I made up my mind to sever all ties forever; to turn my back and let you drown in your own pool. It was when Richard told me he had met your future husband that I knew you were in safe hands. You were naughty, my darling little one, not to have told me he was a brilliant musician, a man of considerable influence who could assist you in navigating the turbulent seas you are sure to face. Darling, I must meet this man of yours. We will have much in common, much knowledge to share. You are indeed lucky to have found such a one.

From what I hear there are many fine voices in your company, young voices which need nurturing, voices that should be protected from those in a position to exploit them. They will have need of your Lana's expertise. I will be free to come to Toronto sometime early in the new year. Perhaps your husband would arrange some master classes?

Richard told you of my operation. The inner torrent began during your last visit. When you left, my insides were in dreadful pain. I was rushed to the hospital close to death and cruelly slit open by those butchers. They could find nothing. It's a miracle I survived.

Dearest one, you must forgive your Lana for wanting so much for you. We will begin again and put all misunderstandings behind us. I will give you more freedom, and you will not question and doubt.

I hope there is still a place in your heart for your Lana.

I remember this letter was at the bottom of a small package delivered to our Cabbagetown front door in mid-December. When I saw the return address on the outside, icicles began to form in my circulatory system, sending chills throughout my body. With bitterness, I wondered what Usova was up to now. Could it be another attempt to woo me back? From the size and weight of the parcel, I thought it more likely a bomb which would blow me to bits when opened. I put the package at the back of the hall cupboard behind the coats. I wasn't ready to deal with this woman who seemed determined to eat me alive, nor was I sure I ever would be again.

The course I had been charting for myself since my last session with Usova had been wrought with doubt and insecurity. I had tried to replace her expertise with that of Arturo's. I thought he could keep me on the right track. His ear was equally acute and he had perfect pitch. I was sure he could detect the least stress on the voice; but could he advise me how to correct any vocal problem I might encounter? I knew he could coach me to make sure I was musically and stylistically correct, but was his ear sufficiently fine-tuned to problems concerning the voice? Besides, when our relationship began, he made it clear he would be my husband and not my mentor. If we were working together on the same opera, he would treat me no differently than the other artists. In other words, I was on my own. He assured me it was better for the marriage that way.

Music rehearsals had begun for the upcoming opera performances in February. I was given the significant role of Prince Orlofsky in *Die Fledermaus*. It was a role which suited me well. I was tall and slim. To be convincing visibly would be no problem. Although the main aria, *Chaçun a son gout*, lay high for me, I thought if I carefully placed the aria, note by note, in the voice, it should give me no trouble. I threw myself into the role with enthusiasm. The part is essentially that of a bored, spoiled Russian prince. It was easy for me to sound Russian—I had Usova's heavy accent firmly planted in my ear. There was much dialogue to master. To make the prince as authentic as possible, I began to artificially lower my speaking voice in order to sound more like a man. All went well until we began to rehearse in the theatre. To be heard in the back row, I began pushing on my vocal cords without realizing it. Because singing is an extension of speaking, forcing the speaking voice lower began to affect the upper register of my singing voice. I could feel my throat tighten while struggling to keep the sound even. No matter how hard I tried to support it, my voice refused to flow freely.

What would Usova advise? I kept thinking of my last lesson and how she had coerced sounds from my throat I never thought possible. I knew what Eva would have said. "Forget about technique. Go out there and search. Search within, and your talent will take care of the rest." I decided, as Usova was now out of my life, I would have to rely on the knowledge she had already imparted and follow Eva's advice.

Two required props for Orlofsky were a monocle and a long cigarette holder, both of which caused me problems. I was not a smoker, yet was required to smoke thin black Russian cigarettes. They were very strong. It took much practice before I could manage without breaking into fits of coughing. It was equally hard on the others. Because of the foot-long cigarette holder, the smoke drifted closer to their throats and noses than it did to mine.

The monocle was an even greater challenge; I had difficulty keeping it in place. My cheekbone didn't extend sufficiently to form a ledge for the eyeglass to sit on. At the beginning, to keep the monocle where it should be, I would scowl deeply in an effort to pull my shallow brow over it. Even then it would fall off at the most inopportune moments.

"Orlofsky, must you make those awful faces; you call that acting?" came the frequent comment from the middle of the darkened theatre during rehearsals.

Eventually I hit upon the idea of putting spirit gum on the rim of the monocle; just enough to make it tacky so it would hopefully stay in place yet release when I raised my eyebrow to make a dramatic point. Too often it would stay when I didn't want it to, and I would have to pull it off by its long black ribbon, taking a bit of skin with it. Sometimes the top edge would fall free, leaving the bottom of the monocle dangling from my cheek. I was thankful this never happened during a performance.

I had completely forgotten about Usova's parcel when, shortly after Christmas, Arturo asked me if I had heard from her since her operation. It was only then I remembered putting the package in the back of the hall cupboard.

When I sheepishly removed it from its hiding place, Arturo's face had that quizzical expression reserved for behaviour he deemed questionable and unaccountable. From a sense of humour hidden in the deep crevices of every fibre of his being, he smiled and asked, "How long has it been there?" Then he added, "Is it ticking?"

"We had a slight disagreement," was all I offered as an explanation while slowly and somewhat fearfully opening the box. It contained a solid brushed brass ashtray. I burst into laughter, knowing her aversion to smoking. Spinning around in my head were Usova's words when her sensitive nostrils detected the smell of smoke on my breath in Salzburg. "Darlink, you've been smokink! People in my studio do not smoke."

"What's so funny?" Arturo asked. "I'm sure it'll come in handy; besides it's quite good looking." Arturo was turning the ashtray over to see where it had been made.

"It's obviously meant for you, not me." (Arturo, more often than not, had a cigarette dangling from the side of his mouth, even when talking. It was his trademark.)

I was about to discard the wrappings when I noticed the letter at the bottom of the box. I began to read aloud the first few sentences. When I came to the part—"Your last visit disturbed me beyond description," I stopped and, folding the letter, put it into my jacket pocket. I'd read it later. "The rest wouldn't interest you," I told Arturo. He could see I was upset but, as usual, he didn't question my reason for not continuing.

Reading the letter later, it wasn't long before a wavy line of disbelief followed by a multitude of conflicting emotions took over. If I continued working with Usova, would she again try to swallow me up? Could she defuse her own temperament sufficiently to humour her ill-behaved pupil? The real question was, did I still need her? My recent vocal problems with the eccentric prince in *Die Fledermaus* assured me I did. The time had come to try and loosen the weave of misunderstanding that had tightened around our relationship, even though the cloth had been warped from the beginning. A letter was due! It would be candid, nothing hidden! Truth without malice—well, not the whole truth; I couldn't exactly tell her I didn't answer her letter sooner because I shoved her parcel behind the overshoes in the hall cupboard and forgot about it. Besides, what was the truth? I still wasn't sure.

I trolled deeply into my troubled sensibilities. How to begin?

January 5, 1954

Dear Lana,
   Forgive the delay in answering your letter of December 15 but with Fledermaus rehearsals and Christmas, it's been a very busy time, and I wanted to make sure I had a clear head before trying to dispel the many misunderstandings that have piled up since the outset of our relationship ...

There I go, immediately on the defensive; this was no way to begin! I ripped the paper up and watched the small pieces float airily down into my wastepaper basket like flakes of snow. I began again.

January 5, 1954

Dear Lana,
   Thank you for the ashtray. Arturo, as a smoker, greatly appreciated it.
   You accused me of not telling you about Arturo. I wanted to tell you; in fact, I tried to tell you, but like a bird about to take flight, I was shot down before my feet left the ground.

No, no, no, this is no time for recriminations. I scrunched the paper up and it joined the other bits in the basket. This certainly wasn't proving to be easy. I tried once more.

January 5, 1954

Dear Lana,
   It is my hope that we can continue to work together. I realize it hasn't been easy for either one of us in the past, but before we begin again, it must be understood that I need to have freedom to deal with my personal life as ...

I stopped. This approach would be sure to ruffle her feather boa.

After several more tries, each time watching the paper drop into the fast-filling basket, I decided I was getting nowhere. I'd give it one more shot and, regardless of the results, mail it. I'd put as much as possible in Usova's own words. I'd make it short and to the point—no more mincing around.

> January 5, 1954
>
> Dear Lana,
>
> We will begin again and put all misunderstandings behind us. I will try not to question, and you will give me space.
>
> The master classes you ask for are under the auspices of the Academy and consequently out of Arturo's control.
>
> I've begun rehearsals for the upcoming opera season, which opens February 28. I've been given the role of Prince Orlofsky, which I am enjoying greatly.
>
> Arturo joins me in sending greetings and looks forward to meeting you in the not too distant future.
>
> Love from your devoted pupil,
> Jessica
>
> P.S. Thank you for your surprise gift of an ashtray! Arturo, as a smoker, loves it.

When the impending opening night of *Die Fledermaus* loomed closer, I immersed myself ever more deeply with a purity of purpose. The prince gradually came bobbing to the surface, rising from the depth of my creative instincts. I crowded my vocal concerns into a shadowy corner and hoped I wasn't putting my voice in jeopardy. It must have been adjusting to my sometimes harsh treatment, for the stage director and the conductor were pleased, but would Usova be pleased? I suspected not.

The day of the performance, a telegram arrived.

> FEBRUARY 28, 1954
> DARLING LITTLE ONE WE EMBRACE YOU WITH OUR WHOLE HEARTS AND WISH YOU A WELL DESERVED TRIUMPH STOP ALL MY THOUGHTS ARE WITH YOU THIS EVENING STOP WOLFGANG SENDS HIS BEST WISHES STOP GREETINGS TO ARTURO
> LOVINGLY
> LANA

Opening night was an unbridled success. My reviews were cloaked in praise over a skeleton of caution.

> One of the most delightful surprises was the performance of Jessica St. James in the role of Orlofsky.—She drew all eyes to her and gave the part utter credibility—Gasps were heard when she first began to sing in the voice of a woman.—She mustered an impressively deep speaking voice but surprisingly

light singing voice and frequently sacrificed beautiful singing for characterization.

Another critic wrote,

> Miss St. James has forsaken much of her vocal talent to bring the role of Orlofsky to life and this she does with amazing clarity.

The cautioning of the critics about putting my singing voice on the sacrificial block did not go unnoticed, however, at the time I believed the sacrifice worth the wager. I was to learn that nothing is worth that kind of gamble. The singing voice must be at all times nurtured, pampered, and cared for like a precious, fragile plant.

Because of the success of the festival's production of *Die Fledermaus*, C.B.C. decided to do a telecast of the opera in May. It would again be performed in English and not the original language of German.

Having the television performance of *The Consul* already under my belt, I was familiar with the many difficulties of live television. I learned quickly, one is at the mercy of the little red light on a camera. In *The Consul*, the director had decided the secretary was a major player in the drama and, consequently, the red light was frequently searching me out, even when I wasn't singing. On the other hand, in *Fledermaus* I was surprised while viewing the replay to discover that the camera would often be elsewhere when I was singing my heart out.

The orchestra was parked in a basement two miles away. We singers were above ground in two separate studios, each in different buildings. We counted on the wills of a conductor and two directors to keep it all together. Despite all this, I enjoyed working in the medium and was far less nervous than performing on stage, even though the broadcast was live.

In order to be believable on camera, the powers that be decided the role of the prince called for a moustache and goatee. These were specially ordered from Hollywood. A few days before the broadcast, I was expected to rehearse wearing the extra growth to make sure it looked authentic. Each hair had been separately sewn on fine nylon netting. When I first applied them to my upper lip and chin and looked closely in the mirror, I could have sworn the hairs had a life of their own, living healthily off the nourishment supplied by my young skin. It would fool any camera an inch away. I was amused when I later heard, that even my father hadn't recognized me during the broadcast. He asked my mother when I was going to appear, immediately after I had finished my big second act scene.

This attempt at realism had its drawbacks. Frequently, when touring with the opera later, I was prevented from using the women's washroom by overzealous stagehands.

Soon after the TV broadcast of *Die Fledermaus,* I received a call from the music director of the Shakespearian Festival in Stratford, Ontario, asking me to audition for the upcoming performance of *The Beggar's Opera* by Kurt Weil. They wanted me to try out for the role of Mrs. Peecham.

As Stratford was close to Lake Huron, where I had spent my summers as a child, I thought it would be a good chance to introduce Arturo to one of my favourite haunts. I knew he would enjoy the beach and swimming, and I would have a place to lay my head if we rented a cottage there. I jumped at the chance.

I was determined this time to be well prepared. The better prepared, the less nervous. I couldn't afford another fiasco like New York. I asked a stage director friend to help me stage the three arias I had chosen: one of Polly Peecham's and two of Mrs. Peecham's, thinking it wouldn't hurt to prepare two different characters. I'd focus on the action so I wouldn't have time to think about nerves. My friend cleverly interspersed dialogue with the singing. He carefully blocked where I should go, when I should sit, when I should stand, and how best to deliver the dialogue. By the time he finished with me, I was completely at ease with both characters. I had no trouble with the singing; it lay in the middle range of my voice. I arrived at the audition full of confidence, secure in what I had to do. I was excited, my adrenalin pumping.

The audition took place in a large rehearsal space in an old warehouse in downtown Toronto. There was a small stage of sorts. I was greeted with friendly smiles from the three directors, one of whom I knew. Though there was a pianist at my disposal, I had brought an accompanist with me because my presentation was too complicated to try to explain to anyone I hadn't rehearsed with. I sang all three arias, one after the other without a break, for they kept nodding for me to continue. I acted through each number, moving about the stage as if in a performance. I was almost enjoying myself.

When I finished, they clapped and I heard even a brava. They called me over to where they were sitting. They asked me if I would be available all June, July, and August.

I nodded, trying to remain cool, my heart racing like mad. They checked to make sure they had my correct telephone number, assuring me I would be hearing from them soon.

I left the audition floating on air, sure I would be spending the summer working in this most prestigious of theatres.

A week went by. I spent most of it as close to the phone as my busy schedule would allow. Another week went by. Finally, I phoned the one director I knew. I asked him what had gone wrong; why hadn't I heard from him?

"We liked you very much but felt you might be difficult to work with as you seemed so sure of how each role should be played," he said.

When I was invited to sing a role in Offenbachs' *Orpheus in the Underworld* for the festival a few years later, I was grateful I didn't have to audition.

12

Robbed in Rome, Italy

In early June, Arturo asked me if I thought I'd be ready to sing *Carmen* the following February. There was a smidgen of doubt mingled with his optimism. He had come from a meeting with the stage director and conductor; they had been casting the three operas for the upcoming year, and both men believed I was ready. The operas were to be *Carmen, Don Giovanni,* and *Madame Butterfly.*

The idea of singing the challenging and taxing role of Carmen sent a sharp shift in the floor of my stomach. It began to rise then drop. My dream since I first began to sing professionally was that someday I would sing this role. My initial opportunity had been rightly thwarted by Usova but now, like a race horse kept in the paddock too long, I was stomping and chafing at the bit. Up to now, my career had been a series of tiny trips. The time had come to strike out on an exciting voyage; however, the uncertainty in Arturo's voice had lit a flame of doubt, which I quickly tried to stamp out with the memory of the stories told to me by my mother.

When I was two years old and still hadn't taken my first step, a friend had said to my mother, "Alice, I'm so sorry to hear there's something wrong with your little girl's legs. I understand she can't walk."

My mother went into a panic and immediately took me to the family doctor. After examining me thoroughly, he said with a chuckle, "There's nothing wrong with this child's legs; she's just too content to play with whatever's within her reach. I suggest you put her toys on the other side of the room. You'll be surprised how quickly she'll become mobile."

The next day she took my favourite doll and put it as far away as she could. I walked. A year later, she regretted she'd followed the doctor's advice. At age three, I took my first solo flight. I rode my old kiddie-car, which had had years of hard use by my brother, down four blocks of the main street, in traffic, to the local hardware store. I helped myself to a new shiny one, leaving the old battered kiddie-car behind. At age four, I became even more adventurous; I walked a mile down the same main street to the railway station and attempted to board a train to Montreal. Luckily, a porter spotted me and handed me over to a Children's Aid person on duty at the station. In the small city of London where I grew up, it was easy to discover where I lived. The woman soon carted me off kicking and screaming into the arms of my distraught mother.

From then on, I was restrained with a rope tied around my waist to a post on our back verandah. Should I again be restrained? Would Carmen be too great a stretch for my instrument? Was this too big a leap too soon, or was it the time to reach beyond the safe and easily attainable and take a chance?

Though Carmen is one of the most arduous roles in the repertoire of a mezzo, it isn't the most difficult to sing, for it lies beautifully in the voice; besides, I already knew most of it from memory. Yes, now was the time to be adventurous. I would again search deep within and find the creative spring which would bring this quixotic temptress to life, and hopefully my voice would respond favourably to my will.

A timely letter from Usova helped finalize my decision.

Salzburg, Austria
June 8, 1954

Dearest little one,
You are a naughty girl not to have written to your Lana for a long time. Why have I not heard from you? Where are you spending your summer? At this time, Arturo should be on holidays. What plans have you both made?
I really don't know where these weeks I am in Europe vanished: London—Paris—Vienna. I had reached the point when my faithful crowd stuck me (a week ago Saturday) into a compartment of the Orient Express. After four and a half hours, I reached this refuge above Salzburg. The 4,000 feet altitude, solitude, peace, and sleep, sleep, sleep, nothing but sleep, performed the usual miracle. I am now becoming my old self again and am able to catch up on neglected correspondence.
On July 14 I leave for Bayreuth to work with Richard. The premiere of Parsifal *is on July 20. Write to him a good luck note, he will appreciate it. Write c/o Festspielhaus, Bayreuth. I will go back to Salzburg on July 22 and not move till the end of August.*
The first week of September will see me back for a few days in Vienna—afterward Italy, Paris, and a few days in London before taking off for New York. I shall be home the first days of October.
Dearest little one, I give you news of my whereabouts in the hope that sometime during these months your wings will bring you to Lana for another "checkup." It is

time, and I am looking forward to finally meeting your Arturo. Do write and tell me your news.

Let me embrace both of you with my deepest affection.

As ever,
Lana.

I wasted no time in answering.

June 14, 1954

Dear Lana,

Your letter of June 8 was timely, for I just learned I am to sing Carmen next February. As you well know, this will require much work, and I will need all the help I can get. Do you think I am now ready? Will you take me on?

Arturo has a concert in his home town of Fiesole, above Florence, July 15. We thought after that we'd do a little tripping around and if possible come to you in Salzburg around the beginning of August. He has to be back in Toronto for a Pops concert August 20. The tenor they have their eyes on to sing Don José opposite my Carmen will be the guest artist. They want to try him out first before they commit to paper. He's from New York. He is a new find! His name is Victor Jubrensky; have you ever heard of him? I understand he has a great voice.

If it is inconvenient for me to come to Salzburg the first two weeks of August for a daily injection of Usova, could you let me know?

We expect to leave for Europe after the American Fourth of July holiday so we'll have plenty of time in Fiesole for rehearsing and visiting Arturo's friends.

Arturo looks forward to meeting the illustrious Svetlana Usova.

Yours in much need of fine tuning.
Fondly,
Jessica

Before I could catch my breath, there was another letter in the mail box from Madame.

Salzburg, Austria
June 22, 1954

Dearest, darling little one,

Yes—by all means assure your Arturo we will be ready for that elusive gypsy. Lana will make sure you are ready. You will come as soon as you can, right after Arturo's concert. Come to me in my retreat before I go to Salzburg.

Your Mr. Jubrensky must be very new in the field of opera, for if he had done anything of consequence, we certainly would have heard of him.

> *Congratulations, my little one. I have faith in you. Carmen will be only the beginning of your many triumphs.*
>
> *My arms are always open to you both.*
> *Yours,*
> *Lana*

We arrived at the Rome airport noon, July 6, exhausted and ill of sorts after a long overnight flight, having landed first in Gander, Newfoundland, to refuel. (It was still the day of the turbo-prop airplane.) We had a three-hour stopover in Paris before catching our plane to Rome. We planned on a few days in Rome before driving on to Florence. On landing, our irascible mood was fanned by an overzealous immigration official. I had neglected to have my passport changed to my married name. Arturo was travelling on an Italian passport. Short of demanding proof of our marital status, the man's prodding eventually stopped and he waved us through, handing me both passports which I put safely away in my purse.

We rented a car and headed for our hotel. We were grateful there was a detailed map of the city in the glove compartment. With Arturo at the wheel, we drove to the centre and stopped in front of the Fountains of Rome to get our bearings. On the map our hotel appeared to be only a few blocks away, but the arrows of the one-way streets were all pointing away from our destination. Undaunted, we set out. A few minutes later, we found ourselves back at the fountains. We searched the map again and this time decided to try a different direction. Minutes later, we were again in front of the same fountains. Our tempers, already simmering close to the surface because of fatigue, burst through their thin covering. "If you'd gone the way I told you to in the first place, we might be at our hotel by now," I murmured under my breath, vitriol oozing from every word.

Silence! Arturo clearly had heard what I said. He quietly and purposefully folded the map, making sure each crease matched. I watched the gathering storm while his face reassembled itself. Then, breaking the tenuous silence, venom searing through his quietly controlled voice, he slowly said, "Give me my passport. I'm going home."

I sat stunned by his childish words. I didn't know whether to laugh or cry. Before I realized it, I was scrambling through my purse searching for his precious document, tears crowding my tired eyes. Without a word, I angrily pitched it at him, and without a word, he left the car, slamming the door behind him. I sat watching as he disappeared behind the fountains, not knowing what to do next. Finally I left the car where it stood, illegally parked.

For two hours, I walked with the hot rays of the mid-afternoon sun beating down on my shoulders, the keys to the locked car securely tucked away in my purse. I was oblivious to the glories of Rome surrounding me, lost in indecision. If Arturo didn't show up again, what would I do? Should I find my way to the hotel and hope he'd eventually show up there? Maybe I should take the car and drive directly to Usova in her retreat near Salzburg, and to hell with my husband.

With these thoughts swirling around in my tired head like wet clothes in a dryer, I circled the outer regions of the monument, always keeping the sound of the fountains within earshot for fear of getting lost in the labyrinth of unfamiliar streets. From time to time, I ventured closer to make sure the car was still there and hadn't been vandalized; or on the off-chance that Arturo had had a change of heart and was sitting on the hood of the engine smoking a cigarette. At that moment, I wasn't sure where he considered home, and I wasn't sure I even cared. For diversion, I counted the number of times I circled the area. On the eleventh count, I saw Arturo leaning against the car, smoking and talking to a policeman. I watched undetected, relieved he hadn't carried out his threat. Suddenly, the policeman let out a great guffaw. No doubt with his usual employment of wit, Arturo had made a good story out of what for me was a very stressful incident. He saw me when I stepped into view and slowly began to walk toward the car. Still chuckling, the policeman left, but not before he had given my husband detailed instructions on how to get to our hotel. By the time I reached the car, we were both laughing shamefully at the ridiculousness of our behavior.

Because of the one-way streets always leading away from the hotel, it was necessary to take a lengthy detour. We finally arrived a half-hour later, exhausted and resolved from then on to face what might come with a more receptive attitude.

Having been well taught the "international language" by Usova in Salzburg, I was able to bribe the concierge at the hotel into selling us two tickets to the sold-out performance of the opera the next evening. It was Bellini's *Norma,* to take place outdoors at the Caracalla, the ruins of the old Roman baths. The title role would be sung by a then-relatively-unknown singer by the name of Maria Callas. Anyone who had ever seen this electrifying diva perform would know it wasn't so much the voice that made her great; it was the aura of greatness she created. Each note, each word, had a force to be reckoned with. I was aware we were witnessing a historic occasion which would be engraved in a rich layer of my memory forever.

The rest of that first day and the next, Arturo led me to drink from the wells of antiquity surrounding every street of that magnificent city. Our last evening, while sitting at a street-side cafe sipping coffee, it was difficult not to overhear an

American lady loudly expounding on the evils lurking in every corner of Rome, particularly on a corner where a bank stood. "They wait outside every bank. When you come out, they will follow you as long as it takes. The moment you're distracted, the purse is gone," she warned.

We made an early start the next morning. I had succumbed to the seductive pressure of an Italian couturier; I had bought an expensive concert gown, which had to be altered and paid for. As well, there was the hotel to be taken care of. It was before the onslaught of plastic charge cards, and I thought it judicious to save my traveler's cheques for future expenses such as the cash that had to be left on top of Usova's piano daily for the two weeks of lessons. This meant a visit to the bank to draw on my letter of credit.

Walking from the bank, the words of the American lady from the night before were still ringing in my ears. With my purse pressed tightly to my chest, I walked crab fashion, my eyes covering my back side until I reached the safety of the car and Arturo. I quickly depleted my stash of lire, paying the couturier and the hotel bill. We then set off for Florence; but first I had one last errand to take care of. I had heard that the Pope would be blessing all things wanting sanctification, from his balcony over the square in front of the Vatican, that morning. I had promised Maria, who cleaned house for us back in Toronto, that I would bring her a rosary from Rome. I thought it would be twice as treasured if it had been blessed by the pontiff himself.

At eleven o'clock, we joined the throng of thousands in Saint Peter's Square. I kept one arm firmly wrapped around my purse, and with my free hand, I held the rosary high, waving it above the sea of heads in front of me while the Pope made the sign of the cross. The American woman's voice followed me all the way back to the car. With relief, I relaxed into the front seat, making sure all doors were locked. We were still in Rome; one couldn't be too careful!

The next stop was a gas station. By this time, it was almost noon, still time to make Florence by evening. We were little more than a block from the gas station after filling up when we heard the dreaded thump, thump, thump from the rear of the car. We were in the middle of a wide avenue. We limped over to the side and sat, uneasiness spreading through our veins. We had been warned by a friend before we left home—*Beware of a flat in Italy!* When you stop somewhere, even at a stop sign, they knife your tire, then rob you.

Arturo got out of the car and went in search of help. It was too hot to sit inside, so I closed the windows to within inches of the top. I carefully put my purse with passport, letter of credit, all our traveler's cheques, and a few lire into the centre of the front seat. I got out so I could have a better view of the whole area, making sure before I stepped away from the car that it was securely locked. There was no building, not even a bush or tree for anyone to hide behind; in fact, there was nothing in close proximity. We could have been the only people in Rome. Everything was shut down from twelve to two for siesta.

I waited for what seemed an endless length of time. Finally in the distance I saw Arturo walking towards the car—alone. He had been to two gas stations and numerous stores. All were shut tight.

We looked at the rear wheel and shook our heads. Neither one of us had ever changed a tire. We took what we thought to be the necessary equipment from the trunk of the car and set to work. It took many minutes before we discovered how to put the jack together. We bungled on. A young boy of about ten or eleven suddenly appeared from out of nowhere and slowly inched his way toward us, seemingly wanting to help. I tried to shoo him away, sensing he might be up to no good. He backed up enough to be out of my reach and remained motionless, staring down at us.

Arturo and I took turns loosening the bolts and removing the faulty tire, with one of us always keeping a wary eye on the boy and our surroundings. When it came time to put the spare tire on, it required our full attention. We both knelt down on the pavement and, with much effort and full concentration, lifted the tire in place. A car drove by; the first car we'd seen since we began our arduous task. It slowed down to wave to us and drove on. Being friendly tourists, we waved back as we tightened the last bolt. I unlocked the car door while Arturo put the ripped tire and jack into the trunk. I stared at the empty seat in front of me. I was sure I had carefully put my purse in the centre so it could not be reached from either window; besides, how could any hand squeeze through that few inches of space, even a child's? Had the heat got to me? Was this a phantom of the mind? Did I put it somewhere else? I carefully searched the car. By the time I finished, the boy was already a distance down the street. I took off after him at marathon speed. With the aid of my long legs, I easily overtook him. I grabbed him by the collar and dragged him back to the car, his arms flailing as he yelled Italian oaths in protest. I threw him into the back seat and turned to my husband, who was standing at the side of the car, a stunned look on his face. He knew nothing of the purse, for he had been securing everything in the trunk when I took chase.

"What's going on?" Arturo asked with the usual amused half twist to his mouth.

"Ask this little twit where a police station is. My purse is gone, and I think he had something to do with it."

Arturo's expression was one of disbelief. "Impossible. No one but the boy came near the car, and he obviously doesn't have it."

"Well maybe we should go ask the pope." The thought had crossed my mind that perhaps God had something to do with it.

I was relieved the police station wasn't shut down like the rest of Rome and glad Arturo spoke Italian. There was one policeman on duty. He asked the usual: Where were we born? Where did we live? When were we married, and how did we meet? Nothing about how and where we were robbed. I still had the boy by the collar.

"My wife is positive this youngster is somehow guilty," my husband said kindly in perfect Italian. "She thinks he should be questioned."

The policeman looked the boy over, said what a fine looking lad he was, patted him on the head, and let him go.

With map in hand, Arturo asked the way to the Canadian Embassy.

At the Embassy, we were greeted with the kindly but bored attitude of "here we go again." Obviously being robbed in Rome was on the list of "musts" for tourists.

We began to nail together the facts of the robbery to an assistant. We got no further than the flat tire when, as if reciting from the same script, he took over: "… and a young boy appeared and wanted to help. When you're busily engaged in changing the tire, he signals to someone nearby. A motorcycle passes, slowing down enough for his passenger to put a long stick with a hook on the end of it, through the opening in the window and snatch the object away without ever stopping. They're very clever the way they do it."

"We never saw a motorcycle," I interjected. "There was only a car which slowed down to wave."

"That's all it takes."

The assistant then told us of a priest who, a few days before, had been standing in a crowd in front of the Vatican to be blessed by the pope when his cassock was knifed up the back and all his money taken from the belt around his waist without the priest's knowledge. He continued, telling of another time when a Canadian tourist went to the hotel parking lot to get his car. He tried to start it, only to discover the engine of his Volkswagen had gone. I could tell the Canadian Embassy was used to dealing with all kinds of emergencies, for, by the next morning, I had a new passport. For the same reason, the American Express was most cooperative; they issued new traveler's cheques immediately, without question.

13

Primitive Existence in Sardinia

Now that we had our new currency safely tucked away, this time in Arturo's wallet in his breast pocket, we directed our car north toward Florence. Once over the Ponte Margherita, we followed along the Tevere River to the A-1, the main artery running north and south through the centre of Italy. The picturesque landscape was dotted with ancient ruins, but they only flickered at the side of my vision, for my mind was elsewhere. Like a pebble dropped in still water, I could feel the concentric rings of excitement enveloping me as I thought of the two weeks we would be spending in Arturo's birthplace of Fiesole. I knew so little of my husband's past life. I knew he had no siblings; that he had lost his mother and father when he was in his early teens (though he never said how they had died); that he had gone to England to live with an uncle and was educated there, at Oxford and the Royal College of Music. Through his years in England, he never lost touch with his childhood friend in Fiesole, Giovanni Baronni, who was now the dean of music in the School of Fine Arts where Arturo's concert was to be held. All else was a mystery. Since our marriage, I had been suspended in a locked closet of unknowing. The thought of piecing together the puzzle of his past was compelling.

Throughout the five hour drive, we spoke little, both of us lost in the reverie of our own thoughts. The rolling hills of the Tuscan countryside sped by virtually unnoticed, and we soon found ourselves at the outskirts of Florence. We circled the city; the winding five mile drive to Fiesole took us uphill through olive-clad slopes, past luxuriant gardens and long lines of cypress trees.

On our way to Villa Luna, where we would be staying, we drove by the school. It looked strangely quiet and lonely in the golden late afternoon light. After a few minutes, we turned onto the laneway leading to the Benedettine retreat, where we would be spending the next two weeks. Villa Luna was nestled comfortably in the hills overlooking Florence. Its pale yellow plaster façade and terra-cotta colour shutters made its appearance homey and welcoming. Along the length of the second floor of the two-storey structure were French doors behind small wrought iron balconies. I could hardly wait to settle in and rest my hot tired body after our taxing days in Rome.

The villa was run by sisters of the Benedettine order as a quiet refuge. The guests were treated to three meals a day, a simple clean and quiet room, and lots of friendly atmosphere. We checked in, and Arturo immediately left for the school to pick up a schedule of the rehearsals, which were to begin the next day, and to find his friend Giovanni.

Before I had time to look around, he was back. "Don't unpack. We're leaving." He said this as casually as if he was telling me he was going for a walk. In his hand was a letter in Italian, which he translated while reading aloud.

"Dear Turi—You'll find me in Sardinia, where the beautiful green, blue, purple water of the Mediterranean meets a beach of the purest white sand this side of heaven; so the guide book says. It is hopefully going to help restore my sanity. Two days ago, the lid blew off the School and we had to cancel the July 15 concert. Sorry, old boy! It was the usual thing—the orchestra musicians wanted more money, the school board had no money in their coffers, so the musicians walked out, refusing to negotiate. I tried to reach you in Canada, but you had already left. Why don't you join Mirella, my five year old boys, and me? I understand it's a bit primitive but hopefully a good place to cool off. The address is 26 Via Roma, Golfo Aranci. Hope you can make it! Looking forward to meeting the new bride! Ciao, Giovanni."

For the last five hours we had been driving in a stifling car under an unrelenting sun, and there was promise of more heat to come. The mention of the cool waters and white sand beaches of Sardinia sounded irresistible; besides, at that moment, we had no better place to go. There were three weeks to fill before I was to be with Usova in Salzburg.

What surprised me was how cool Arturo was concerning the cancellation of his concert. He seemed almost relieved to leave Fiesole. For my part, I was disappointed not to have the chance to sleuth my husband's origins. Despite this, as was my nature, a new adventure was not something I wanted to avoid.

According to our map, the only way to get to Sardinia was by ferry from Civitavecchia, a five-hour drive back down the coast directly west of Rome. Arturo made a phone call to a tourist agent he knew in Florence, hoping it would still be open at seven o'clock. Because of the two-hour siesta midday, most businesses remained open until eight in the evening. We found out the next ferry left at midnight, arriving in Sardinia at six in the morning. If we left immediately, because of my husband's inclination to speed, we should be able to make it on time.

The drive to Civitavecchia, though in the darkness of a moonless night, was intrinsically more pleasant without the scorching sun sending its searing heat through our open windows. We arrived as the ferry was letting down its gate to discharge one dilapidated, ancient pickup truck and to load the few cars waiting to board. Six o'clock sharp the next morning, we arrived at the little port of Olbia. Our first glimpse of Sardinia was far from encouraging. In the early morning light, it looked bleak and desolate. The scattering of buildings around the dock were as grey as the overcast sky above. The few people silently waiting for the ferry to disgorge its cargo were dressed in varying shades of grey as well. The coastline was dotted with dark cliffs that had little vegetation on top. We were surrounded by a symphony of grey.

Golfo Aranci was only a half-hour drive away, but by the time our car had been unloaded and we were able to scrounge a little breakfast of hard Sardinian bread and coffee from a food hut, it was eight o'clock before we arrived in the little fishing village. It was a good thing we filled up with gas on our way to Civitavecchia, for we were told there were few gas stations on the island, particularly on the north-east side where we would be staying.

We drove through Golfo Aranci before we realized we had passed it. Retracing our steps, we found the village to be a collection of no more than thirty or forty little dwellings, all the same shade of bleached pink and made from the earth they were sitting on. As there was only one dirt road running the length of the village, we thought it must be Via Roma. To find number twenty-six was a greater challenge. Above each door in large black numbers was written 4950515253. We had stopped our car, wondering what to do next, when a tall, strikingly good-looking man came out the door of a nearby dwelling the size of a one-car garage. After straightening up from having to bend almost double to get through the small opening, he saw Arturo, who had stepped out of the car.

"Mio dio-nessuno! (My god-no!)" The words came out with a loud explosion of air and certainly didn't sound welcoming. Both men stood looking at each other. Then, as if drawn together by a huge magnet, they embraced effusively with a great burst of laughter. Giovanni was a head taller than my husband, and his handsome face was fully visible over Arturo. My eyes met his, and he smiled the warm smile of an Italian sunrise meeting a new day. "Turi, so this is Jessica. You old devil!" he said in English.

Was he calling Arturo a devil because of my apparent youth or because of my appearance, I wondered? None the less, because of his smile, I took it as a compliment. Tentatively, I got out of the car and offered my hand in greeting. He gently pushed it aside and gave me a big hug instead. One couldn't help but like the man!

A few minutes of conversation with Giovanni, and we understood why the welcome hadn't been more enthusiastic. He, his wife, and twin boys were sharing their little house with two other families. Their outhouse was available to all villagers. One could get water from the community tap in the village square from six to nine in the morning only. The water was carried home in large urns on the heads of the women. There were no fresh fruits or vegetables except for a meagre crop struggling to survive in the parched earth at the back of each house. The luxury of fresh meat came once a week when a local cow was slaughtered. There was fish every Sunday when the fishermen came home with their weekly catch. The only things in abundance were bread, pasta, and children. Golfo Aranci had not yet advanced to the twentieth century.

When the initial shock of our arrival had subsided, Giovanni invited us in to meet Mirella and the boys. Over coffee, we would decide our next move. Although they both spoke a little English, most of the conversation was in Italian. Giovanni had much to explain to Arturo due to the cancelled concert, so I was able to observe our hosts in their tiny habitat. Mirella, with her long black hair casually falling around her suntanned face and over her bare shoulders, was as beautiful as her husband was handsome. Her eyes were like swatches of translucent brown velvet, alert and friendly. Her nose by itself could be called large, yet with her generous mouth and prominent jaw to balance it, the total effect was striking. The boys were identical twins and had the best features of each of their parents. They all had Italian charm in abundance. Like the sun above them, they radiated warmth. Because of Mirella's and Giovanni's erudite and sophisticated appearance, they seemed strangely out of place in their primitive habitat.

We were sitting on well-worn stools on an earth floor around a large, crude table. There were no other pieces of furniture in the room. We were close to the back door, or I should say opening, for there was no door. Through the opening I could see a large pit surrounded by rocks where I later discovered Mirella performed her magic with what little food was available. Though there was barely enough room for the table and six of us, the other inhabitants of the house managed to squeeze by in an unending flow, and with gaping mouths would mutter *scusa* and *prego* as they padded up the stairs to their over-crowded living quarters above. To the right as one entered was a small room which I took to be the only bedroom. Obviously there was no space for guests.

Eventually it was decided, as we had paid the grand sum of fifty dollars to get to Sardinia, we should stay for at least another couple of days; besides, I wanted to delay the inevitable as long as I could. Uneasiness had begun to play on me at the thought of the subsequent meeting between Usova and Arturo, remembering her reaction when I told her I was to be married. Would there be an unbridgeable gap between them? If she was indifferent, cool, and abrupt, as she had been with Eva at Irma's concert in Salzburg, he would retreat behind a curtain of ice. If she lathered him with honeyed words, he would instantly recoil and cut her short with his sometimes scathing wit.

"Will we be sleeping on the beach? There's certainly no room for us in your mud hut." Arturo's voice was laced with the kind of sarcasm that flows freely between close friends.

"There's a hotel at the other end of the village a few minutes walk from here. That is, there's a sign saying hotel. We've yet to check it out." Giovanni then added, as if he'd had second thoughts, "You're sure you're up to this? There's a ferry back to the mainland at midnight."

"Look, we're here; let's make the best of it. If there's a hotel nearby, then that settles it," I said with one thought in mind: to postpone as long as possible the imminent meeting between the two forces guiding my destiny.

Because our arrival had taken the proprietor of the hotel by surprise, he seemed not to know what to do with us. The hotel had reopened a few months ago and we were their first customers. We had the choice of two rooms. We chose the one closest to the bathroom. There was no bath, just a basin and toilet. We soon regretted our choice, for the only toilet served the patrons of the hotel bar as well. It was flushed by pouring a nearby bucket of water into it. The proprietor flushed it to demonstrate. Unbeknown to us, it was the only water for that day. And the next would not be available until six the following morning. It wasn't long before we preferred the Baronni's outhouse to the much-used hotel toilet. Although our bed was a double, the mattress was only a single, leaving a foot of open spring on either side. We clung close in spite of the hot Sardinian nights rather than risk injury on the rusty, irregular coils.

After we checked into the hotel, our hosts walked us down to the beach close by. There was a huge expanse of the whitest, finest sand I had ever seen. In the bright morning sun, it was blinding. The locals were convinced of its healing qualities; that it could cure rheumatism and arthritis. By eleven o'clock, there were already mounds of sand with heads protruding out one end, feet out the other.

The temperature had already risen to a high level. We changed into bathing suits and fell into water so clean, so clear that when we looked down at our feet, it was like looking through a crystal prism reflecting extraordinarily brilliant hues of purple, turquoise, and blue. This alone was worth the visit to Sardinia.

Our time in Golfo Aranci soon fell into a pattern—days on the beach, meals with the Baronnis. I never learned to trust the hotel cooking.

Wherever we went, we were stared at with curiosity and suspicion. The people had learned to accept the Baronnis because they were Italian. Though the name Moretti was Italian enough, I was Canadian and Arturo now lived in Canada. The village had been an allied naval base during World War II. This had disrupted the locals' quiet existence, and they still didn't trust foreigners. Why would we come to a primitive village like Golfo Aranci if we didn't want something sinister? At the beginning, I wondered as well.

Golfo Aranci had for years been known to be a centre for malaria. After the war the Marshall Plan dictated that the village be sprayed with DDT yearly until it was free of the malaria-carrying mosquito. Starting in 1949 each house was sprayed, the year printed in bold numbers over the door—49-50-51-52, the last year being 1953.

When I first met Giovanni, I decided to try to engage him as often as I could in conversation about my husband's early childhood. Arturo came into my life somehow burdened by his past. It would help me to understand the man he now was if I knew what had come before. I had no desire to possess my husband, to pry into the happenings of his former life for curiosity's sake; I wanted only to draw closer to him. Whenever I tried to delve beneath the surface, to dig deeper into the well of his inner self, I was met with silence. He immediately changed the subject. It was as though, if he revealed too much of himself, he would be vulnerable to hurt. What made him this way? I felt the clue lay in the dust of the past.

The perfect opportunity to learn more about his history came shortly after we arrived in Golfo Aranci. We were on the beach. Mirella had left moments before to get lunch for the twins. Arturo was under the shade of a nearby tree, deep in the orchestral score of Beethoven's opera, *Fidelio,* reviewing the Leonora Overture for his upcoming Pops concert in Toronto the following month. Giovanni had buried himself in the sand to test its therapeutic qualities. It was the perfect time to approach him; he couldn't escape me. I stood beside him drying myself after countless dips in the exhilarating water of the Mediterranean. I looked down; his eyes were closed.

"Can we talk?" I asked. "Is this a bad time? Are you asleep?"

"Mmm."

In spite of his groggy reply, I sat down. Undaunted, I began again. "You've known Arturo a long time, I guess?" I tried to make it sound offhand, as if fabricating conversation for its own sake.

"Si," he answered sleepily.

Silence! I could see a different approach was necessary, direct and to the point. "How did his mother and father die? Arturo has told me nothing."

There was another long silence. I wasn't sure he'd heard me when the grains of sand slowly shifted and began to fall from the top of the mound in silver streams. He raised his shoulders and back and rested his weight on his elbows and forearms, which were stretched behind him. I watched the rivulets of sand fall from his sun-bronzed chest and marvelled anew at his good looks.

"*Dio mio.* You really are serious, aren't you?" There was a wide grin on his face. He paused as if trying to translate his thoughts from Italian to English. "Your husband has always been a very private man." Then he added with a laugh, "But I want to assure you he has nothing questionable to hide; at least, not that I know of."

He pushed the rest of the sand aside, stood up, and moved away so the leftover grains wouldn't fall on me as he dusted them off. He came back, carefully and slowly spread his towel, and sat down beside me. "Okay, where shall we begin?"

I looked back over my shoulder; Arturo was fast asleep. "Try the beginning."

Without hesitation, Giovanni began to unlock the alignment of closed doors which had always faced me, and I was able to put together, piece by piece, the puzzle.

When Mussolini suspended the government of Italy and took power in 1928, Arturo's father was the editor of a newspaper in Florence. Mussolini had begun his career as a journalist, first in Switzerland, then Austria. On his return to Italy, he became editor of a socialist daily in Milan called *Avanti*. Soon after World War I, he broke with the socialist party and founded his own paper, *Il Popolo d'Italia,* in Milan. From the outset, Arturo's father and Mussolini were political enemies. His father watched Mussolini's steady climb up the ladder to complete power with dismay. He had always viciously opposed *Il Duce* in print whenever he could. Mussolini on taking power became determined to silence his outspoken critic. Arturo's father was continuously warned by the Fascist secret police, but he chose to ignore them.

Arturo and Giovanni were twelve years old when the Fascists came to power. Both boys studied piano with Arturo's mother, a well-known concert pianist. One evening, as Giovanni was finishing his lesson with Signora Moretti, the secret police burst into the home and seized Arturo's father. He was never heard from again, presumed murdered by the black shirts.

Frightened for both her own and Arturo's safety, Signora Moretti fled to her brother in England. Shortly after this, she took her own life, unable to face the future without her husband. Arturo remained with his uncle and family.

From the outset, he felt ill at ease and lonely in England. He had nothing in common with his two male cousins. His uncle, a professional musician, immediately recognized the young Arturo's unusual musical talent and brilliant mind. The uncle was determined Arturo should have the best education England had to offer. Frequently that came at the expense of Arturo's cousins. This caused much jealousy, and the boys set out to make life impossible for Arturo. To protect himself from the many indignities suffered at the hands of his older cousins, he withdrew into himself. He had never come to terms with the deaths of his father and mother, both of whom he adored. He found solace only in his music.

When World War II began in 1939, Arturo was twenty-two years old. He had already graduated from Oxford and the Royal College of Music. He was much in demand as a coach and accompanist for singers at the Royal Opera House. He was now financially independent, and life looked full of promise. The day after war broke out, the English government ordered all German and Italian citizens in the United Kingdom to be rounded up and interned. Alarmed, Arturo fled the country. From then on, Giovanni lost touch and his letters to England were returned. A few years after the end of the war, in 1945, Arturo showed up at the opera house in Milan where both Mirella and Giovanni were lead singers. When he arrived at La Scala, Arturo's talents were quickly recognized, and he became the *meraviglioso ragazzo* (wonder boy) of the company. Little by little, Giovanni and Arturo's friendship continued where it had left off. It was then the account of those unknown years emerged from out of the ashes of the war.

When Arturo escaped England, he went to Switzerland, which was neutral. While there, he married a young Polish pianist at the beginning of a brilliant career. She had been in Switzerland giving concerts when war broke out. Due to her Jewish background, she dared not return to Poland where Jews were being slaughtered like cattle by the Nazis. In 1948, three years after the end of the war, she returned to her native Warsaw for a series of recitals. Once behind the Iron Curtain, she became a captive of the Communists, who refused her a visa to travel outside the country. Arturo tried in vain to get the Swiss government to intercede and to either secure her release or arrange for him to travel to Poland. With constant promises from the Swiss which never materialized, he had to be content with her infrequent letters. Finally, frustrated, he decided to take matters into his own hands. He would return to his native Italy, where he might have more success.

At La Scala, Arturo was the foremost *répétiteur* with an occasional conducting appearance to keep him happy. Despite this, he could see his chances were minimal in Milan. He had his heart set on becoming a conductor. All opportunities at that time were jealously coveted and securely entrenched in the hands of the old guard. In the meantime, letters from Poland became fewer until they finally stopped. Arturo became desperate with no help forthcoming from the Italian government. Then in early April 1951, a telegram arrived notifying Arturo of his wife's tragic death in a motor accident.

From then on, he became submerged in a vacuum of despondency. It was then that time and chance, the twin offspring of destiny, came to the rescue. A search had been put out from Toronto, Canada. They were forming a new opera company and were looking for someone, preferably young with experience in the Italian repertoire, to head it. Arturo had been recommended for the job, particularly because he spoke perfect English. He saw this as the opportunity he'd been hoping for and took the leap into the relatively uncharted waters of Canada.

Sitting beside Giovanni in the hot sun, soaking up with fascination the recounting of my husband's earlier years, my eyes caught sight of Mirella in the distance sauntering along Via Roma, a large basket in her hand. The boys had hold of her long wraparound skirt and were stretching it out behind her. They looked like little pages attending a queen. Mirella's long tanned legs were covering the ground faster than I would have wished, for I wanted to hear more. I wanted Giovanni to tell me about the School of Fine Arts where he was Dean. Before he could go on, Mirella was beside us with her basket full of sandwiches, fruit, and wine; things she magically produced daily from the meagre harvest of Golfo Aranci.

Each morning over breakfast, Giovanni would beg us to stay another day, and soon a week sped by in a languid, pleasurable existence. By the time we departed, even the locals accepted us, sure we presented no threat to their future. I learned to love our simple existence with one drawback: the plumbing. My whole intestinal tract had rebelled. I was never able to come to terms with such elementary arrangements.

Saturday night was movie night in the little village. A screen made from a white sheet was hung on a stone wall behind a simple wooden platform in the square. Benches from a stack kept under a makeshift shed roof at the side of the open space were set out in neat rows. Our last night, Giovanni suggested to the villagers that instead of the usual movie, we put on a concert. It was July 15, the night Arturo was to have conducted in Fiesole.

The hotel had an old upright piano in the bar, compliments of the U.S. Navy, leftover from the war. Though several notes were missing and it hadn't been tuned since its arrival, the piano was better than nothing. With the help of a wrench, Arturo was able to bring the keys that were playable up to the correct pitch. He and Giovanni mounted the instrument on a wide wooden plank and dragged it to the square with the aid of the village donkey, with Arturo on one side and Giovanni on the other to make sure the piano remained steady. The donkey, which had been resisting vigorously the whole three hundred yards along the rough earth surface of Via Roma, made the trip lengthy and hazardous. By the time the piano was placed in front of the platform, Arturo, Giovanni, and the donkey were all exhausted, pouring with sweat, and much in need of a drink.

The programming presented no problem. Mirella and Giovanni had a myriad of material with them that they were reviewing for a concert tour in the fall. I had my *Carmen* score in hand, ready to be pulled apart by Usova in a few days. Arturo had years of experience stashed away and could pull from the crevices of his incredible musical memory an unending supply of Italian folk songs, opera arias, and duets. We only had to select what we thought would best suit the occasion.

A short rehearsal was planned the morning of the performance. We began before the intense heat of the Sardinian sun beat down on us. It was decided Mirella and Giovanni would start with Mimi and Rodolfo's opening duet from *La Bohème*. When Arturo hit the first notes of the introduction, the malfunctioning keys thumped with an out-of-tune twang, the lower ones sounding like croaking frogs, the upper ones as if the poor piano had a severe case of laryngitis. We burst out laughing while he struggled to make music from the anguished instrument. Throughout Mirella and Giovanni's singing, Arturo did his best to avoid the offending keys. When it became my turn, with a devilish smile on his face, his fingers would search out all the defective keys they could find. Then, he would thump loudly several times a wrong note to make me appear off-key. By the time we finished the rehearsal, I was ready to strangle him!

Mirella had a collection of colourful Italian wrap-around long skirts she wore over her bathing suits—her Sardinian uniform. With a borrowed red skirt over my black bathing suit and my large gold hoop earrings, I felt the result should pass for Carmen. The closer we came to the time of the concert, the more we began to wonder if the locals wouldn't prefer their weekly movie. Finally at seven o'clock in the evening, the square began to fill up. Streams of children with their parents shuffled in and quietly took their places on the benches. By the time the concert was to begin at eight, there were over two hundred expectant faces staring at the platform, patiently waiting for something to happen.

Below the diminutive stage, Mirella and Giovanni's two boys took turns shining their flashlights on the music so Arturo could see, as the dim light of twilight began to fade. Leaning over the back of the upright, I watched Mirella and Giovanni spin their spell while the diffused light of the old, empty projector did its best to make them visible. The tiny village reverberated with the glorious sounds of Puccini's music, brought to life by two accomplished performers. I envied Mirella's dramatic beauty, with her thick black hair pulled tight into a large knot behind her head, her perfect body at its best in her aqua bathing costume and matching wraparound skirt. Giovanni, looking elegant in his white polo shirt and black jeans, captivated his audience with his lyrical tenor voice and affable personality. Watching them perform, unease began running rampant in my nervous system. The more I watched, the more I felt unready to share a stage with such seasoned pros. It wasn't so much the audience that made me nervous, it was the thought that I might disappoint and embarrass my husband in front of his friends.

When their singing stopped and the burst of approval died down, I leaned forward over the back of the piano and whispered to Arturo, "I can't go on after that. I'll look like a rank amateur, and I certainly can't sing French to these people. Signal for Giovanni to begin his next number."

My husband only smiled and, with the aid of his perfect memory, began to play the few bars beginning the recitative of Orpheo's aria, *Che faro*, rather then the scheduled *Carmen*. Repeating the notes, he nodded his head for me to commence. As if on automatic drive, I began to sing while mounting the two steps onto the platform. "*Euridice—Euridice.*" By the time I reached the centre of the little stage, the energy generated by Arturo's accompaniment began to seep into my veins. I felt the music saying to me, "We'll show them. You can do it." His support was always there, encouraging me to give more, to sing my best. This was the first time of many when we performed together that I felt a heady intoxication which happens when two people are as one. When we finished, even the boys were cheering. After that, the challenge of singing with Mirella and Giovanni became an exciting adventure. Mirella and I sang the flower duet from *Madame Butterfly*. She and Giovanni sang all of the arias and duets from the same opera. The concert ended with the quartet from *Rigoletto*, Arturo supplying a croaky baritone voice from the pit. We must have been a success, for even the infants remained still until the applause and cheers woke them up; then they too joined in the general din.

Like the click of a camera shutter, the picture of our visit to Golfo Aranci settled in my memory to be collected permanently in life's album.

14

Bayreuth—Arturo Meets Usova

It was as if someone had taken an eraser and rubbed from my memory the events of the next few weeks. When and where did we finally meet up with Usova? I searched among the letters left in the shoebox. There was a photograph half-hidden under the yellowed pages. It was faded, as if taken in a fog. On the back was written, in Usova's large, resolute hand—*July 21, 1954, lunch at Neues Schloss.*

Only fragments of this occasion have survived in my memory. In the hope of squeezing from the photo more particles of the past, I carefully scrutinized each detail. Usova, Arturo, and I are sitting at a table on the sun-drenched patio of the Schloss, with its impressive facade in the background. It must have been an off hour, for behind us are rows of empty tables. Standing by Madame's chair is a balding waiter staring into the camera, his hands behind his back, his white jacket stretched to the full over his portly stomach. It is cool, for Arturo is wearing a windbreaker and Usova a V-neck cream-colour sweater over a paddy green blouse. On her ears are her signature large emerald earrings. She is looking down, her prominent eyelids in their covering of green iridescent eye shadow glow through the mist of the faded photo. She is helping herself to what looks like a mixed salad. It's hard to tell her age in the photo; in the shade of an overhead umbrella, her face looks remarkably free of wrinkles. She looks to be in her late fifties, however, engraved in a layer of memory is the image of an older woman in her mid-sixties. Gone too is the long hair swept up in tiny curls on top of her head. In its place is a smart, short haircut, probably the reason for her younger appearance. To me, the most revealing thing about the photo is that we look to be thoroughly enjoying ourselves. Arturo is sitting on one side of Usova, looking directly at her through dark glasses, a broad grin on his tanned face. Usova's prominent teeth are exposed in a wide smile. I am on the other side of her, my chin resting in my cupped hands with my elbows on the table, looking blissfully happy. The longer I study the photo, the more the shadows clouding my memory dissipate.

I recall, we arrived on the Italian mainland early in the morning of July 17, having taken the overnight ferry from Sardinia. We headed our car north from Civitavecchia, hoping to reach Milan by evening. Arturo had not been back since he left for Canada a year and a half earlier, and he was anxious to touch base again with his past associates. He wanted to make sure his ties with La Scala Opera House remained intact. We spent only one night in Milan, as the opera house was closed for the summer and most of his colleagues were busy throughout Europe and North America at the various summer festivals. Because Usova was to be in Bayreuth from July14–22, we decided to catch up with her there instead of later in Salzburg. At this point, I wanted to get the meeting between Usova and Arturo over with as soon as possible. My continuous worry over the inevitable was beginning to spoil my holiday.

After a long drive through the Alps and a night in Innsbruck, we drove into Bayreuth as the extended shadows of early evening stretched out on the road in front of us. The first thing we had to do was find Usova. I thought the Festspielhaus would certainly have her or Richard Alexander's address. Recalling her expert wrangling technique in Salzburg, I was sure she could scrounge two tickets to Richard's opening performance in *Parsifal* the next night. In Bayreuth, the houses were always sold out well in advance.

Though Wagner was not one of Arturo's favourite composers, he had never been to Bayreuth and was anxious to check out the renowned acoustics of this remarkable opera house. Without hesitation, my car found its way to the Festspielhaus, driving along *Tristan Strasse*, past *Lohengrin Strasse*, past *Hollander Strasse*, where I had stayed two years before, and on to *Tannhauser*, where we parked the car. From there, a walk around the opera house in Richard Wagner Park and up *Siegfried Wagner Allee* brought us to the front entrance. There was little doubt we were in the land of the Wagners.

Near the entrance of the large, sprawling red brick structure was a small group of animated people who looked as if they were all talking at once. In the centre was a stocky little figure in a smart white pantsuit; her bright green spike heels struggled to raise her to the height of the others surrounding her. When I saw the hennaed head, I took my husband's arm and drew him back behind a nearby shrub; I wasn't ready to face Madame yet, for I knew the first meeting would be crucial. I had to plan it well.

"What's your problem?" he said, peering through the foliage of the bush. When he saw the red head, he guessed what my problem was. "Grow up! *Mio*

Dio, you are such a child; are you really so frightened of that little creature?" Then, with a humourless laugh, shaking his head, he added, "Good God, she's half your size."

"That little creature is loaded with explosives, so beware," I countered.

"Thanks for the warning. I'll be sure not to light up when I get near her."

One by one, the group began to peel off, and Usova was left alone. She had her back to us and was about to enter the Festspielhaus when I sauntered casually out from our leafy cover. "Lana," I called, "I'm glad we've found you." She stopped, and I ran up to her.

"What are you doing here?" A smile was slow to appear; obviously I had caught her off guard. "Come, darlink, give your Lana a kiss." She took hold of the lapel of my jacket and pulled my face down even with hers. She gave my cheek a quick peck; then she saw Arturo. The constraint in her voice immediately turned to honey. "So this is the maestro." She walked over to him, arms extended, her face glowing with friendliness and the kind of charm she reserved for members of the opposite sex.

Arturo stood his ground, hands in his pocket, ready to stem the tide of effusion. With a wicked grin on his face, he said quietly, "Madame Usova, I think you and I have much in common."

She had expected an embrace or at least a friendly handshake. Being used to people gushing over her, she was unprepared for this controlled, reserved treatment, and she obviously felt it bordered on rudeness. She stopped and her extended arms fell to their sides. The smile disappeared as quickly as it had flashed on her face. I sensed a deep freeze taking over. "Yes, and what is that?" she asked tersely, ever ready for a loop in the yarn in which she could insert her needle.

"Well, to begin with, we both have to deal with a sometimes difficult child." The grin was still on his face.

She looked at him, her penetrating, questioning eyes at half mast, not sure how to take this self-contained stranger. Then, slowly, the charm returned. "And, what else?" she asked, almost coyly.

"And we both want only the best for her." Arturo put his arm around my shoulders and gave them a tight squeeze. The worst was over. From then on, there was a cautious cushion of respect between them.

Usova arranged for us to stay three nights with Frau Schmidt, where I had stayed before. She also managed to get us house seats for *Parsifal* the next night, though not together. For several years after its premiere in 1882, *Parsifal* remained Bayreuth's exclusive property, with the exception of concert versions which took place throughout the music world after Wagner's death. He wrote *Parsifal* to be performed in Bayreuth exclusively because of its religious subject matter. Not until 1903 did the first stage performance outside Bayreuth take place at the Metropolitan in New York. Cosima Wagner, Richard Wagner's widow, went to court to try to prevent its appearance but lost.

Opening night in Bayreuth was always a grand affair. Luckily, I had with me my extravagant concert gown purchased in Rome, and Arturo had his white tux, which was unused due to the cancelled concert in Fiesole. We both easily passed Usova's critical eye.

The performance began at five with hour-long breaks between acts when one either dined in the festival restaurant, walked in the park or, to quote a member of an earlier audience, "watched the French flirt, the Germans drink beer, and the English read the libretto."

Like many people, we went on foot to the theatre. It was but a short half-mile from Frau Schmidt's, but we were relieved it wasn't raining, for it had been threatening on and off most of the day. In the dull late afternoon light, the theatre looked even more unprepossessing than I had remembered. Locals often referred to it as having "the charm of an Octoberfest beer tent and the elegance of a railway station." As we approached, the brass ensemble on the balcony above the front entrance sounded, summoning the opera-goers, alerting them that the performance was about to begin.

Inside, because of the extensive width of the auditorium and there being no centre aisle and little leg room, we excused ourselves while stumbling over knees, searching for our seats, which were in the centre and several rows apart. The minute the curtain went up on the mammoth Bayreuth stage, revealing a slightly raised circle of light, centre stage, I was spellbound. The Knights of the Grail were kneeling in prayer around the circle. In the darkness behind were shadows of huge, century-old trees extending to the top of the high proscenium, with sunlight playing in and out among their large trunks. There was nothing on stage except the Knights. This dramatic effect was created solely by lighting behind a scrim. Particularly memorable was the scene in Klingsor's castle tower. One could hear the voice of the magician coming from the blackness near the top of the proscenium as Kundry emerged through a bluish vapour from a pit on the stage below. Staring into the blackness of the upper part of the scrim, I was suddenly aware of a pinpoint of bright green light where Klingsor's voice could be heard. Throughout his singing, I watched, transfixed, as the light gradually grew in size until it became a face—or was it a face? Yes, a face—and then shoulders. By the time I saw the whole body, his long monologue had ended, and the action below had changed to the flower maidens dancing in brilliant sunshine in a flower garden. All was done with lighting. This was 1954—surely Wieland Wagner was well ahead of his time in the art of stagecraft.

When I had seen *Parsifal* at the Met in New York in 1952, the Blumen Mädchen had bounced, not danced their way across the stage, each one weighing close to two hundred pounds. I had mistakenly thought in order to sing Wagner, one had to have a huge voice and physique to match to project over the large orchestra. In Bayreuth, with the orchestra hidden under the stage and the incredible acoustics, the slim singers had no trouble being heard.

Richard as Amfortas was memorable. Both his suffering and his rich bass-baritone voice touched every fibre of my being. The Kundry of the evening was Martha Mödl, famous for her portrayal of one of Wagner's most dramatically difficult and taxing female roles. She squirmed and writhed about the stage like a boa constrictor, her every pore sexually charged. I have heard she wore no underclothing on these occasions, as she found it too restricting when performing with abandonment the erotic gyrations demanded of her.

During each intermission, Usova collected us and, with her usual sense of purpose, took us on her rounds between courses to make sure we met all the important personages she thought might further our careers. It was almost midnight before the opera ended. By that time, Arturo and I both had such severe cases of "chapel bottom"—we were numb from the waist down. We had been sitting through the long performance on the hard cane seats, a test of fortitude well worth the discomfort. Every performance I have seen of *Parsifal* since, has paled by comparison. In the hands of the brilliant director Wieland Wagner, grandson of Richard, combined with the acoustical marvel of the theatre his grandfather conceived, the opera was memorable.

The next morning, while we were eating Frau Schmidt's large breakfast of German sausage, cheese, fruit, and breads, Madame phoned. We were told to meet her at ten o'clock in front of the Festspielhaus; one of her children was auditioning for the Wagners. They were casting for the 1957 festival, and she wanted me to witness what would soon be in store for me. She ended with her usual "and be sure not to be late."

It was a beautiful, cool sunny morning. We left the car at Frau Schmidt's and strolled up *Hollander Strasse*, along *Tannhauser*, through the park to the front of the building. We planned it so we would arrive on the stroke of ten, as ordered. Usova was already there, pacing in circles. "Hurry children, they have already gone inside."

Her reference to my august and sophisticated husband as a child brought a devilish smile to his face.

"Don't you dare," I hissed, certain he was about to respond with a double-edged barb.

We followed Madame through the door like grade-school children following the head mistress on a field trip; Arturo appearing to enjoy his new role enormously. Once inside the theatre, there was enough light to make out the features of the three well-established divas; each one sitting patiently waiting her turn to sing. They were all sufficiently revered artists to be hired on their reputations alone. In the centre of the theatre were the three Wagners: Wieland and Wolfgang, both grandsons of Richard, and their mother, Winnifred. We were about to sit down in the back row when Usova spotted her protégé. "Darlinks, you sit here; I will sit with my child for she will need me to hold her hand and give her courage."

The first diva, I had heard singing Martha, in *Faust,* at the Metropolitan in New York. This time she sang the important role of Brangaene in *Tristan and Isolde.* Out of her throat poured dark mezzo tones of pure bronze. To me, it was perfect singing. Only minutes into the audition, there was a terse *"Danke schön, die nächste Dame bitte,"* (Thank you, next lady please.) from one of the Wagners.

The next one to sing suffered the same fate. I began to realize how far from ready I was to impose my ill-prepared gifts on such illustrious personages as the Wagners. Was I in too great a hurry? After all, each one of these divas had at least ten years of professional experience behind them. I felt humbled.

Usova's child fared better. She was asked if she would be available to sing the role of Eva in *Lohengrin* in the summer of 1957. Usova was obviously pleased, for when she stood to leave, she turned in our direction and nodded as if to say, you see what happens when you are a pupil of Svetlana Usova's. With a self-satisfied grin on her face, she put her arm around her "child's" waist and left the theatre.

After showing Arturo the orchestra pit and as much of the theatre as I dared, we wandered out into the bright sunshine. We were discussing our next move when we heard a familiar voice calling from behind. "Darlinks, would you join me for lunch? There's a restaurant I want to explore. It is the other side of town, so we will need your car." She was alone. Her famous pupil had departed.

It was over lunch at the Neues Schloss that I watched the relationship between Arturo and Usova develop from a tentative game of chess, wherein each player manoeuvres skillfully over the board, using carefully thought out and well-calculated moves, into a kindredship of mutual admiration and respect. Small wonder I looked happy in the photo taken from my shoebox!

Usova was delighted we had shown up in Bayreuth; it meant we could drive her, and she wouldn't have to take "that tiresome train" to Salzburg. She would pick up her mail at the Zistel Alm, her retreat on the Geisberg, before descending into the city.

During the drive the next day, I watched with fascination from the back seat the drama being played out between the two participants in front. Usova played on my husband as if he were a rare Stradivarius violin, treating him with the utmost respect while trying to coax from him the results she hoped to achieve. She spoke at length of the fragility of the singing voice and the unscrupulous, ignorant teachers bent on destroying one of God's most precious gifts to mankind. For the most part, Arturo quietly let her talk on, well aware of her manipulative attempts, but she had met her match. With his words well-peppered with humour and witticisms, he managed to throw her off base and, with evasion and chicanery, thwart her endeavours to get him to help her set up shop north of the U.S. border. She believed him to be in a position to foster a truly prodigious school for the making of great singers. She insisted it was his duty to seize the opportunity to have at his side the "messiah" in the art of singing. I was relieved when we finally arrived at the Zistel Alm, for I began to worry my husband might eventually be seduced, knowing Usova's unflagging tenacity.

The first thing Madame did was pick up her mail. Because we had left the address of Madame's retreat with the company in case they wanted to reach Arturo, there was a letter for him. Usova handed it to him before going back into the hotel to collect the belongings she had left behind while in Bayreuth. Sitting in the car waiting for her, Arturo opened the letter. It was from Max Fremstad. When he finished the letter, he handed it to me. Reading it, I could feel each word filtering into my veins and arteries, erupting into anger and hurt.

July 17, 1954

Dear Arturo,
 I hate to bother you in your well-deserved vacation, but the president of the board gave me your address and insisted I should write you. I do so reluctantly but as the news is rather good and there is nothing which will give you headaches or worries, I shall get immediately to the point.
 Tanya Taylor, from the Met, has accepted to sing four Carmens, consequently Jessica will sing the three other performances. She has accepted the same fee as the other imports, plus travel expenses. The only trouble is that she had previously signed with the Cosmopolitan Opera Company in San Francisco to sing Carmen there on February 28, with rehearsal February 26. In order to save the entire problem, I came to the conclusion that we open the festival with Carmen on February 24. Taylor can then go to San Francisco the next day. (She has promised to arrive

in Toronto a week before opening night and she will return from San Francisco for the other three performances on March 2.)

There is much angst from our temperamental conductor regarding the suitability and capability of our "unknown tenor," but we will have to wait until after your concert in August to see if the tenor meets with maestro's approval. If not, we will hope and pray we can find a replacement at this late date. Please drop me a line of your approval as soon as you can.

All the best to you and Jessica for a wonderful continuation of your holidays and my regards to Madame Usova.

Most cordially yours,
Max Fremstad

When I finished reading, I reached forward and dropped the letter on the seat beside my husband. I could neither think nor speak clearly. It was the first I'd heard I would be sharing the role of Carmen, and the thought of it being with a seasoned performer from the Met threw me into a fit of terror. I knew my every sound and action would be compared with hers. If I failed to live up to others' expectations, it could end my career. The same people who once loved you could instantly turn on you because of a missed step. I tried to turn down the volume of my interior turmoil. Gone was the fragile confidence acquired by basking in what I thought to be past glories. The reality was, I wasn't ready to sing Carmen, and certainly not with this unexpected additional challenge.

"Why wasn't I told I'd be sharing the role?" I was surprised how flat and strained my voice sounded.

"Did you honestly think you'd be able to sing seven performances in two weeks? Even the most seasoned performer would think twice." His retort was laced with sarcasm.

"You might have picked a company member instead of an accomplished diva. I bet she gets opening night as well." Outrage was quickly taking hold, and I felt the full force of blame gathering. Why didn't he tell me this before?

"There isn't anyone else." He laughed without humour. "Look, it's time you faced it. You're in the big league now. School is out—over with." I could tell by the tone of his voice the subject was closed.

I should have withdrawn right then; told him to get someone else to play his other woman, but I didn't, for so badly did I want the role that ambition swept away all caution.

"The air in this car is not healthy. What goes on when Lana's back is turned?"

The sound of Usova's voice caught us both by surprise. We had been so absorbed in our own turbulent thoughts that we hadn't heard the car door open.

With a smile to Usova, Arturo filed his irritation and got out of the car. He took her suitcases from the *Gepäcksträger* while I sat silently in the back seat, arms crossed, dejected and pouting. We began to wind our way down into Salzburg along the Gaisberg-Autostrasse, strangers in a haze of silence.

"Which of you will tell Lana what this is all about?" Her voice sliced through the thick air in its usual commanding way. We both sat like pieces of sculpture, waiting for the other to respond. "Well, I'm waiting." I could see her easily provoked impatience surfacing. My husband weakened first.

"Madame Usova," he began slowly and cautiously, "do you consider it wise for a comparatively inexperienced young singer to tackle seven performances of *Carmen* in two weeks?"

Her reply was instant. "Darlink, it is Lana, please. What are you trying to tell me? Be more precise."

There was a charged silence. I leaped into the fray, knowing how Arturo must have reacted to such a combative command. With deliberation, I began punching each word. "What he neglected to tell you was that I am to share the role with none other than Tanya Taylor from the Met, and that I get second billing."

You cannot squeeze blood from a stone. I have seen what this lady does with poor Carmen. She has no class, a voice of little consequences, and a great deal of nerve." Her words flowed like dark sticky toffee. "No, darlink, you have nothing to fear," she repeated.

From my perch in the back of the car, I could see the corner of Arturo's eye crinkle behind his dark glasses and the side of his mouth twitch up. "I can only hope your expert opinion of this particular artist isn't shared by the general public. If so, we're in deep trouble, and it is I who should be frightened."

She countered with an almost inaudible, "We shall see."

But this incident created a fissure in my relationship with Arturo that, for my part, never quite healed. I found his lack of communication concerning my career difficult to accept. Eva had warned that being married to a conductor wouldn't be easy, particularly if he happened to be artistic director of the company.

We dropped Usova at her apartment on Joseph Messnerstrasse around noon and, in a few minutes, we arrived in front of the Kurtz's apartment on Rainerstrasse. For the past two years I had been in frequent touch with Trude and Herman Kurtz through letters. They had insisted we stay with them while in Salzburg. They wanted to "look my husband over" to see if they approved.

My lesson the next morning had an inauspicious beginning. We weren't five minutes into it when I could see this was going to be yet another pothole in the ill-paved road I had travelled with Usova over the past two years. I was unsure if I should mention, up front, my concern over the upper register or wait to see how it sounded. When I sang in Golfo Aranci, my voice felt good. The damage done by forcing the speaking voice lower appeared to have corrected itself. Perhaps by now the problem had disappeared.

As usual, she began with a few warm-up scales. We hadn't reached the *E* below high *C* when she stopped. From her seat at the piano, she lifted her heavy green eyelids high enough for me to see the white under the iris. *"Lieber Gott,* what have you been doing to this beautiful voice of ours?" There was a deep sigh. "You have trampled down the ground Lana had so carefully tilled. I shall once more have to take the hoe and shake the earth loose." Another deep sigh! "You do try my patience so, little one."

We began again, this time from the *A* in the middle of my voice. She struck two chords above it, then two below. I had to repeat these five notes over and over until they were perfectly placed in the mask and even throughout. Using five notes at a time, she moved up and down my voice until the two octaves from *A* below middle *C* to *A* below high *C* were placed to her satisfaction. Throughout the exercise, like a sergeant major, she barked out commands, "Relax—out of your throat—further forward—use the cavities of your face—shoulders down—relax—your neck is stiff—open your eyes—the jaw, relax it—look in the mirror—darlink, see how cramped you are."

By the end of the hour, I couldn't help but admire her remarkable ability to distill technique into a series of commands, critiques, and adjustments. The voice soon began to respond to her punishing treatment. Eventually she was able to once more put the trolley back on its tracks.

The second lesson commenced with work on the *Carmen* score. I knew the role from memory, having learned it to perform in Massachusetts two years earlier. I was able to stand free of the music and concentrate on placing each note carefully in the voice while Madame filled in for her husband, accompanying me in her halting fashion on the piano. "The interpretation will come later," she said.

We arrived almost at the end of the first act without problems. When I began the Sequidille, I was stopped at the third bar. "Darling, each note in that run is as important as the next; now do it again.... No, no, I don't want to hear any *H*—again." For most of the week, the lesson began with this aria. Psychologically, it would have been better had she laid it aside and worked on another section of the role, for the aria evaded me no matter how hard I tried, but she was determined to perfect it before we went further. It soon became an *idée fixe,* and at the sound of the first chords, my throat would constrict. I began to hate to sing this aria that always, in the past, had given me great pleasure.

My last lesson consisted of dialogue, largely one sided. The minute I entered the studio, Usova sat me down on the settee in front of the crook of the grand piano. "Today we talk, we do not sing," and she sat down beside me, our knees touching. Her face gave no indication of what we would talk about. "In the past you have managed with ease to bring to life the characters you have performed because of your gift for comedy and for acting. These have been superficial creations, partly because you looked the part and partly because they were superficial characters." I was about to argue when she frowned her displeasure. Then, with her penetrating eyes she searched my face. "You will find Carmen very different. You must dig much deeper this time. You will use your voice to colour each sound with meaning as you would in speaking. Though you sing in French, you must feel each word as if it were your own language. The French in your Canada will expect to understand what you are singing about." She leaned forward, her face close to mine, her voice soft, exuding sexuality. "You will create a fearless, vibrant, passionate temptress. Men must inhale you over the footlights." She sat back. "Oh, what a Carmen I would have made had I the right voice—the right appearance." A look of reverie came over her face then quickly disappeared. "But that was not to be. You will be my Carmen for me." She took my hand, and her piercing eyes again bored holes in mine. "If you are not careful, your looks could work against you. You are tall and slim. Your ladylike English upbringing will be hard to shed, for you are very much a part of all that went before." She paused. "On the other hand, if used properly, your height could be a great advantage. A tall Carmen could be an imposing Carmen. You must infuse every fibre of your being with a magnetic current. Then, *liebling,* you could be—" and she put her fingers to her lips and blew an imaginary kiss into the air above "—*grossartig* (magnificent)."

She moved closer, and the increased pressure on my knee filled me with uneasiness. I recalled with dread her attempted seduction over a year ago. I instinctively pulled away. Sensing my discomfort, she put her hand on my knee to anchor it. "Darlink, you will park all your inhibitions at the stage door before you enter the theatre." She shook her head with impatience. "Carmen knows nothing of inhibitions; she is a gypsy, an earth being, amoral, not immoral. There is a fine line which you must walk. She is not a slut. There are as many Carmens as there are singers who play the role, and you will play her your way, with energy, with conviction, and with class." She took both my hands and squeezed them hard. "I believe in you, little one. I believe we can one day be a great Carmen, but it will take work. You have yet much to achieve."

She stood and went to the front of the piano. She flipped over the top pages of her schedule book, which lay on top. "Let me see, I return to New York the first week of October. You will come to Lana for at least a week out of each month until Christmas. You will not again stray from the fold. It takes too much out of Lana each time she has to coax the voice back into shape. Beware little one," she warned, shaking her finger at me, "one day it might stray too far and be lost forever."

I left the lesson with the usual mixed emotions. I was elated over the high expectations she had of me but still had deep misgivings over her domineering persona. Doubt kept creeping through the thin surface of my self-esteem, chipping away at my confidence. Would I ever be master of my voice, able to detect problems and correct them before they became intractable? Would I ever be able to cut the umbilical cord and be free of this unrelenting mentor?

During my sessions with Usova, Arturo spent his time wandering around the Festspielhaus, hoping to meet former colleagues from Milan. Each day he scrutinized the list of performers beside the box office in case there was a familiar name. Though Usova invited him to attend each lesson, he refused to be witness to my "torture," insisting it best he remain uninvolved. We always met for lunch and spent the afternoons searching for my old haunts and discovering hidden corners I had missed. Before I knew it, our week in Salzburg was over and we were saying *Aufwiedersehn* to the Kurtzes.

Our last evening, we treated Usova to an expensive dinner at the Goldener Hirsch; she wanted to see what celebrities were in town.

The restaurant was full to overflowing when we arrived at eight o'clock. The people going to the opera had already left, and the later diners were loudly chatting in every language conceivable. It sounded like a meeting of the United Nations. We were glad Frau Kurtz had made a reservation for us, but we soon realized it was unnecessary, for when the maitre d' saw Usova, his face lit up like a roman candle. She had reached into her purse and pulled out a fifty schilling note.

Flashing a playful smile she said in a syrupy voice, "Kurt darlink, is my favourite table available?"

With an appropriately reverential bow, the maitre d' answered in his most courtly German, as if addressing royalty, "Dear Madame, you know if it wasn't already taken, it would be yours, but please wait here, I'm sure I can find one to your pleasure."

Kurt soon returned and led us through the dim, candle-lit room. Usova followed close on his heels, her head held high, weaving her plump little body through the tables as though she was leading the victory march in Verdi's *Aida*. He stopped at an empty table in the centre, directly under the only ceiling light in the room. Usova smiled and nodded her approval. The minute we were comfortably seated and studying the menu, in her usual fashion, she took charge.

"Kurt, we will begin with champagne and the caviar, yes, and the venison and whatever comes with it. We'll finish with the *Salzburger Nockerln* and espresso for three."

I was surprised Arturo settled for champagne over his usual scotch, knowing he disliked the bubbly nectar as much as I.

Usova then got down to business. Much to her frustration, she had so far been unable to force a commitment from Arturo regarding her involvement in saving young Canadian voices. Her persistent, pernicious provocations had bounced off his wall of silence like an echo in a canyon. Now that she held him captive, she thought it worth one last attempt, this time resorting to bribery. She lifted her glass of champagne and, looking directly at him, her penetrating eyes saturated with charm, murmured, "Maestro *Salute*—To the future of our young talent!" She put her glass down. She reached across the table. She took Arturo's hand while he was butting out a cigarette in the ashtray in front of him and said earnestly, "Darlink, Canada is a young country full of promise for the future. You have an opportunity to build a school unique in the world which would attract young talent from around the globe. New York is already tainted. The city is full of charlatans who know nothing of training the voice. They feed their pupils only what they want to hear. These poor children grow fat on cake and cookies and are charged exorbitant fees...." Arturo withdrew his hand when he saw a short, balding, middle-aged man lean over Usova's shoulder.

"*Küss die Hand gnädige Frau. Willkommen* (welcome)," he said, taking the hand Arturo left free and bringing it to his lips. "We have been looking forward to your arrival with much anticipation."

"Herr Maestro Bergfeld, what a delightful surprise." With her German sounding even more Russian than her English, she began discharging her thick dark treacle. "I'd like you to meet my two very talented friends, Maestro Arturo Moretti and his charming wife, Jessica St. James—one of my star pupils. They are visiting from Canada. You'll soon be hearing much of both of them. Maestro Moretti is the artistic director of the National Opera Company in Toronto. At this very moment, we are making plans for a school to train the finest young talents in the world for the operatic stage." She turned, directing her beaming smile toward us. "Darlinks, I would like you to meet a most important gentleman, Maestro Bergfeld of the Salzburg Festival."

With little more than a side glance, the Herr Maestro stiffly nodded his head and mumbled, "*Guten Abend*," then turned his full attention back to Usova. It was obvious he felt any artistic endeavor coming from the backwoods of Canada wasn't worth acknowledging.

Despite the slight, Arturo gallantly jumped to his feet, motioned to the waiter to bring another chair, and said quietly, in his most beguiling Italian, "Maestro, it is an honour. Will you join us?"

The maestro, seeming neither to hear nor see Arturo, again kissed the hand he still held and murmured, "Dear Madame, I would love to join you, but unfortunately I have friends waiting at another table and I'm already late."

When Usova was sure Herr Maestro was out of ear range, she leaned across the table and, as though launching a conspiracy, whispered, "His conducting is as uninspiring, dull, and stiff as his demeanor, but his importance in Salzburg is considerable, so it is good you have met him."

"I don't think we made an everlasting impression on your most important conductor," Arturo scoffed under his breath. If Usova heard him, she brushed the remark aside.

"Now, what was I saying? … Oh yes!" she continued, as her probing eyes again bore down on my husband with considerable force. "Darlink, this school has long been a dream of mine. Through you, I finally see it coming to fruition…. Ah, I see our venison has arrived. We talk later."

Our table was surrounded by three white-jacketed, white-gloved young men, each carrying on his shoulder a platter covered with a silver dome. As though performing a Schubert trio, on cue from the lead waiter, they lifted the covers.

During the meal Usova talked endlessly of the plans she was conjuring up whereby she would arrange to have Arturo conduct, wherever possible, her illustrious pupils. She would make him famous! "If we are to succeed, it is important you be well known. I will see to it that you conduct for my children all over the world," she said grandly with a sweep of her champagne glass.

"My dear Lana," Arturo interjected quietly over espresso, "I am not the whole cheese. I am but a small slice in the opera department of the academy."

"Darlink," and the familiar oil began to ooze from each word, "If the cheese is potent enough, even a little slice can permeate the air. We will again talk when I return to New York in the Fall."

15

Toronto—Arturo's Concert with Victor

It was good to be home again. Our Cabbagetown row house looked as inviting as ever except for the garden below the front window, which resembled a shaggy, mangy animal; the red impatience looked like flaming sores peeking through the matted foliage. It would take much weeding and trimming before the bed would return to its former glory. The crab grass from my neighbour's front lawn, which I had so carefully purged from the garden before leaving for Europe, had once more taken over. Creeping Jenny was thriving, covering the low-growing juniper. The periwinkle was bursting its boundary, spreading out over the flagstone walk. There would be much to occupy me in the garden while Arturo spent long hours slogging over his scores in preparation for his prom concert on the twentieth. He would have to reacquaint himself with music he hadn't conducted since his Italy days, layering the dynamics and honing the articulation of the orchestra; reviewing the phrasing and bowing. Not only would he have to mark his own scores, but he would have to spend long, tedious hours surrounded by dozens of orchestra parts, indicating the up and down bowing of the strings so they wouldn't look like a poorly trained corps-de-ballet waving arms and legs about at random. The markings were done in pencil and had to be erased afterward before the rented material could be returned. He worked on the dining table because its eight-foot length was the only surface large enough for the task. After each of his concerts, we had extra roughage in our food because of eraser droppings, which somehow always managed to escape my frequent dustings.

The program was to begin with Beethoven's "Leonore Overture" from *Fidelio*. This would be followed by Florestan's aria from the same opera. After intermission would be excerpts from *Carmen*; the overture followed by the flower aria so our temperamental maestro, Bartoletti, who would be conducting the opera performances in February, would be able to hear the proposed tenor, Victor Jubrensky, before agreeing to hire him.

Though it was general seating at Varsity Arena, where the proms were held, I understood there would be a reserved seat for me beside Maestro Bartoletti. He would be anxiously waiting to critically assess the tenor's capabilities to make sure the poor man lived up to his high standard of performance. I too was anxious. Like a fearful bride in a pre-arranged marriage waiting for her first glimpse of her groom-to-be, I prayed the tenor wouldn't be short and fat. As I was five-foot-ten in stocking feet, no matter how well he sang, we would surely make an odd looking couple.

By the time I got to Varsity Arena, the orchestra was already tuning up. I scanned the folding chairs in front of the makeshift stage and saw a lady's arm reaching above the full house, energetically waving a glittery silver scarf. "Yoo-hoo, yoo-hoo, we're down here," called a high-pitched voice. I recognized Bartoletti's American wife and headed in her direction. I no sooner reached my seat beside the maestro when my husband appeared from behind the bleachers and onto the crowded stage. He paused, obviously trying to decide which way to proceed. The orchestra players seemed to take up every inch of the platform, leaving him no space to find his way to centre stage.

"*Mio dio*, he'll have to fly to get to the podium," said Bartoletti as Arturo's silver head began to weave gingerly toward us between the harp and first and second violins. Because of the awkward entrance through the orchestra, there was a slight scowl on his face before it lit up in a radiant smile. He nimbly mounted the makeshift, small podium and bowed. The clapping continued until he turned to the orchestra and raised his arms. The minute he signalled with his baton for the overture to begin, there was a surge of electrically charged energy. For a pickup orchestra playing in an arena with appalling acoustics, the sound was amazingly rich. As always happened when I watched my husband conduct, I became fascinated with his left hand. It's a rare conductor who uses this hand with as much grace of movement and with such clear enunciation. The slightest movement of his fingers caused a change in the response of the entire orchestra. The hand is the extension of the musical mind; the conductor is the one that makes things happen. I sat back with complete confidence that the orchestra was in the hands of a master and let the glorious sounds of Beethoven wash over me.

When the overture finished and the enthusiastic clapping died down, Victor Jubrensky strode onto the stage. He manoeuvred his way through the players with the grace of a dancer, his large body seeming to float on top of his strong legs. There was something strangely familiar about his bold stride, but when he turned to address the audience, the face was that of a stranger.

During the introduction to Florestan's aria, I studied Mr. Jubrensky closely. He was a large man, about six feet in height. His head was covered with short, dark, curly hair. His prominent jaw, wide neck, and large rib cage promised a big, dramatic voice, and there was about him an aura of confidence bordering on arrogance. The aria is known to be perilous for a tenor. In the opera, Florestan is lying on a dungeon floor, and his first note is a high *G* sung mezzo voce. *"Gott, welch Dunkel hier."* I have heard many a good tenor struggle with this opening phrase. At least this tenor could tackle it standing up. The initial sound was not promising; it was as if there was an obstruction in his throat that he was trying to push through. I looked sideways at Bartoletti. His thick lower lip was protruding more than usual in a pout, his eyes were closed, and he was shaking his head. I knew right then the poor tenor hadn't a chance, but as the aria progressed and Jubrensky began to warm up, a strong rich voice and charismatic stage presence emerged. It was a pure, ringing dramatic tenor sound that cut to the heart of the listener, but there was something about the occasional unrefined note that seeped through my skin and spread out in my memory, even though the face remained an enigma.

Though Mr. Jubrensky broke all accepted performance rules, it was this originality that made his interpretation exciting. Arturo was with him all the way. It was obvious they felt comfortable working together, that they breathed together. When the aria was finished, I heard a hissing sound at my side, followed by an outburst in Italian. *"Mio Dio, devo lavorare con quest'uomo?"* (My God, and I'm supposed to work with this man?)

Thankfully, the audience didn't share Bartoletti's opinion. The clapping was loud, long, and encouraging. Though Jubrensky's exit from the stage was as graceful as his entrance, I couldn't help but notice he favoured his left side as he walked. A splinter of time passed through my brain almost too quickly to register. Where had I seen this man before? During the short intermission, while half-listening to the maestro's wife, Lola, incessantly chattering in a southern drawl, this question never left me. It wasn't until after intermission, when Jubrensky began to sing the flower aria from *Carmen*, that my memory unfolded like a fan. Of course, my New York taxi driver! No wonder the face was unfamiliar; it had been totally overgrown with hair. Only the eyes and the tip of the nose had been visible. This was indeed him. I marvelled how, in less than two years, he had been able to tame such a raw and relatively unrefined sound. My mind immediately reverted in time to that surreal taxi ride in New York City at night in the fall of 1952.

"Until we meet again," had been his last words. The picture of the bar on Lexington Avenue and our unrestrained rendition of all the duets we could conjure up came vividly alive. I began to laugh, quietly but uncontrollably. A frown came over Bartoletti's face, and I felt a sharp jab in the ribs.

"*Basta!*" he hissed. "*Silenzio!*"

"Honey, what were y'all laughin' at when that poor tenor was singin' his heart out?" Lola drawled while we searched our way backstage to try to find Arturo and Mr. Jubrensky after the concert. I couldn't think of a quick explanation, so I mumbled something about thinking I had met the tenor before under most unusual circumstances.

When we entered the reception room, Victor Jubrensky had his back to us and was surrounded by women, most of them wives of the opera board. Lola immediately pushed her way through the bevy of females and effusively draped herself all over the tenor. Bartoletti followed her, a half grin on his face, conveying a mixture of pride and apology for his aggressive wife. I burrowed my way to my husband and gave him a congratulatory peck on his cheek. I remained by his side, sure Mr. Jubrensky wouldn't remember me and, if he did, he certainly wouldn't admit it under the circumstances.

Obviously, Arturo felt the poor man needed rescuing, for he called out loudly enough to be heard over the din of the crowded room, "Victor, when you can escape from all your admirers, come over here. I'd like you to meet my wife." At the sound of Arturo's voice, the circle of women opened up.

Victor Jubrensky took a few steps toward my husband and stopped. "Holy shit, I don't believe it!" He remained where he stood and began to laugh a wonderful, ringing tenor laugh that came from his gut; then I too began to laugh.

"You *do* remember!" I managed to sputter.

"You two have met before?" Arturo's eyebrows rose in a quizzical look, not sure if he should join the laughter or be worried.

"How could I ever forget that night? It was because of you I decided to become a professional singer." His voice rang out over the general hum of conversation. There was instant silence, and all heads turned our way as Mr. Jubrensky wrapped his large arms around me in a bone-crunching hug, lifting my defenseless body high enough off the floor to make my feet dangle loose. When I was set free and able to catch my breath, I knew an explanation was expected. I had no idea what to say to dispel the questions reflected in the faces around us. In moments of indecision, I usually thought of food.

"I bet you're starved," I said. "Why don't you join us for something to eat? We can go to the Park Plaza up the street."

This was directed at Mr. Jubrensky, but without missing a beat, Lola drawled, "Sounds divine. We'd love to."

Over food and drinks, Victor proceeded to make the best of a good story. As if still driving his taxi, he filled his audience of four in on every detail of that crazy evening; how he had picked me up at 10:00 PM in front of Grand Central Station; how we had emptied his friend's bar singing opera duets until midnight. He went on to say that that was the moment he knew what he wanted to do with his life. He had become terrified at the thought of the empty, unstructured stretch of years in front of him and, for the first time, had found something that spoke deeply to him. The joy of making music with someone else was beyond anything he had experienced before. It even beat making love! The next day he sought out a renowned teacher whom he hoped would take him on. From then on, he was determined to become "the best damn tenor around."

Arturo was so captivated, if he'd had a contract handy, I'm sure he'd have signed Victor up right then and there.

One reviewer in the paper the next day was equally impressed.

> Tenor Victor Jubrensky met the challenges of the evening splendidly in his two numbers: Floristan's aria from Beethoven's Opera, *Fidelio*, and the flower aria from Bizet's *Carmen*. Despite a shaky beginning, he sang with intelligence, musicianship, and dramatic involvement. His ringing, robust sound showed tremendous potential.
> The gifted conductor Arturo Moretti was excellent in his meticulously detailed and passionate reading of both scores. His rendering of Beethoven's "Leonore Overture," with its gradual building to an exciting climax, was masterful. As well, Moretti served the needs of the tenor in both arias with sensitivity.

Victor Jubrensky went home to New York City the next day with a contract to sing seven performances of Don José in Bizet's *Carmen* the following February.

16

Preparations for Carmen Begin

The gruelling but gratifying preparations for the role of Carmen began in October. Until then, I had been relearning and memorizing the music and, with the help of Usova, placing each note into my voice. Music rehearsals with Maestro Bartoletti commenced early in the month, with two sessions weekly with me alone. A few weeks later began the ensemble rehearsals. The roles of the smugglers, El Dancairo and El Remendado; Carmen's friends, Frasquita and Mercedes; and the captain of the dragoons, Zuniga, were all sung by members of the company. The toreador, Escamillo, and Micaela, Don José's childhood sweetheart, were imports like Don José; they would join us after Christmas. The prima donna, Tanya Taylor, would arrive mid-February, a week before opening night on the twenty-fifth. I, thankfully, would be doing all rehearsals up to then.

At that time, my confidence was fragile. I was overly aware of my shortcomings, imagined or real. My voice was not fully mature, not lush and sexy as a Carmen voice should be, and not always reliable. Nervousness frequently plagued me and, at such times, my support would fail, making the high notes sound thin. This was my first attempt at a major role; I hadn't yet learned where to conserve both voice and energy and where to let caution go without damaging my instrument. This knowledge can only be gained through experience. The thought never left me that I was up against a formidable adversary, a seasoned performer by which Carmens were frequently measured.

In the second act, there is a dance sequence where Carmen is expected to display a credible command of flamenco dancing. Most performers of the role settle for a sexy walk, leaving the castanets to the orchestra. I was determined to do better. From early childhood, I had danced in one form or another. I saw no reason that, if I took the challenge seriously, I couldn't master the technique of flamenco dancing in four months; but where to find someone who could teach me? I began with the yellow pages. There was only one person listed, a Senorita Carmencita. I thought the name promising. Because her studio was east on the Danforth, near the beaches, it would require a long bus ride, but I had no choice; I phoned. "Sure, you can start anytime. How about once a week, eh?" a very Canadian voice said.

The next day I arrived in front of a well-aged red door opening onto the street. Great chunks of paint were missing exposing at least three different colours underneath. A small sign directed me to the second floor. Each step creaked in protest while I mounted the steep flight of old, unattended stairs. At the landing above were three doors to choose from, with no indication what lay behind them. The one to the left was slightly ajar, so I chose it. I put my ear close to the opening, but there was no sound from within. At two o'clock in the afternoon, I thought this strange for a dance studio. I knocked and instantly heard the heels of a woman's shoes click their way toward me. The door was opened by a plump, middle-aged woman, the most un-gypsy-like creature I had ever seen.

"Excuse me, I'm looking for Senorita Carmencita's dance studio." I was sure I had chosen the wrong door.

"And you are Jessica St. James?" There was no smile of welcome on her face. In fact, there was no expression at all. Her face was like a mask of dough covered on top with the dried leaves of a cornstalk pulled tight into the nape of the neck. The dull eyes were of indeterminate colour. The chin seemed to recede into the upper part of the full neck. Her sloping shoulders, sagging breasts, full hips, and rounded stomach had no waist to relieve their fullness. This was not what I imagined the body of a flamenco dancer should look like. Only the slim legs and red Spanish dancing shoes looked the part.

She turned, and I followed her into the studio. The room was approximately forty feet long, with a dirty, unpainted wooden floor. There was nothing in the room but a stretch bar with a large mirror behind it at the far end. Various size posters of flamenco dancers were dotted around the pale green walls. I couldn't help but wonder, because of the studio's shabby appearance, if I was her only pupil.

"Tell me, why do you want to study flamenco dancing, eh?" Her voice was as expressionless as her face. I suppose because of my height, she considered me as inappropriate a candidate for Spanish dancing as I thought her to teach it.

"I will be singing the role of Carmen in late February, and I'm expected to be able to dance and play the castanets."

"This is not something you can digest in one meal. This is an art that takes years of feeding with the right nutriment." She said this with some degree of disdain but quickly tempered her curt reaction with a deep sigh, "Yes, well, we'll give it a try, eh." I don't think she could afford to discourage any potential pupil.

"A few years ago I studied ballet with Boris Volkov." I told her, wanting her to know I wasn't starting from scratch. "And I've taken a few lessons in ballroom dancing."

"Yes, well, we'll see. Have you proper shoes, castanets? You can't expect to practice in what you have on."

I was wearing an old out-of-date summer suit that had a mid-calf circular skirt and short jacket. Under the jacket, I wore Arturo's shirt tied at the waist. I thought this ensemble the most appropriate thing I owned to swish the skirt and move my legs like a flamenco dancer. I had bought a pair of Spanish dancing shoes that laced up my ankles at Cappezio's on Yonge Street. The only castanets I could buy were cheap ones made of plastic. I took my shoes out of the bag I had bought them in and took my castanets from my purse. When she saw them, there was another deep sigh, this time followed by a shake of the head.

"Oh dear. Well, go behind those curtains in the corner and at least change your shoes." She pointed to the frayed drapery beside the stretch bar. Behind it was a cot, two chairs, and some shelves. Could this be where Senorita Carmencita slept? I began to feel sympathy for this little woman.

She stood me before the large mirror. She raised both of her fleshy arms, her thumbs and middle fingers all but touching, the other fingers stretched toward heaven. She struck a pose; one arm curved in front of her body, the other above her head. She turned her chin and arched it to one side. Though I knew what she was attempting, the position looked ridiculous on a woman of her shape. I strangled the temptation to laugh. Then came a succession of taps that sounded like a machine gun; stamp-ball-heel-heel-stamp-ball-heel-heel. I watched her little feet, fascinated. They were beating a rat-tat-tat faster than I thought feet could move. She turned a complete circle, not stopping until she was again facing the mirror. "This is your basic step." She repeated the sequence slowly several times. "Now you do it."

Stamp-ball-heel-heel, stamp-ball-heel-heel, I clacked with my feet. She seemed pleased. By the time I had finished an hour of stamping and having my head pulled in various awkward positions, my body stretched on the bar, my arms manoeuvred in ways I didn't think possible, I was stiff and sore from head to foot, but I could hardly wait for my next lesson in a week's time.

"Next week you bring your music, eh? We'll try putting the foot work with the beating of the castanets. I suggest you do the stretches I showed you daily for at least a half hour; the foot work as well. I hope you don't live in an upstairs apartment or they might ask you to move."

Did I detect a slight smile on the mask-like face as she made this attempt at humour?

The next lesson began with the castanets.

"You'll have to find a better pair than these; they'll be okay to practice on for the time being, but their sound is awful. They have to be made of special hard wood." She took a pair from the pocket of her full black and red gingham skirt. I watched as she carefully looped the two cords attaching the two discs of wood, over her thumbs; one loop below the knuckle, the other above. The castanets lay loose, hanging in front of her palms. With her right hand raised shoulder height; beginning with her little finger, she did a strong, fast drum roll over the castanet. With her left hand waist high, she cracked the wooden discs together using her two middle fingers. It was then I noticed her long nails covered with bright red polish. I looked at my own undernourished ones.

"Do I have to have long nails to make that sound?"

"It sure helps," was her only comment.

She threaded my thumbs through the cords of my castanets. I managed the left clap, but the roll with the other castanet eluded me. "Um, senorita, would it be possible for me to roll with my left hand and beat with the right? I'm left-handed." I stumbled over "senorita." I never did get used to calling this faded, dumpy, middle-aged Anglo-Saxon woman by what I thought to be an exotic Spanish title.

"Sure, let's try, eh?"

You couldn't exactly call my roll precise, with each finger making a separate click, but it was a beginning.

Senorita then showed me how to practice by rolling the fingers of my left hand against the palm of my right without the castanets, making sure they made a continuous, even roll. "This is to strengthen and improve their flexibility," she said.

For the next four months, I executed this exercise in the bus going to and from my various lessons and rehearsals and whenever I was sitting with my hands free. It almost became a nervous tic. It took the better part of a month before I managed a continuous, even roll, rhythmically stamping my feet at the same time. My plastic castanets were eventually replaced by beautifully hand-carved wooden ones my mother bought during a trip to Spain. After four months of patient but strenuous effort on both our parts, Senorita Carmencita eventually turned me into a credible flamenco dancer.

When I arrived for my final lesson, there was a notice on the door of the building: "Premises condemned. Occupants have moved." I tried the door, but it was locked.

From that day to this, guilt, which has festered into deep shame, haunts me, for I finished my lessons with Senorita Carmencita owing her money. Unlike Usova, who insisted on payment upfront, she was content to collect her pittance at the end of each month or whenever the student could afford to pay her. That last day, I had the cash in hand. I remember making half-hearted attempts to find her after that. I phoned, but the number was no longer in service. If I had searched the yellow pages from time to time, I might have found her, but I didn't. I reasoned, she had my telephone number; if she needed the money, she would have called, but I knew in my heart this wasn't necessarily so. I should have tried harder.

About the same time I began working with senorita, I set about improving my limited high school French. We would be performing the opera in its original language, and I was worried Maestro Bartoletti's French was as broken as his English. I knew I would need outside help, for I wanted my French pronunciation to be as perfect as Usova expected it to be.

My friend Joyce, who was singing the role of Mercedes in our production, shared an apartment with two actresses. There was Donna, who had rented the crazy apartment in New York with Joyce and would soon have her own talk show on television at two o'clock every weekday afternoon; and Henrietta, who was an exchange student from France. Henrietta was enrolled in a University of Toronto drama course to improve her English.

Henrietta offered to take me through the *Carmen* score in French, word by word. She used her tape recorder to tape the complete role, speaking into the mike with feeling and conviction as if she was performing on stage. I would play her tape through, listening carefully; then, trying to mimic her voice, I would speak into my own tape recorder, paying careful attention to each inflection, each change of colour, each nuance, until, on replay, I sounded as French as she did. It wasn't easy and took great concentration and many months before I was happy with the results. She had no idea how the words should fit the score, as she couldn't read music. She deserved great credit, for her interpretation exactly matched the dramatic intent of the music. It was amazing the effect this work with Henrietta had on my portrayal of the role. I began to feel each word as if it was my own language.

Next on my list was finding someone to design my costumes. Usova warned me about the folly of leaving this up to our local company. "Darlink, don't underestimate the importance of costumes. How you look has a great deal to do with how you feel and how the audience feels about you. If you look the part, the first battle is won. Young opera companies usually dress their performers in sacks rented from agencies accustomed to amateur theatricals. You must make sure you have your own, designed specifically for your attributes."

For this, I turned to the man who designed the *Fledermaus* costumes for our television performance. They had been spectacular.

Staging rehearsals began in December, and I was again looking forward to working with the brilliant Max Fremstad. When the company had formed three years earlier, most of us were shy on stage experience. I marvelled at how this astonishing man was able to turn us from raw talents into immediate and credible professionals. He had guided me through all my past roles, squeezing out creative juices hidden deep within, always feeding my confidence along the way. On the other hand, there were often those less fortunate who, in spite of exceptional voices, lacked aptitude for the stage. He would diminish these poor souls to cinders by imitating their awkwardness and exaggerating their defects, yelling cruel insults with every move. At such times, I was grateful I was able to escape his acerbic tongue because of my acting ability.

At the beginning, all went well. I was captivated as he demonstrated Carmen's actions, sex oozing from every pore of his oversized body. Even with his obvious scoliosis of the spine, he was able to move with amazing agility and grace.

As in the past, it wasn't long before he began arriving late for rehearsals, sometimes keeping me waiting for over an hour. Most rehearsals took place in the rehearsal hall at the academy because the company had no home of its own. There were chairs lined up outside the hall where I could be found sitting daily, waiting.

One morning Arturo happened along on his way to his office. "What are you doing here? I thought you had a rehearsal over an hour ago."

"I did," I said grimly.

"Oh, I see, he's late as usual," he said flatly, his mouth looking as if it had been drawn on his face with a red felt pen. He turned and headed down the hall toward the staff room without another word, wearing a look that had the glitter of steel shavings.

I had complained frequently to my husband over the past week about Max Fremstad's tardiness. It was a mistake I was to deeply regret.

Within minutes Fremstad appeared from the direction of the staff room, face puffed and purple, blowing oaths from his nostrils like a wild horse.

"*Dieser arrogante Scheisstrottel!* (That arrogant shit idiot!) No one speaks to Max Fremstad like that.... No one—*nie wieder.*" He barged by me and out of the building like a ship breaking ocean ice. After that, all stage rehearsals were conducted as if I didn't exist. I was to rock rudderless in a rough sea, struggling to stay afloat.

When Arturo arrived home that evening, I wasted no time in confronting him. "What on earth did you say to Max this morning?"

"Only what he deserved," he said indifferently, heading for the kitchen to pour himself his accustomed before-dinner drink.

"And what was that?" I persisted, following after him.

He poured a jigger of scotch, casually dropped two ice cubes into the glass, and turned, his face expressionless. "If you must know, I said balls." This was said in an annoyingly non-committal way while he walked by me and into the living room.

"Balls—meaning what?" I was stunned. He must have said more to have generated such anger from Fremstad. I wanted to question further, but I knew from his brusqueness the subject was closed.

From then on, when staging schedules were posted outside the rehearsal hall, my name never appeared. Despite this, I was always careful to show up in case they were rehearsing a scene where Carmen might be needed.

The morning after Max and Arturo's set-to, there was a music rehearsal of the second act quintet with Carmen, her friends Frasquita and Mercedes, and the two smugglers. Joyce was already there, talking to Bartoletti. When she saw me, she wasted no time in reaching my side. "I'd have given anything to have been a fly on the wall in the staff room yesterday," she whispered, squeezing my arm tightly.

"What are you talking about?" I said in mock surprise, loosening her grip with difficulty. It hadn't taken long for whatever happened between my husband and Fremstad to become gossip.

"Your husband must have told you about the fight he had with old Fremstad. It was about you." There was a smile on her face as though she was savouring a delicious dessert.

"He mentioned it, but you know him, on such occasions he tells me little; I just get good at reading between the lines," I said, as if it was irrelevant.

Joyce licked her lips, preparing to fill me in on the lurid details, when we were cut off by the drumming of a fist on the piano.

"*Silenzio!* We begin," said Bartoletti.

"Tell ya later," she whispered, "over lunch."

Max Fremstad was a formidable personage and commanded the utmost respect at all times, whether deserved or not. He could be affable and charming as long as no one crossed him. Only at one's peril did one humiliate Max Fremstad!

Over lunch later, Joyce recounted what had happened, giving every little detail its due. It was morning break and the staff room was full. Fremstad was at a corner table casually sipping coffee with the accompanist when Arturo walked in. Fremstad saw him and, in a jovial voice, called out, "Tell your wife I'll be there shortly."

Arturo walked directly to the table and stood beside Fremstad's chair, looking down on him, saying nothing. Sensing a storm brewing, everyone in the room stopped talking. Like a ribbon of steel, Arturo's quiet, even voice cut through the stillness. "Get your balls off that chair PDQ and tell her yourself—and, at the same time, you might try apologizing for keeping her waiting for over an hour. And in the future I will expect more professional behaviour from you."

No one moved. It was like preparing for a photo with an old-fashioned camera, when no one dared breathe. Finally Max pushed his chair out from the table. Slowly unwinding his portly body, trying to stretch it to reach over Arturo's head, he stood. He removed the cigar from his mouth, butted it purposefully in the ashtray, glared at my husband, and, with his head held as high as his scoliosis would allow, walked from the room, his face blazing red. All this was done in slow motion, like running a movie reel at half speed. It was minutes before chattering resumed. Even then, it never rose above a sotto-voce until Arturo left. This was related to Joyce firsthand by the accompanist who sat through the whole scene, mouth open, not daring to move. She had never heard anyone speak to the great Fremstad in such a manner.

Things began to change radically for me when Victor Jubrensky arrived on the scene early in the new year. It was obvious Fremstad liked him from the start. In body, they had much in common; they were both large and moved their bulk around with amazing dexterity, despite both having a slight scoliosis of the spine. Victor responded to the stage director's way of working with enthusiasm and agreed with his interpretation of the role of Don José.

However, things were different in Bartoletti's camp. From the outset, there was trouble between Victor and the maestro. Each had his own deep-seated idea of how the role should be sung. Bartoletti was steeped in tradition and Victor, with his unique imagination and free spirit, had no intention of being strapped into a strait-jacket. To make things worse, he had no respect for the maestro, whom he considered a stupid man saved only by his operatic instincts.

As for me, I was eternally grateful to Bartoletti for helping me through a difficult situation. His knowledge of the singing voice was largely intuitive, but he knew how to make the sound talk in vivid colours of light and shade: deep amber, cold silver-blue, and warm brilliant gold. He introduced me to the full genius of Bizet's music, giving each note a life of its own, a reason why the great master had written it as he had. He gently nursed my voice through problematic passages, never allowing me to force the sound, showing me where to save and where to let go. He kept the orchestra in check, making sure it never overpowered my voice. Above all, he believed in my ability. He never lost faith in me, even at the end when the going became tougher. It was because of this man I was able to persevere through the storms of constant rejection and personal unpleasantness displayed by the stage director.

The first stage rehearsal for Victor was the evening he arrived in Toronto. Max Fremstad had assembled the whole cast, chorus included, so they could meet Micaela, Don José and the toreador, Escamillo. It was called for seven o'clock, as most of the cast held day jobs in order to survive. The rehearsal was to begin with the act one chorus, skip Carmen's aria, and continue until the end of Micaela's and Don José's duet. "We won't need Carmen," Fremstad announced when he began to block the opening scene outside the cigarette factory in Seville. I stayed.

The next evening, act two quintet until the end of the act was scheduled.

"We'll omit Carmen's dance and go to Don José's flower aria," Fremstad said after blocking the quintet. "The understudy can sing Carmen's few lines."

"It's okay, I'm still here. I'll sing them," I said with a voice full of good will.

After the rehearsal, Victor came over to me and took my arm. "Let's go have something to eat."

At eleven o'clock, Murray's in the Park Plaza Hotel was still open but almost empty. Joyce was sitting with a few of the cast members and beckoned for us to join them. Victor took my arm and carefully steered me to a table in the far corner of the large restaurant. "I want to talk to you—alone," he said, hanging his full length coon coat on a peg behind him before sitting down.

After ordering a full breakfast of eggs, bacon, sausages, muffins, and French fries, he looked at me with questioning eyes. "What's with you and Fremstad? He treats you as if you had a contagious disease—no, worse, as though you weren't there."

I told him how my life had become suddenly shambled by a few angrily spoken words by my husband to Fremstad. When I told him what the words were, he let out a great guffaw. Then, just as quickly, he became serious. "That really would be laughable if the consequences weren't so shitty. Uncle Victor will sure have to do something about this."

"Please, please, Victor, I beg you to stay out of it. It'll only make things worse if you say anything to either of them. I'm a big girl. I'll just have to learn to live with it."

"Okay, I guess you know what you're doing, but ..." He paused, a deep scowl on his face, his lips working their way around a thought. "I know what we'll do. Any of the scenes between the two of us, I'll simply insist we do the complete scene even when it includes your action alone, like tonight with your dance sequence. Watch me; I'll make his fuckin' life miserable. Just make certain you show up for every rehearsal 'cause you can be damn sure that old bugger will use the understudy every chance he gets." He paused, shoving a large scoop of fried egg into his mouth. Gesticulating with his fork in my direction, beating time with each word, his mouth full of a mixture of egg and saliva, he continued chewing and went on. "I have another idea. They've given me a studio at the academy to use whenever I want. We can go over the scenes which need brushing up when we're both free."

And so began an innocent solution to my problem with Fremstad, which I soon realized was the wrong road to be travelling on. Though Victor was careful to keep this arrangement strictly avuncular, we were both naïve to think the rest of the world would view it this way.

It was reliable Joyce who put me back on track. "I don't know what kind of hanky panky you two are up to," she said to me after a rehearsal several weeks later, "but from where I sit, it doesn't look healthy. The two of you continually disappearing into a practice room alone; everyone's talking about it."

I noticed too that as far as Arturo was concerned, we were skirting dangerous territory. The atmosphere around the house was degrees cooler. He had become withdrawn and irritable. Was he jealous of Victor? I couldn't believe this sophisticated, mature man would be plagued with doubts about his wife's constancy. I dared not tell him Victor was helping me cope with Max's dastardly behaviour by coaching me with staging directions I never received. If I did tell him, he would surely complicate an already difficult situation by tearing another strip off Fremstad's sleeve. No. Until the end of the engagement, I would take one day at a time, cope with a difficult situation as well as I could, and immerse myself in the role and give the performance of my life!

From then on, I had to be content with Victor prodding Fremstad on my behalf. I knew Maestro Bartoletti would make sure I had my fair share of orchestra rehearsals after the diva arrived from New York.

True to her word, Tanya Taylor touched ground in Toronto one week before opening night. From then on, all stage rehearsals took place in the Royal Alexandra Theatre, and I became a spot on the wall.

Madame Taylor was a woman of little stature. She was medium height, medium weight, with medium brown hair and a singing voice of little distinction, but as I watched her rehearse on stage from my perch in the darkened theatre, I was amazed at the authority she projected. She radiated an immediate electric current. She had carefully and thoroughly worked out little bits of stage business which added immeasurably to her characterization of the role. No movement was extraneous. Nothing was left to chance either in acting or singing. She made me acutely aware of my own deficiencies. She was indeed a no-nonsense Carmen to be reckoned with.

From the outset, Victor Jubrensky and Tanya Taylor were kindred spirits. Victor sensed Taylor's prowess as a performer and knew he could learn a great deal by putting himself in her hands. For her part, she was captivated by Victor's eagerness to learn and recognized his raw talent. Watching them rehearse, conflicting emotions of insecurity and admiration encompassed me. Fear coated the inside of my mouth. Should I back out now before it was too late and let Miss Taylor sing all performances? I knew, of course, this was impossible. She would be singing Carmen in San Francisco immediately after opening night here and would not return until the last three performances. There was no escape; I must watch and learn all I could from this exceptional performer.

A few days after Tanya Taylor arrived, Joyce's friend Donna called. "I have a spot on my afternoon two o'clock TV show Wednesday; could you do me a favour and fill it for me? It's only a half-hour. Is there any stuff you could do that doesn't need an accompanist? Then I could ask you afterward about your *Carmen* performance."

I didn't need much persuasion. My dance sequence with castanets would be perfect. It was the right length and a good chance to perform in front of an audience of who knew how many. I arrived an hour beforehand to be made up and change into my gypsy skirt, Arturo's shirt tied at the waist, and dance shoes. I showed Donna what I had in mind, and she said "That's perfect."

We had taken our places on the set five minutes before show time when suddenly Donna excused herself. It was only her second show; nerves had taken hold, and her digestive system had suddenly rebelled.

"You'd better make it fast then," said the cameraman.

Minutes went by. I waited. People in the studio ran around like electrified mice, calling Donna's name. The little red light on the camera lit up, and a finger from behind it pointed directly at me. With difficulty, I managed to wipe the fear from my face and replace it with a smile. I saw the cameraman's hand wildly beckoning me to begin. I had no idea what he wanted me to do. Donna was still nowhere to be seen.

I got slowly from my chair and took my castanets from the pocket of my skirt. Words began tumbling from my mouth, and I could only hope they made sense. "Um, I might as well begin by introducing myself," I stammered, trying to sound casual while struggling to put the red cords of the castanets over my thumbs. "Um, my name is Jessica St. James, and I'll be one of the two Carmens singing next week ... um ... in the opera of that name at the Royal Alex." Another pause; then I heard myself calling for a chair and somebody to sit in it. From out of the darkness of the studio, a hefty, bearded man appeared wearing a bright plaid shirt and carrying a metal folding chair, his face hidden behind a black, unkempt mane. It never occurred to me that he was probably a member of the stage-hand's union, not the actor's union. There could be repercussions.

"Sit there," I whispered, "and leave the rest to me." In my best theatre voice, I continued, "You are Don José, and you went to prison for Carmen. You have just been released. This is Carmen's way of thanking you." I circled his chair as if stalking prey. His head lay on his chest, hair still covering his face. It was like trying to seduce a faceless dummy. I began to sing. *"Je vais danser en votre honneur, et vous verrez, seigneur, comment je sais moi-même accompagner ma danse. Je commence."*

My heels and castanets began to beat out Bizet's Spanish rhythms, the adrenaline started to pour, and I forgot about Donna, about the little red light, and about the thousands who might be viewing the show. I was off, wound up like a mechanical doll. "La-a-a-a-a-la-a la-a ..."

When I finished dancing I caught sight of Donna, wild-eyed and disheveled, making her way onto the set. There was panic written all over her face.

"You wanted to ask me questions about the upcoming production of *Carmen*?" I said, walking over to join her, casually trying to fill the pregnant silence. For the next fifteen minutes, I conducted my own interview. Donna looked shaken to the core and incapable of functioning beyond the occasional, "Go on," and, "Really, that's interesting." When the little red light went off, I knew my ordeal was over.

"Whatever happened?" I demanded, then launched into a diatribe, mostly to get rid of the pent-up steam accumulated over the last nerve-wracking half hour. Donna promptly burst into tears.

Through sobs and recriminations, she pieced together what had happened. The lock had seized on the door of the cubicle in the ladies' room. She had banged and screamed, but her efforts had gone unheeded because of the building's sound-proofing. Finally the director went looking for her. He couldn't get the door open, either, so he had to find the set carpenter to take the door off its hinges. By the time she was set free, she was hysterical; sure her short career was over.

When I was leaving the studio, the cameraman approached me. "Where do you hail from? You sure as hell don't come from Canada."

I suspect he meant this as a compliment, but I took it otherwise. Depreciation of all things Canadian at that time permeated the CBC. The network's rumoured slogan, "It may not be good but it's Canadian," always filled me with fury. "With that kind of attitude, it's obvious *you* are Canadian," I said scornfully over my shoulder while walking out the door.

The day after my TV appearance, a letter arrived at my husband's office, hand-delivered.

February 19, 1955
Royal York Hotel

Dear Maestro Moretti:

I have been in Toronto now for four days and have yet to be approached by any of your media, either press, radio or television.

Yesterday, while resting in my hotel room after lunch, I turned on the television only to see your wife on a popular afternoon talk show being interviewed about her upcoming performance of Carmen.

I find this incredible! You have gone to the trouble of engaging someone of international prominence to sing the role, and you have your wife, who is filling in while I am in San Francisco, do the publicity.

Maestro Moretti, not only is this gross stupidity when you could take advantage of such a coup for the company, but it is a complete lack of courtesy, and smacks of nepotism of the worst kind.

Please inform all media that I am available to them any time and will expect to hear from them soon.

Tanya Taylor

I discovered this letter years later among Arturo's papers. I had been innocent of its existence. I remember thinking, when reading it for the first time a few years ago, how deeply hurt my husband must have been, for nepotism was the last thing he should ever have been accused of. He had always been careful to detach himself completely from my career. He would have been pleased if I had been given the lesser role of Mercedes, Carmen's friend. Because he was head of the opera company, he was only too aware of the difficulties our respective positions provoked. It was Fremstad and Bartoletti who convinced him I was ready to take on the role, and he knew nothing about my TV broadcast until after the fact.

17

Usova's Master Class

Not long ago, when I was searching my shelves for a particular book, my eyes fell upon *Inside Russia Today* by John Gunther. Why was this title engraved in a special layer of my memory? When I took it from the shelf, an envelope fell out. I turned back the cover of the book. On the inside was inscribed in Usova's unmistakable hand, "Xmas, December 18, 1954—To Arturo, with deepest respect and admiration, Lana."

I picked up the envelope and removed the letter.

> *My dear Maestro:*
>
> *I was thrilled to have finally met you this past summer in Bayreuth and Salzburg. What a lucky girl our Jessica is to have captured the heart of such a brilliant man.*
>
> *I have reserved the week of February 20–27 from my busy schedule so that I can be in Toronto to hold my "little one's" hand and give her courage before her first Carmen performance on the 26th. At the same time, I shall make myself available for a series of master classes for your opera department. Ask Jessica to let me know how many students to expect. My sessions are usually two to three hours in length.*
>
> *The enclosed book,* Inside Russia Today, *was written by a close friend, John Gunther. He is an exceptional author, and I'm sure you will find the subject matter as compelling as I did.*
>
> *Christmas greetings and warmest affection to you both.*
>
> *Yours, Lana*

The picture of Arturo's face while reading the letter flashed before my eyes. He knew full well Usova's manipulating ways, and I could see his lips stretch into a wide grin. He was well aware, too, of her international fame. He considered it an added feather in his already generously plumed cap to have her give master classes at the academy's opera school. It was obvious to him that such an arrangement could be beneficial to them both.

I picked Usova up at Union Station the morning of February 20, 1955. Toronto looked pristine in its thick layer of freshly fallen snow. She had hoped to take a plane the night before but because of a severe snowstorm, no planes were flying; she had to take the overnight train from New York City instead. The clock said nine, and I was one of a large crowd waiting under the great arched ceiling for passengers to arrive.

The first to emerge was a tiny figure in spike-heeled, red Cossack boots with a large Russian-style fur hat placed on her head at a jaunty angle. Her short body was swathed in a full-length mink coat, which almost covered her boots. She had managed to collect, en route, two handsome young men, each wearing a hard-earned smile and carrying a large suitcase. I wondered how long it had taken them to succumb to her charm. She walked like a general followed by his lieutenants. Despite her short legs, she strode with authority and a sense of purpose; a personage to be reckoned with. It was minutes before the next passengers began to appear.

"Look at that mink coat on tiptoes. Do you suppose she's some sort of movie star with those good-looking guys following her? She sure looks important," said a young woman at my side.

I broke from the crowd and hurried toward Usova, hoping to guide her out of the building before the rest of the passengers filtered through the door. After my quick peck on both her cheeks, she introduced me to her young companions, calling each by name. I hurried our small group through the crowd to the exit and a waiting taxi.

Before stepping into the cab, Usova took the hand of the tallest and most handsome of her cavaliers. "You darlink boys, I don't know what I would have done without you." Her Russian accent flowed like the Volga on a warm sunny day.

The young man put her red-gloved hand to his lips and gallantly murmured, "Dear Madame, the pleasure has been all ours."

She got into the cab and, before closing the door, cooed, "Remember now, it is dinner at Sardi's when I return." She flashed a teasing smile, exposing her prominent teeth. "You have my telephone number!"

For someone who had spent what probably was a sleepless night, she was unusually talkative and full of life. She even offered up gossip about Richard and his latest amours. She told me Irma had married a young violinist who was not nearly good enough for her and then began to talk about her husband, "Wolfie," who at this time of year was thankfully in California most of the time. Her domineering and authoritative self slipped off her like an oversized jacket, to be replaced with a prattling Usova I had never seen before.

While we drove up Jarvis Street and turned east onto Wellesley, she commented on how much Toronto reminded her of her beautiful Russia with its snow piled at the side of the streets in high banks. When the taxi stopped in front of our little row house, my eyes turned in the direction of the park at the end of our street. It looked like a field of diamonds with the bright sunlight twinkling on the snow. The limbs of the trees were all bent down like little old men carrying big white sacks on their backs. All the blemishes of the large metropolis were hidden under several inches of fresh white snow. The city looked beautiful.

"And this little doll's house is where you live? I had rather imagined you and Arturo in a grand penthouse." She sounded disappointed. Then she added, blowing derision from her nostrils, "Hmm, how sweet." Was she wondering if the three of us would be sleeping in the same room?

"You needn't worry; the house extends well into the back of our lot," I said. "There's more room than appears from the front."

Underneath my bravura, I wondered if Arturo had been right. He had been uneasy about Usova's visit for more reasons than one. First, he felt our house too small for Lana's overpowering persona. There would be no escaping her, and she would be very high maintenance. He was sure our little guest room and en suite bathroom, though charming with its arched dormer window adding extra space to the sleeping area, would be too confining, and the stairs to the second floor too much for her short, sixty-plus legs. "I'm sure she would be happier at the Royal York Hotel," he had said.

I could see now I had been too quick to reassure him otherwise. I had argued that, judging from her uninviting apartment in New York, she cared little about her surroundings, and she must be used to stairs because of the number she had to climb at her rented studio in Salzburg. Besides, she insisted she wanted to stay with us.

After I paid the taxi driver and he deposited Usova's large suitcases on the sidewalk, I opened the gate of the wrought iron fence. I was glad to see Arturo had shovelled the snow and put salt on the flagstone walkway and steps, for with the least coating of ice they could be treacherous. I worried Madame's spike heels could easily catch in their uneven surface, so I reached for her arm.

"Darlink, your Lana is not yet decrepit," she said with a hint of annoyance. "She still can balance on her own two feet." Then she struck out with assurance, mounting the steps like a teenager.

While I struggled with her suitcases, I hoped Arturo had already left for the academy. Usova was sure to remark on our "diminutive little nest," inciting a look from my husband, of, "See, I told you so." This would be followed by a double-edged barb in my direction, given his ill-humour these past weeks.

When I finally got her bags and Usova safely into the vestibule, I called Arturo's name. I was thankful to be met with silence.

The stained glass window above the front door filled the entrance hall with the yellowish-orange tones of a sepia print, a welcoming relief from the cold outside. Looking through the French doors leading to the sunken living room, I could see my husband had been busy inside, as well; at the far end of the room, a fire crackled merrily in the old iron fireplace, casting a warm, undulating glow. Covering the surrounding walls were large geometric paintings of musical instruments. Above the fireplace was a dramatic abstract portrait of my husband conducting, painted by a close friend.

The previous owner had opened up the house, removing walls on the main floor to create a flowing space from one room to the next. Visible was the grand piano in front of a wall of books in the next room: Arturo's sanctuary. The other walls of the study were carpeted with photos of musicians, friends from the past and present; these were interspersed with drawings of costumes and designs for stage sets of operas we had been involved in. The furnishings had been carefully chosen for their comfort and simplicity to complement rather than detract from the paintings. It was without question the home of musicians.

"What a charming house. You are happy here, are you not, little one? I mean, with your life in this city?" Her query implied "this city lacking in culture."

"Of course. We have both made a great life for ourselves here. Why would you ask?"

"Because I detect a worried look on that sad little face. Darlink, worry is like a boil which should be lanced immediately, before it sends its poisons through the whole system. We will talk later! For the moment, Lana is tired and wants to be alone."

"Come, I'll show you to your room and bring the suitcases after," I said, not bothering to try and convince her all was well, knowing it would be a useless exercise.

When we reached the bottom landing of the stairs, she paused. I had Kokoshka's sketch of Eva hanging in the most prominent spot I could find; it could be seen from both the living room and the top of the stairs.

"His work is so harsh and uncouth," she said, as though smelling a dead cod that had been too long on the beach. I could see her eyes sharpen with jealousy, and I suddenly realized there was no picture of Svetlana Usova gracing our sanctuary.

The guest room was at the opposite end of the hall from the master bedroom. Opening the door, I saw the sun was pouring through the dormer window, bathing the room in a cheery glow. Usova seemed pleased with her diminutive quarters. "It's like a small cocoon. In a few hours, Lana will emerge from its protective walls a radiant exotic butterfly."

Arturo arrived home at his usual hour of six; in the meantime, there had been no sound from the guest room. Usova had had no lunch, and I worried she might have expired, that her chest had again filled with lions. I was about to tell him of my concern when she appeared at the top of the stairs, attired in mink from the top of her head to her ankle, the tips of her red Cossack boots peeking out from under like a two-pronged tongue.

"Darlinks, Lana is hungry. She will take you both to dinner. There was a little café on the corner; I saw it from the taxi when we turned into your street this morning." She started down the stairs, and I was relieved her red-gloved hand was firmly gripping the banister, for the treads of the steep, hundred-year-old stairs were uneven. "Come, it's a lovely evening. I need cold, clean air to sweep away the cobwebs. From my little garret window, I could see the street has been cleared. We will walk to the restaurant. It will make me feel as if I am back in Russia."

When she reached the lower landing, she walked directly over to Arturo, and before he had a chance to prepare himself for her avid assault, she took hold of the collar of his coat, pulled his head down to her level, and firmly planted a kiss on his mouth. "Maestro, darlink, take my arm. We will talk over dinner."

Though it was only a quarter past six, the popular little French restaurant was already full. As we opened the door, the smoke-drenched air mixed with the cacophony of voices exploded from the entrance like exhaust from an old, diesel-powered truck.

"Lana, you wanted a change of air. Is this what you had in mind?" my husband quipped.

"With all these people, the food has to be good," she said, ignoring his comment while forging her way into the crowded vestibule. Cutting through the din with the clicking of her spike heels on the wooden floor, she sailed past the people waiting in line to be seated. Her well-trained eye immediately spotted the maitre d'. She motioned to him with a nod of the head while reaching into her purse. "You will find us a nice quiet corner like a good boy," she cooed, giving a beguiling, toothy smile to the aging grey-haired man while handing him a five-dollar bill.

"Of course, Madame, I will see what I can do."

He soon returned with a "this way please," and Arturo and I followed the clicking heels to the back of the restaurant as the glare of the waiting customers bored holes in our backs. I hoped no one recognized us.

After ordering our drinks and food, Usova, as was her wont, took charge of the conversation, directing most of it toward Arturo. He sat back, saying little, puffing on one cigarette after another, adding immeasurably to the already polluted atmosphere hanging heavily over us. My throat started to feel as if it had been scrubbed hard with sandpaper.

Usova began where she left off during our final dinner the previous summer in Salzburg at the Goldener Hirsch—that is, with bribery. "Darlink," she began with her most honeyed voice, "Lana has been hard at work in New York on your behalf. Maestro Rosé of the City Center Opera seems very interested. He has asked for your résumé. Will you prepare one so Lana can take it back with her when she leaves?" She paused and, with a self-satisfied smile, went on. "No, you'd better prepare two. Sir Roland Dunn of the Met is also interested."

Arturo had just butted his cigarette in an ashtray in front of Usova when she took his hand. Leaning close to him, never taking her penetrating eyes from his, she said in a low voice, as if sharing a much coveted secret, "Both these institutions are badly in need of conductors of your caliber."

I saw the corners of my husband's lips twitch upward in a sardonic grin, poised for a withering remark. I was grateful the waiter appeared with our food.

Usova, who had had no sustenance all day, immediately tucked into her lumpfish caviar in sour cream blinis, a specialty of the house, and the subject was closed for the present. From then on the conversation took on a more practical turn. "Now there are people of importance I should meet; people who could help us in establishing our school. Best I should be introduced as soon as possible."

"We'll discuss that later," my husband said, determined to change the subject. "First things first. I should go over the schedule for tomorrow with you." The rest of the conversation centred on the master classes—where they would take place and number of participants.

Arturo had arranged for Madame's three master classes to take place at Eaton Auditorium, the only space available that was large enough. The first session was to begin at noon the next day; the subsequent two would be on the following evenings so those who worked during the day would be able to attend. In each three-hour class, there would be eight students participating, with all others attending as observers.

When we arrived a half hour before the first session was to begin, the auditorium was almost full. Arturo and Usova went backstage while I took my seat in the middle of the auditorium. The program listed the participants for all three sessions. I was surprised to see Victor Jubrensky's name on the list. He was to be the last of the day's participants. I had barely finished reading his name when he was at my side. He took off his coon coat, rolled it up, squashed it under the aisle seat which I had saved for my husband, and sat.

"Hey, I reserved that seat for Arturo. What are you doing here anyhow? Aren't these classes for students only?" I muttered.

"Don't worry, I'll be leaving during the break. In the meantime, he'll be stuck backstage. Now, to answer your question, I thought the old girl might be useful to me in New York. I asked your husband if I could sing in today's class, and he said he saw no reason why not as long as I paid my forty bucks."

There was a grand piano centre stage and, at the right side, a small oriental rug with a table and uncomfortable looking chair. Shortly, Arturo came out from the side of the stage to introduce "the great Svetlana Usova, diva extraordinaire, teacher of many of the world's most acclaimed singers."

I could see his eyes searching for me to see what seat I had kept for him. When he spotted Victor at my side, a frown flashed on his face and quickly disappeared again. There was a pause while he rearranged his thoughts; then, with well-practiced ease, he proceeded to pile accolade upon accolade to make sure we all understood we would be in the presence of greatness. He was a master performer. After one particularly extravagant statement, he removed his glasses, took out a handkerchief from his pocket and wiped the glass clean before continuing on to the next lavish remark. He wanted to make sure his audience had time to fully digest each word of praise before putting his glasses back on.

"He sure knows how to lay it on with a trowel," was Victor's aside.

There was loud applause when Usova appeared onstage, her red hair looking brighter and her face paler than usual under the harsh light. She seemed to have lost weight as well, for though you couldn't call a short, plump figure dashing, she looked very chic in her black, mid-calf Chanel suit and her green silk blouse that accentuated the colour of her eyelids and her large emerald earrings. In her usual commanding way, she walked to the table piled with information about the participants and sat. My mind instantly floated back to that day over two years ago when I first sang for her and how terrified I was.

"My God, she could scare the ass off a donkey," was the comment at my side.

With timidity, the first candidate, a tenor, came onto the stage, not sure whether to first give his music to the accompanist or approach Usova. With a warm smile, she beckoned him over. She took his hand and pulled him down so his head was level with hers. She whispered into his ear, and he burst into laughter; then, in her deep Russian voice, she said so we could all hear, "Now you go over and sing for me "*Si. Ritrovarla, io giuro*" from Rossini's *La Cenerentola*, and we will see if you can keep a tune. Relax, my dear boy, Lana won't bite. Enjoy your singing and make me enjoy it as well."

"I'd give anything to know what she whispered to him," Victor said. "He's a different guy from the one that crept onto the stage like he was tongue-tied in the crotch."

"Shut up," I hissed angrily as I nudged Victor's arm with my elbow.

When the tenor finished singing the aria, the observers in the hall gave him a hearty clap of approval, but there was no such pat on the head from Usova. Her reaction was indifferent. No one was sure if she approved or thought he should try something else for a living.

"How old are you?" Usova asked.

"Twenty-two, almost twenty-three!"

"Yes, well, there is much work yet to be done on your technique, your breathing, the placement of the voice. It is like a pyramid. Your nose is the point. It is the only way you can get around all those words. This is killing stuff you are singing. Now let us try the recitative again but first—" she turned toward the back of the stage "—we need water here for the singers. It is very dry in this hall. We must make sure these throats are well-lubricated."

When water was eventually deposited on Usova's table and the student had sipped from one of the glasses, he began again. He got no further than the first three notes. "No, no, more *appoggiatura*—again!" This time he managed to get only two notes out. "Roll your *R*s on prrronto! In the mask! More concentrated sound! Stand up straight, shoulders back—again." He began once more. This time without stopping him, like a sergeant major, she barked out commands. "No *portamento*—pay attention to the music—three-eighth notes, not a quarter—now do the run up to *C* again—think bull's eye, put it in your nose, the sound is too breathy. Get the lead out of your voice." Her watch was propped up in front of her and, at the end of twenty minutes of steady drilling, she stopped. "We have seven more students to go, and I must watch my time. Thank you, you have the seed of potential within you, however you must work hard to make the flower and fruit ripen. Now, next student please."

"Shit, that poor bastard! That probably cured him of ever wanting to sing again. Is this what she puts you through?"

"Shush." Victor was really beginning to annoy me.

The next aspirant was a petite soprano of twenty-one years. Her choice of aria was "*O mio babbino caro,*" from Puccini's *Gianni Schicchi*. Although she had a pretty voice, she indulged in romantic sentiment to a fault.

"Have you a father?" was Usova's first question when she had finished. "You must understand when you sing this aria that Lauretta knows how to work her father. She has no intention of killing herself; she knows she'll have her own way. You must sing this with artful cunning. Leave the saccharine at home to sweeten your tea or coffee."

There was a ripple of laughter from the audience. Usova waited until they settled, then plunged on. "Now, sing it again, this time with more intensity." The poor girl got no further than *O mio*. "No, no, no. Feel the arc of the music. You hit the *M* too hard. The *O* has to be more forward—support, support—it's a double *B*. They would boo you off the stage in Italy. You must keep the air flowing. You are grabbing with your throat; loosen your lips. Why do you make those funny faces? Come over here." She reached for her purse and took out a silver compact. She opened it and handed it to the student. "Sing that complete phrase again. See—see what you are doing with your mouth? You don't do that when you speak. You look like you're chewing a tough steak."

Usova went on without let-up for twenty minutes, when finally the student's ordeal was over, and she was able to retreat to the safety of backstage.

The next two entrants, a baritone and a mezzo, suffered the same uncompromising fate; then there was a break of ten minutes. I was relieved Victor had to report backstage so they would know he was in the building; it was good to be rid of him. I had found it hard to concentrate on what was taking place on stage because of his constant facetious remarks.

After the break, the next student was a tall, slender bass, sporting a scraggly black beard, obviously first growth. "And what have you for me?" Usova said with an encouraging smile.

"I have the bass aria, "*Il lacerato spirito*" from Verdi's *Simon Boccanegra,*" the student said with confidence.

"How old are you?"

"Nineteen."

The smile quickly disappeared. "I see." There was a pause; then shaking her head, she said angrily, "You should not sing this role for at least another ten years." Under her breath, but loud enough for the front few rows to hear, she added, "Why do these so-called teachers allow such abuse of a young, healthy voice?" Then loudly, "What else have you brought?"

"Nothing."

"You have nothing else you can sing?" she persisted caustically.

"I have no other music with me." There was defiance in his voice.

Usova turned and addressed the audience. "It is not for me to tell these young people what they should or should not sing; it is the first thing a competent teacher should advise." She paused long enough to make sure her displeasure was felt by both the audience and student and with a show of impatience, she sighed. "Come, if I am to hear the voice and see if it is properly placed, then I have no other choice, but I will not comment on the interpretation."

The student handed the accompanist his score and went over and leaned against the crook of the piano. He appeared relaxed and in command. Without visibly taking a breath, he opened his mouth. A deep sound of pure gold flowed from his open throat. I could feel the skin on my arms tingle and crinkle. It was impossible to believe such a mature sound could come from one so young. He sang with perception and intensity, enunciating each word clearly. To me, his performance was flawless. I searched Usova's face for any sign of emotion, but it revealed nothing; it was a stony mask.

When the young man finished, there was a burst of applause. Usova sat still, not taking her penetrating eyes from the student's face until the clapping died down. She took her time before speaking and, when she did, she spoke slowly, her heavy Russian accent punching out each word. "My advice to you is to waste no time in searching out someone who can properly and carefully guide you. If you do not soon find such a person then you will become—what do you say?—a flashing pan when you could have a long and successful career. You should not be singing Verdi; it should be Mozart."

There was no hint of praise in her voice for this exceptionally talented student.

"Next please." She looked down at her list. "I believe we now have a mezzo."

While she bulldozed her way through the next two aspirants, I became increasingly aware of how destructive Usova's methods were. This was not the way to bring to the surface the best in any student. There was no doubt in my mind that, as a diagnostician, she was brilliant. She could detect the smallest sickness in the voice and knew what medicine to prescribe if the problem was curable. But if in the cure, the patient lost the desire to carry on, what good was the medication? Surely an injection of encouragement and confidence would serve a student better than large doses of bitter medicine.

The last participant was Victor Jubrensky. He strode onto the stage with assurance. With a slight bow of acknowledgment to Usova, he gave his music to the accompanist and took his place in the crook of the piano. From the outset, it was obvious he was not a student seeking instruction or criticism; he would be giving a performance.

When he finished singing the flower aria from *Carmen,* there was a resounding round of applause sprinkled with a few bravos. With that look of steel I recognized so well, Usova said slowly, slicing through his ego with her sharp tongue, "My dear sir, you must make sure your head does not compete with the size of your feet." There was sudden laughter from the auditorium, and she instantly put her hand up for silence. She was in no mood for levity. "The first thing you must learn is humility. I needn't tell you, you have a voice of great potential; I think you already know this. But it is like a diamond which must be honed; it needs chiselling and shaping before you can call yourself an artist. You are far too quick to put your own signature on a composer's work and often at his expense. Like an architect who builds a building, you must start from the bottom and build up, not from the top down. You must know exactly what you are doing and why. You must at all times honour the composer. In your hands, God has bestowed a gift; it is up to you what you do with it. I have nothing more to say to you."

Victor stood riveted to the ground, speechless. I could see by the expression on his face that he was clawing at his brain cell to try and come up with something clever and appropriate. Usova looked hard at him, her stare green slits of metal. For moments their eyes met, each seeming to paw the ground, eager to lower their horns and attack; then, slowly, Usova stood and faced the audience, leaving Victor to retreat unceremoniously from the stage.

I was sure Victor would now think twice about using Usova for his own gains. With her uncanny intuition, she saw through him immediately. If anyone was to be used, it would be Victor. Given the chance, Usova would make him world class and then bask in his glory.

"Before we leave today, I would like to thank everyone for coming and showing support for these young singers," Usova began. "You have just heard that Canada has a great natural resource in its talent, but like any natural resource, it needs moulding and shaping into a saleable product. You must make sure these young people have access to world class teachers, even if you have to import them," she paused to make sure her point was getting across, "or this river of talent will dry up or simply flow to foreign lands."

She walked around to the front of the table and began again. "Few areas of art have been subjected to as much—what do you say in English?—ah, yes—quackery as the development of the singing voice. In many cases, it has been Lana's fate to try to restore youthful luster to an already damaged voice, a difficult if not impossible task. It is absolutely necessary a young student finds the correct teacher from the beginning, before bad habits are formed." She turned and picked up the pitcher of water from the table, slowly poured a little of the liquid into an unused glass and took several sips. She put the glass back on the table and, with purpose, walked to centre stage.

Watching her, I couldn't help but think how each movement was made for effect, calculated to emphasize the importance of her words. What a performer she must have been on the operatic stage!

"It was Lana's good fortune from the outset to have been put into the hands of Maestro Dimitri Andreivitch Ousatov by my great friend, the Russian bass, Feodor Chaliapin. I was in my late teens when I began to study with this exceptional maestro. Not only did he furnish me with a solid technique, but he played a considerable role in my artistic development. To me, he was a god. To him, I owe my in-depth knowledge of the workings of the voice and my understanding of the composers and the theatre they wrote for.

When this great man passed away, he bestowed on me his legacy of teaching. I became his disciple. It has been Lana's quest—no, her resolve—ever since, to pass on his method of teaching to as many corners of the earth as there are opera houses. God has sent to me many of the world's greatest talents to shape. To Him, I shall be eternally grateful, for it has made my crusade one of never-ending fulfillment."

She turned and went back to the table to pick up her purse. Facing the audience again, and with her Russianness at its most appealing, she added, "You have been a wonderfully attentive audience." She paused. "Not one cough did I hear." She paused again. "Thank you, *merci beaucoup, molte grazie, danke sehr, bolshaya spaciba*. I have enjoyed myself very much and hope you have as well." There was silence as she turned to leave the stage, then the whole auditorium erupted into applause and as one rose to their feet with loud bravas.

My husband appeared from behind the curtain with a wide grin on his face, clapping heartily as well. He kept his rhapsodic words of thanks to a minimum, sure they would appear anticlimactic under the circumstances.

The next few days were taken up with orchestra rehearsals, dress rehearsals, and the introduction of Usova to personages she felt could be useful to her. Sleep had become for me a country to which there was no entry. Nerves had begun to play their dissonant chords of doubt and misgivings. It didn't help that Arturo was increasingly distant. Whenever we spoke, the crackle of static was in his voice. None of this escaped Usova's constant scrutiny, and finally the promised "talk" came the evening after her second master class, while we were sipping tea before turning in. We were sitting at the kitchen table when she suddenly reached over and took both my hands in hers, her gaze boring deep holes into my psyche.

"The time is overdue. We must talk." She gave an extra squeeze to her already tight grip. "You are worried that you will fail; this is natural, for you are facing the biggest challenge of your young career. You are aware you will be compared with this other Carmen, of course; but my darling little one, you must see that Tanya Taylor has limited capabilities. Her looks are common, her voice is common, and her Carmen is a vulgar tramp. You must not make the error of trying to imitate her. You can't make yourself into a slut, so don't even bother trying. You will shed your fine English upbringing. You will leave those inhibitions at the stage door with the doorman. You are fortunate to have found Lana to guide you. Just remember all that she has taught you, and you will make her proud. Now, enough of Carmen—there is something else nibbling away at you. When I saw you and Arturo together that first evening at dinner, I sensed the same cold current of charged air I felt while getting into the car outside the Zistel Alm this past summer. This is not the time for added stress. Whatever is upsetting you, Lana must get rid of this infection immediately before it further spreads its poison."

With difficulty, I freed my hands from her firm grip. My downcast eyes began to study the fingerprints and coffee stains on the glass tabletop which had escaped my notice when mopping up after breakfast. I could feel Usova's unrelenting eyes scrutinizing me, trying to draw out the contamination.

"Well, I'm waiting. Lana is tired but will not leave this chair until she knows the problem."

I continued staring at the stains, hoping they might help assemble my thoughts. How much should I tell Usova, knowing her tendency to incinerate whatever is offered? The last thing I needed was another explosion. Could I tell her of my problems with the stage director and Victor's part in it? Tell her how I was aware jealousy was eating away at my husband's heart but I dared not relieve his pain for fear he would again lash out at Fremstad? Tell her I planned to explain everything to Arturo after we buried *Carmen*? Could I trust her to say nothing that would further inflame my husband and our already fragile relationship?

"Well?" Usova repeated.

I took a deep breath and began.

When I finished, there was silence; then, with a long-suffering sigh and a slow shaking of the head, she said, "Oh, my darling little one, you must quickly develop a thicker hide if you want to survive in this business. You are fortunate your problem lies with the stage director; he has only made things a little difficult temporarily. The conductor could do much more damage. The orchestra could shred you to bits by playing *fortissimo* to your *pianissimo*, *largo* to your *presto*. Put all this rubbish out of your mind; besides, it does no harm to make a husband occasionally jealous. When it is all over, he will be more attentive. Now, you will concentrate solely on giving the performance of your life. Be assured, my lips are sealed. Enough said. To bed, for we both shall need all the sleep we can get."

For the first time in weeks, I slept soundly that night. The poisons had been spilled, and I dreamt only of success upon success.

The next evening was my dress rehearsal. The final dress would be Tanya Taylor's, the night prior to opening night. Even though my rehearsal was only a partial-dress (lighting had yet to be set, makeup and costumes yet to be completed), I felt relaxed and fully in control. I felt good in my costumes as well.

Usova had brought with her a beautiful Spanish shawl, which she presented to me the morning after she arrived. "I wore this for my last performance in Moscow. I have treasured it ever since, waiting for a Carmen worthy of it. You will wear it over your first act costume."

The shawl was emerald green, with a long silk fringe of the same colour. It was richly embroidered with large, deep red roses and looked stunning over my full skirt of brown cotton and off-the-shoulder white blouse, drawing out the green of my cummerbund. My problem was, I hadn't had time to practice with it before the rehearsal. A shawl can be worn many different ways. It can be used to advantage, accentuating the action, but it must be carefully planned beforehand. To play it safe, I decided to drape it casually over one shoulder for the time being and make sure to work with it before opening night, but it kept slipping off, hindering any natural movement. Finally, in desperation, I began to improvise, waving the shawl at random, using it as a "come on" to members of the dragoons as a bullfighter would to a bull. Obviously, the action fell short of its intended goal.

"*Lieber Gott*, what do you think you are doing? You look like you are sending distress signals. Get rid of that goddamned piece of rag," roared Max Fremstad from out of the blackened theatre.

Retreating backstage through the cigarette factory door after singing the "Habanera," I hurriedly descended the stairs from the upper platform of the set. I wanted to get rid of the offending garment before my next entrance minutes away. When I reached the bottom, Usova was already there. Her eyes were bulging, and she was shaking with rage. "That man is a stupid, arrogant, bad-mannered boor; here, give me that shawl." She grabbed it off my shoulder, muttering, "That idiot has no imagination. None. Never mind, we will work with it. If used properly, it could be most effective." She folded the shawl lovingly over her arm and, without another word, went back to the front of the house.

During the rest of the rehearsal, Fremstad loudly barked out light cues in German. Often we would be plunged into semi-darkness or totally bathed in brilliant, fluctuating colours of blinding light. At one point, the poor stage manager became so rattled that the curtain came down prematurely in the middle of Micaela's third act aria. On this occasion, Fremstad's oaths could be heard outside the Royal Alexandra Theatre and onto King Street.

Throughout the rehearsal, Maestro Bartoletti was kind to me; always supportive, never drowning me out. Usova afterward called it over-indulgence. However, he showed no such courtesy to Victor, frequently giving him a hard time. He directed the orchestra through Don José's difficult passages at a funereal pace, leaving him gasping for breath. Near the end of our second act scene together, Victor had had enough. He stopped singing and yelled over the orchestra, "Get the bloody lead out of your ass. Are you trying to kill us up here?" To me, he hissed, "That shit-head doesn't know his brass from his oboe."

Maestro stopped the orchestra, put his baton on the score stand, and disappeared into the pit, his lower lip protruding in a pout.

"There will be a ten-minute break," Fremstad yelled.

At the end of the break, the maestro was back in place, still sulking, and the rehearsal continued, even slower than before.

When we left the stage after act three, Victor grabbed my arm as I was about to go up the stairs to my dressing room to change costumes. He was in an ugly mood, which didn't surprise me after his ongoing tug-of-war with Bartoletti. "Would you kindly tell that Russian bitch to get off my back?"

I stopped dead in my tracks. I had been expecting a diatribe over the maestro's tempi. "What are you talking about?"

"While you were onstage this last act, the old witch barges into my dressing room like she's Jesus Christ and says to me—" Victor proceeded to give a masterly imitation of Usova's broad Russian drawl "—'Darrlink, you keep singink like this and, in less than a year, you vill have no voice. Only Lana can save you.' Christ, who does she think she is?"

I couldn't help but laugh; the picture of Usova trying to snare Victor was only too vivid. "It's your own fault. When you sang for her, you wanted her opinion; now you've got it. Besides, she's probably right."

"Well, you can tell her for me to keep her goddamned opinions to herself." And he stormed up the stairs to his dressing room, looking as though he couldn't wait for the last act when he kills Carmen.

Usova's only remark at the end of the rehearsal was, "Now that that is over with, you will concentrate on making Lana proud."

Opening night was a grand affair. The theatre was full of black ties and elegant gowns. The air bristled with excitement and anticipation. This was the first time the young company had boasted such a prestigious star as Tanya Taylor. With the combination of one of the most popular operas in the repertoire and a world-renowned Carmen, the place was sold out.

I wish I'd stayed home! Sitting between my mentor and my husband, watching Madame Taylor, fear enveloped me from head to foot, and I could feel the rivers of perspiration rolling down my spine. My digestive tract started to twist and groan in agony like a boa constrictor that had swallowed a lawn mower. I was miserable!

From the moment Carmen appeared in the doorway of the cigarette factory, all eyes were riveted on her. She was a bewitching, fascinating creature, exuding sex. It mattered little that she was no beauty; such was the extraordinary electrical current she projected. Was she born with this star quality, or did she acquire it along the way? All I knew was that I didn't stand a chance compared with this great diva. The audience was continually on its feet, yelling bravos, often holding up the performance for minutes. I could see Bartoletti look at his watch constantly, worried he might go overtime, which could be costly. He made up some of the lost time at the expense of poor Don José; I never heard his flower aria in the second act taken at such a clip. When Victor finished singing, the crowd was again on its feet, prepared to give him a long and loud ovation. Bartoletti signalled for the orchestra to keep playing, cutting the clapping and bravos off in their infancy. There were no dragging tempi that night. All was taken at a sparkling tempo.

The curtain calls at the end of the performance were thunderous. When Victor appeared in front of the curtain, this time Bartoletti had no control over the unconstrained bravos he received.

Usova's comment about Miss Taylor's performance was predictable. With scorn oozing from every word, she sneered, "That poor dear has such a small talent! It is surely a lesson in what confidence can accomplish."

I wondered why she didn't use the tool of confidence in her teaching when she saw what it could accomplish in a performance, instead of always grinding this necessary component into small bits under her spike heels.

The reviews the next day were glowing in all papers; particularly for Tanya Taylor.

18

Ill-Fated First Performance of Carmen

"Nothing is more risky for a young, rather inexperienced singer than to have to make his or her attempts at an ambitious role in the full glare of an important opera house," wrote Tito Gobbi, the world famous Italian baritone in his memoirs My Life. In my case, he could have said, "In the full glare of a hometown audience."

I awoke early, having tossed and turned all night like a log adrift in an angry sea. One minute I was soaked in sweat, the next shivering from the cold air gusting through the open window. Arturo was still unused to central heating and insisted on fresh air at night regardless of what was taking place outside. My throat ached; it hurt to swallow. "Oh God," I thought. "Not now; the last thing I need is a cold."

I could hear ice pellets bouncing off the window as if it was being attacked by woodpeckers searching for grub. The roads were sure to be ice-covered and treacherous. With luck, few would be adventurous enough to brave the elements tonight to witness what for certain would be my downfall. My restless sleep must have disturbed my husband, for when I rolled over to check his side of the bed, the sheets were empty and cold. He probably was asleep on the couch in his studio, where he had slept frequently these past few weeks. I glanced at the clock. It was only six.

Lying on my back, I began to take deep breaths using my yoga training, hoping it would induce sleep. Starting at my toes and working up to my head, I concentrated on relaxing every muscle in my body, but the tension wouldn't let go. I must have eventually dozed off, for when I woke again it was nine o'clock.

The house was silent; I could hear the ice storm still raging outside. There was no sound coming from behind Usova's closed door when I walked by it on my way to the kitchen. There were four tell-tale cigarette butts in the ashtray on the kitchen table, and the smell of cigarette smoke still lingered in the air, so I knew

Arturo hadn't been gone long. Under the ashtray was a note in his difficult-to-read handwriting: "Good luck tonight. I'll be watching hockey. See you later—"

Arturo had been enslaved by the game of hockey since accompanying the president of the board of the opera company to a playoff game shortly after he arrived in Canada. If an important game came up during an orchestra rehearsal, he would put his transistor radio under the podium so he could keep track of the score. If it was during a performance, he would put the radio in the green room so he could check on the score each intermission.

Even though his absence had been noticed at my rehearsals during the last month, it never occurred to me I would have to compete with hockey on the most important occasion of my career.

I made coffee, filled a bowl with cereal, and sat down at the table in disbelief. I could feel tears welling up in my eyes as I stared out the patio doors. The trees and bushes were already covered in a thick icy coat, their branches bent into semicircles of intricate patterns above the glistening, crusted snow. I struggled to pull myself together, rationalizing that if I made a mess of it, better Arturo not be there. I know he would suffer shame stoically and quietly and shrink further into his protective shell.

Warming my hands around the cup, I began sipping the hot liquid. It felt good sliding down my raw throat. I forced myself to eat, knowing I would need all the sustenance I could keep in my queasy stomach.

After breakfast, I tackled the problem of Usova's shawl. She had carefully placed it on the chair by the stairs before going to bed after the dress rehearsal. Her last words had been, "You will wear that shawl; you will not play with it. It is too beautiful to use as a red flag exciting the bull." As usual, she was right; it would be best not to work it into the staging. I would anchor it securely around my shoulders instead. The only way I could think of was to sew elastic ribbon on each side of the shawl to loop around my upper arms. Surely this would keep it in place.

Usova finally emerged around noon. She had her usual bagel and coffee and said we should warm up the voice for half an hour to make sure it was still there.

"A few scales and vocalises will be enough." There was no mention of the shawl.

Because of the inclement weather and my tender throat, I spent the rest of the day resting and going over my score before rustling up a light supper for Usova and myself. I planned to leave for the theatre at 6:30 PM, in plenty of time for an eight o'clock curtain. During supper, Usova asked if we would be meeting Arturo at the theatre, for she hadn't seen him all day. I said, "I don't know" and hoped she'd leave it at that.

The storm had subsided, but in its wake, torn off branches lined the roads as we made our way carefully to the theatre. The pavement was covered in a mixture of salt and ice, making driving precarious. At seven, the parking lot beside the stage entrance was empty.

The stage door attendant, Jimmy, already on winking terms with Usova, greeted us with a cheery, "Good evening. It's sure to be a lousy house tonight; second night always is, and with this weather ..."

While Usova went to the box office to make sure her allotted seat lived up to her expectations—that the seat was conspicuous enough to be seen by performers and audience alike—I went up the few stairs to the dressing room I shared with Tanya Taylor.

Her persona was everywhere. Her black wig was on a form on the table in front of the makeup mirror, her makeup box open beside it, her costumes hanging on a rack nearby. After much searching, I found my costumes tucked away in a corner of the room, squeezed together on several hooks, well out of sight; my wig in a plastic bag on a hanger beside them. It was obvious Madame Taylor wanted no evidence of our shared accommodation.

After checking to make sure all my costumes were in order, I noticed, on the makeup table, several telegrams addressed to me. Beside them was a small vase with a single red rose; under the vase was an envelope with my name on it. I opened it. Inside was a card with a gaudy pink flower covered with sequins and sparkles on the front of it. I knew it couldn't be from Arturo. Even as a joke he would never send such a card. The message inside read—

> *Cara Jessica,*
> *In bocca al lupo! Our thoughts and hearts are with you.*
> *We believe in you—*
>
> *Lola and Luigi Bartoletti*

Tears for the second time that day flooded my eyes, blurring my vision. A deluge of mixed feelings surfaced; disappointment and hurt that the rose hadn't come from Arturo and pleased that Maestro should have such faith in me. The telegrams of good wishes from family and friends did little to abate my mounting uneasiness.

I put Madame Taylor's wig and makeup box under the table, put my own in their place, sat down, and stared into the mirror. A thin, fair, Anglo-Saxon visage with large reddened and frightened eyes stared back. There was much work to be done before those features could be believable as a sexy, untamed, beguiling gypsy. I began with dark tan grease paint. I darkened and thickened my eyebrows, applied black eyeliner to emphasize my eyes, capping them with false eyelashes, and finally enlarged my mouth with deep red lipstick; the rest would have to come from within. I had almost completed the transformation and was putting on my long, dark-haired wig when Usova walked in. She had exchanged her ticket for a seat at the front of the left lower box, as close to the stage as she could get. I feared, like a hockey coach, she would supervise my every move.

There was a knock at the door. "Half hour before curtain," droned the flat voice of the stage manager.

Usova threw her mink coat over Tanya Taylor's costumes, there being no other available hanging space. "Before I leave, we will do a few minutes work." She began to guide me up and down the different registers of my voice. I was thankful my sore throat had not yet adversely affected the sound. I began to pace back and forth around the small room like a circus lion waiting for the cage door to open. Usova reached up and firmly gripped both my shoulders. "Darlink, stop wasting your energy; you will need it and more to get through this evening."

We began again, this time concentrating on what had become my *bête noire*, the first act "Sequidilla". We went over and over each note of the run until they were clearly defined and the triplets clean. Usova was still working my voice when a head appeared through the half-open door. "Ten minutes to curtain; places please."

"Yes, yes, we know," she spat out impatiently. "Darlink, I leave you now. Make Lana proud," and her red hair, emerald earrings, sumptuous bronze lamé evening gown, and casually draped full-length mink coat disappeared out the door.

As I put on my skirt and blouse, a reservoir of stage fright loosened its flood gates. The singer's physical enemy, rigidity, began to seep through like a paralysis. My jaw, neck, and shoulders seized. The mental enemy, fear and doubt, ate away at my innards until I was sure I would throw up. I tried to take my mind off myself. I tried vainly to apply all the tricks that had worked for me in the past. I took deep breaths, exhaling slowly. I studied my score to try to psych myself into the character of Carmen, but always creeping back were the same doubts, the same questions. "What am I doing here? Will my voice behave? Will my memory fail me? Will I suddenly draw a blank?"

I could hear the orchestra tuning up. The overture began. I started to pace again. Soon I heard the children's chorus, "Ta-ra-ta-ta, ta-ra-ta-ta." Their high voices pierced my sensibilities. "Carmen, take your place on stage." The head of the stage manager peeked through the door again and disappeared.

I grabbed Usova's shawl and quickly secured the elastic through my arms. I spun around a few times to make sure it stayed securely on my shoulders and left the safety of the dressing room.

Coming down the few steps onto backstage, I looked up to see Joyce in her colourful Mercedes costume waving from the platform above, her lips mouthing the word "merde." She was ready to make her exit from the cigarette factory onto the stage and was surrounded by the chorus of cigarette girls. There were too many for the ten-by-four-foot-wide platform to accommodate, consequently the overflow spilled down the stairs, which in minutes I would be mounting. Victor was already onstage, his strong tenor voice bouncing off the high rafters above.

It was my cue to begin to ascend the stairs after the girls lit their cigarettes. When the cloud of smoke billowed from above and the girls disappeared out the factory door, I slowly began to climb, the ache in my throat pounding with each step. My breath stuck in my chest like an eel swallowed whole.

"*Mais nous ne voyons pas la Carmencita,*" sang the basses.

I opened the factory door and walked out into the full glare of the stage lights.

"*La voila,*" sang the tenors.

The minute the spotlight rested on me, the adrenaline began to flow and fire began to burn in my veins. I thought only of the beautiful, passionate, heartless gypsy woman I was portraying and the challenge of bringing her to life through the thrilling music of Bizet. Excitement filled my body with sweet sensuousness while I sauntered seductively down the steps of the square toward the fountain centre stage. Sitting on its edge, I took a cigarette from the pocket of my skirt. Before I could light it, a dragoon was at my side to light it for me. I took a deep drag and slowly let the smoke drift from my mouth while sizing up the other dragoons.

"*Carmen, dis nous quel jour tu nous aimeras,*" sang the tenors and basses.

My eyes rested on Don José. Victor, a corporal in the dragoons, was sitting polishing his gun, paying no attention to what was going on about him.

"*Quand je vous aimera—ma foi, je ne sais pas. Peut-être jamais! Peut-être demain! Mais pas aujourd'hui, c'est certain.*" My voice flowed freely from my relaxed, open throat. The soreness had flown away with the tension. I stood, dropped my cigarette, and ground it under the heel of my red Cappezio pump. With a fixed and purposeful look, I slowly sauntered in the direction of Don José. Standing close to him was the fattest dragoon in the unit. I stopped in front of this well-padded chorister and began to sing.

"L'amour est un oiseau rebelle." Like a wolf stalking its prey, I circled him, appraising his bountiful flesh. Completing the circle, I began playfully to scratch up and down his voluminous stomach as I leaned against him. When he went to grab me, I spun around to escape capture. Disaster struck! The back fringe of my shawl became entangled in the buttons of his jacket, and I was riveted to the spot, bound to my corpulent corporal by an umbilical cord. The elastic under my arms did their job well; the shawl remained glued to my shoulders.

I instinctively glanced down at Victor for help. He was sitting close by, his back to the audience, his face a map of contortions. He was struggling to restrain his laughter. I knew there was nothing he could do to help because he was supposed to ignore me, but I instantly hated him for his ill-timed humour.

It's difficult to remain seductive while chained to pounds of flesh. Which ever way I tried to move, my fat friend moved with me. There was no other way; I would have to sing the whole "Habanera" leaning against a pillar of meat. It wasn't until the chorus began to sing the refrain that I had a chance to twist around and hiss at my captor, "For God's sake, get me loose!" But he had frozen like a statue of ice, his arms straight down at his sides, a look of horror on his face.

I had just begun the second verse of the aria, the words falling out of me with no thought as to their meaning, when I felt a sharp pull from behind. I turned to see Joyce, who appeared from among the townspeople milling around the square. She gave the corporal a sound slap on the face and wedged herself between the fat dragoon and me. I heard a rip while she somehow pulled us apart. She grabbed his arm and, with a scowl on her face, shaking her finger at him, dragged him to disappear into the crowd.

But the deed had been done; the spell broken. From then on, I was Jessica St. James, struggling to sing through the aria as well as I could until retreating again into the cigarette factory. My exit from the stage was followed by a dribble of polite applause.

Once inside the factory door, I peeled off the offending shawl and pitched it from the top of the scaffolding as far as I could, not caring where it fell. I never wanted to see it again. The chorus of cigarette girls exited close on my heels, squeezing by me and down the steps to the floor below to await their next entrance. I remained on the platform, my hands wrapped around the railing, my knuckles white from the tightness of my grip. I was shaking from head to foot, fighting back tears. The dreaded "Sequidilla" was coming up next, an aria I had always loved to sing before Usova's assault on it last summer in Salzburg. Since her overzealous scrutiny, each note had now become a tortuous test. My throat again seized with fright at the thought of having to go back onstage. Like a bird, I wanted to fly from my high perch, out the stage door, over the icy streets below, and far, far away. I wanted to be anywhere but where I was.

I looked down to see Joyce pick the shawl up from where it had landed on the bottom step. Suddenly Fremstad appeared from nowhere, bulldozing his way through the mingling chorus. He was enclosed in storm clouds and heading straight for Joyce. His shoulders hunched, a menacing look on his face, I watched as he shook his fist at her. He was obviously giving her a severe basting, but I could hear nothing over Micaela's and Don José's duet on stage. I hoped her quick thinking in saving the day for me hadn't jeopardized her future with the company. She was pointing to the ripped fringe, Fremstad still shouting at her, when the stage manager appeared. He gave a quiet clap for attention and said in a stage whisper, "All right girls, you can start screaming now and get your asses up the stairs PDQ for your next entrance." (There had been a brawl inside the factory; Carmen had stabbed a fellow worker.)

Joyce was spared a further onslaught of oaths. She turned and joined the women of the chorus mounting the steps. When she squished by me on the platform, I took her arm and murmured, "Thanks!"

She smiled and, beneath her breath, mumbled, *"De nada!"* and disappeared through the factory door and onto the stage yelling, *"Au secours, messieurs les soldats."*

Seconds after the women had gone, Victor appeared through the same doorway; "Are you okay?" he whispered with genuine concern while roughly pushing me out onto the stage, down the factory steps, and into the town square, holding my wrists tightly behind my back as instructed to do.

Struggling to gain my freedom, I hissed back, "I just want to get this damn thing over with as fast as possible."

Like a ventriloquist, not moving his lips, he muttered, "At the tempi that old bastard in the pit's taking it, we'll be lucky if we get home by breakfast."

He led me across the stage to the captain of the dragoons, who was standing at the far left, a few feet from the box where Usova was sitting. "There's been a fight, one woman wounded," Victor sang in French while pushing me toward the captain.

"And by whom?" sang the captain.

"Ask her," Victor sang before retreating to centre stage, leaving me to confront Usova's clearly visible stony, mask-like face, her mouth pulled tight into a thin line over her protruding teeth, her eyes closed slits of green. Her obvious displeasure so unnerved me, I missed my next cue, forcing a frantic look and flick of the left hand from the maestro in the pit. Luckily, the next few phrases of singing were no more taxing than a repeat of "tra-la-la," and I was able to believably escape to centre stage and out of range of Madame's visible ire. From then on, I was so conscious of Usova's presence that I could think of little else. My singing of the dreaded "Sequidilla" became laboured, with each run and triplet carefully measured. Instead of flaunting sexuality into the face of Don José, I became someone on remote control, performing without heart, without conviction.

At the end of the act, while leading me up the steps and off to prison, Victor whispered, "For God's sake, kid, loosen up. Ignore the old dragon lady." Then, as prearranged, I pushed him down the steps and escaped offstage.

I hurried to my dressing room. I had no time to dwell on my disastrous performance. I had only twenty minutes to change before act two began. My next costume had many underskirts, making it heavy and difficult to get into with an unreachable back zipper. I would need help.

I opened my dressing room door to find, not the wardrobe mistress, but Usova, her face discharging pent-up recriminations. When she spoke, her voice was slow and even, her accent as thick as borscht. "There is an old Russian saying: 'A crow once shot at dreads every bush.' If you don't pull yourself together and from now on begin to deliver, you will fear all future performances. We will work," she decreed, "I must get that voice loosened up and out of the throat. Now hurry, we have not much time."

"Please, could you find someone to help me change? I can't do it alone," I said with breathless urgency.

"I will help you while we work," she insisted.

"I don't need you to tell me what's wrong. I know what's wrong. At this moment what I need is encouragement." I was surprised at the brittle churlishness in my voice.

"Lana gives no encouragement unless it is earned," she spat back. "You are singing as if you never met Svetlana Usova. Poor Don José," she scoffed, a hissing sound coming from her closed teeth. "You had as much sex appeal as a dead carp. You continue singing in this manner, and you won't get through the performance."

I began hurriedly taking off my cummerbund, blouse, and skirt, at the same time pleading with Usova. "Please, Lana, please. I have no time. Find the stage manager. Tell him I need help, now."

It was as if I hadn't spoken.

"Which is your second act costume? You cannot go on stage in this condition." Her voice was steady, icicles dripping from each word.

"There's no time," I said in desperation.

"We will make time. You will keep them waiting; no matter." She faced me and, gripping both my upper arms, firmly began to shake me. I was surprised at her strength. "Get a hold of yourself." she commanded. When she released my arms, I could see the red stripes where her fingers had been. "Now, bring me your costume."

I went over and took the red dress with the large black polka dots off the hanger, undid the zipper, and stepped into it. I put my arms into the long, tight sleeves and, with difficulty, pulled them over my shoulders. I put my hands around my waist to force the two sides of the back zipper together while Usova pulled it up.

"Now—take deep, long breaths," she ordered. "Relax! Relax your neck! Put your head down! Turn it from side to side! Drop and rotate your jaw! Now, hum, bring that sound forward, into your nose and cheek bones!"

With each successive command, she pushed my diaphragm, worked my shoulders, and took hold of my chin, moving it from side to side. She had just completed the ordeal when the stage manager appeared through the door.

"Carmen, place for act two."

"Lana, will you please go. GET OUT!" I shouted, roughly taking her hand from my chin.

Slowly and deliberately, she picked up her mink from the chair where she had dropped it and, without another word, regally sailed out the door like the Queen Mary luxury liner.

The second act went without mishap, but the damage done in the first was irreparable. I struggled, the cast and chorus struggled, the orchestra struggled, but with the half-hearted response from the house, it was useless. Even the opening of the act in Lillas Pastia's Inn, with its high-energy dancing and colourful costumes, failed to generate enthusiasm. The only number which got its usual full share of applause was Don José's flower aria, which Victor, as always, gave his one hundred and fifty per cent, despite confrontation from the pit.

Usova's seat at the front of the box remained empty. I found this as disconcerting as her presence had been. Had she left? If so, where had she gone? Those questions kept penetrating the thin coat of my concentration.

There was a mixture of concern and relief when she didn't show up in my dressing room during the next intermission. To get through the performance was taxing enough without having the added strain of constant conflict. My costume was a quick change—leather riding boots, culottes, blouse, bolero, and wide-brimmed black felt hat. I had asked Victor to undo the problematic back zipper of my second act dress while leaving the stage.

The third act took place in the mountains outside Seville, where the smugglers were gathered. Midway through the scene, I was sitting on a tree stump watching my friends Mercedes and Frasquita tell their fortunes in the cards. To hear what they were saying, I approached. Curious to see what the future held for me, I reached into the left pocket of my culottes for my cards. The pocket was empty. Had I mistakenly put them in the wrong pocket? I searched the other pocket—no cards! Then I remembered giving them to the props person after my dress rehearsal because Fremstad thought them too pristine. He thought they should be replaced with a more ravaged deck. Distracted by Usova, I forgot to check my pockets before going on stage.

Panic struck! It would be impossible to sing the aria without them; each word I sang related to the card I was dealing. My brain seized. I could neither move nor think. In seconds I would have to begin singing. I sank to my knees between Frasquita and Mercedes. I turned to Joyce, who had just finished singing how rich she was going to be. "Give me your cards, quick. They forgot to give me another deck." I blurted out. Poor Joyce took one look at my panic-stricken face and hurriedly gathered up her cards.

"Jeesus," she whispered.

"Let's see what the cards hold for me," I sang in French while Joyce pushed her cards into my out-stretched hand. I barely had time to deal out two cards before singing, *"Carreau—Pique."* By this time, I was so shaken, the singing of my favourite aria became a tortuous marathon. Mercedes had to finish our trio, sharing cards with Frasquita.

At the end of act four, after Carmen has been stabbed by Don José and my gruelling ordeal was finally over, I quickly retreated to the protection of my dressing room and slammed the door. I wanted no curtain call; I wanted to see no one; I wanted to be alone in my misery and shame. I was glad Arturo had not been in the audience to witness the fiasco. His belief in my talent would have been shattered, to say nothing of the humiliation he would have suffered.

I dropped into the chair before the makeup mirror, tore off my wig, and began to remove my eyelashes when Usova burst into the room like a sudden gust of polar wind. It was as if she had brought with her the raging ice storm of the previous night. She shut the door, leaning against it to make sure no one would interrupt what she had to say. Her coat was half off one shoulder and, through the mirror, I could see the telltale blotches of red on her ample bosom, creeping over the edge of her low cut gown, up her neck, and into her face. Her cold silence permeated the air. When she at last began to speak, her voice was measured and shaking with rage. "So this is how you reward Lana for her years of hard work. I have given you my heart and soul, and in return, you punish me by throwing away what could have been a brilliant career. I believed in you, in your talent, but that is over, finished. You have just ruined your chances forever. In this business, there is no second chance. People do not tolerate failures." She took a deep breath as her hand went up to her frighteningly red chest. "I do not tolerate failures."

I stared silently at her image in the mirror, not knowing what to say. I wasn't sure whether to attack or retreat. "Sorry about the shawl," I said indifferently, trying to change the subject. "I'll see if I can fix it."

"The shawl has nothing to do with it," she shot back.

"The shawl has everything to do with it," I exploded, reeling around to face her. "Without that damn thing, this never would have happened." I paused, took a deep breath, and stared at her. With daggers protruding from my eyes, my lips curled in rage I hissed, "You must have put a hex on it." I was sure my face was as red as her chest.

"Careful how you speak to Lana," she cautioned; then the muscles of her face suddenly relaxed as she slowly shook her head, "Oh, my dear child, to put the blame of failure on an innocent shawl is unworthy." Her voice oozed with oily acrimony. She turned to leave, then paused, her hand on the doorknob. "We are finished," she said dryly, as if speaking to herself, then added, "I will be at the stage door," and left.

Though she had declared we were finished twice before, this time her words had the ring of truth about them. Before, she still believed I could "make her proud." Now, I knew she deemed me hopeless.

I looked into the mirror and began removing my makeup. There was a calm determination in my expression that hadn't been there previously. I felt strangely liberated, as if the chains that had had their stranglehold on me over the past two and a half years had suddenly been severed. I would make it without Svetlana Usova. I knew there would be no making up this time; our turbulent relationship was over.

19

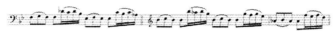

Carmen Redeemed

After the performance, we drove to Cabbagetown in stony silence. The freezing rain had ceased, and the roads had turned to a murky slush. I parked the car on the laneway beside the house; there was no point in putting it in the garage at the back because I would be driving Usova to the airport to catch the noon flight in the morning.

Once inside, she retreated to her room without a word. The embers were still glowing in the fireplace, so I assumed Arturo had only recently gone to bed. I was chilled through and too upset to sleep. I went to the kitchen and poured a small drink of straight brandy to try and warm myself and calm down.

Finally, exhausted, I went upstairs and fell into bed. The debris of my performance began to rain down on me, crowding out the few good moments. Misery encased me with a dark shroud of shame. I had let everyone down: Arturo, Usova, Bartoletti, the cast, and, mostly, myself. I could feel the warmth of my husband's body close by; was conscious of his even breathing, his special scent, a mix of tobacco and scotch. I longed for his arms to enfold me, for him to murmur comforting words of understanding and love, but I knew these were words he would never speak because of his wounded pride; he still believed there was something going on between Victor and me. The tears began to well up in my eyes and spill over onto the pillow. They quickly grew into uncontrollable sobs. Spent, I hoped sleep would push away the pain, but it eluded me. I turned over to face Arturo's back. I gently shook his shoulder, but there was no response. The even breathing stopped, and I could sense the resistance. Like a wounded animal crawling into a deep hole, I quietly turned away and fell into a fitful sleep. The last thing I remembered was seeing a slim ribbon of dawn peeking in between the opening of the bedroom curtains.

When I awoke, the other side of the bed was cold; Arturo must have left for the academy earlier than usual. The house was bathed in silence. I knocked on Usova's door to ask if I could bring her breakfast, but there was no sound from the other side. At ten o'clock, she emerged, covered in mink, her hat slightly askew, as though it had been dropped onto her head from the ceiling. She grandly descended the stairs in silence, leaving her large suitcases in the bedroom for me to carry down the stairs as well as I could without damage to my back or the cases. She stood at the bottom of the stairs, impatiently tapping one toe of her Cossack boot, her glacial eyes following my every move as I struggled down, step by step, one suitcase at a time, until both were safely stored in the trunk of the car.

She dropped an envelope with Arturo's name on it on the little table by the front door before she swept by me. Throughout, her face remained a mask, her eyes more frog-like than usual, her mouth a bright red slash pulled tightly over her teeth.

In silence, we drove to the airport. I pulled up in front of the terminal's United States entrance. Usova remained sitting, staring straight ahead as if mummified. My instinct told me she expected me to speak first, but words stuck in my throat. I got out, collected her suitcases from the trunk of the car, and handed them to a porter. I opened the passenger door, but she just sat, looking out the front windshield. Was she waiting for me to go down on my knees and beg forgiveness?

I mumbled under my breath, "Lana, I'm sorry I let you down." That was all. I couldn't crawl.

She slowly got out and began to follow the porter into the building. She suddenly stopped and turned. Her eyes widened, then hardened into glass marbles. "You have broken Lana's heart," she said, and then she disappeared into the building.

"She has no heart," I thought with bitterness as I got back into the car and leaned across the front seat to lock the passenger door.

Driving home, I tried to thrust my fears into the sunlight and shake them like a duster. I had two more performances, two chances to redeem myself—a matinee the next day and an evening performance two days later. I would expunge the previous night from my mind. I would make it part of the distant past and not let it become part of the future. In years, it would emerge as an amusing event to be wheeled out at party occasions.

When I arrived home, there was a car parked in front of the house with a familiar figure sitting in it. I drove up our laneway as Joyce stepped from the car. In her hand was a paper bag and, under her arm, newspapers.

"You've been waiting long?" I called out, walking toward her.

"No, just arrived. Here—thought you might want this." She handed me the paper bag.

"Come in. Have you had lunch?"

"Can't stay; got *Butterfly* tonight; brought you the papers. The *crits* aren't too bad." Then, after a pause she added, "Considering."

"Thanks a bunch. You can keep them. I'm not interested," I said, indifferently.

"Well, take them anyhow. I'm finished with them." She pushed them into my chest.

"Thanks for rescuing me both times last night," I said, securing the papers in my folded arms so they wouldn't fall into the snow. "I hope Fremstad didn't give you a hard time."

She laughed. "That poor guy didn't have a clue what happened. Ya know he actually almost smiled when I told him about the shawl." She ended with a "See ya," and was back in her car and off down the street.

Entering the house, I placed the newspapers on the little table on top of Usova's letter. I dropped the paper bag onto the floor before taking off my coat and boots, putting them away in the closet. I retrieved the papers, intending to leave them by the fireplace to burn, when I noticed Usova's letter was unsealed. Curiosity took precedence over conscience; I opened it. Enclosed was a detailed account of Usova's expenses. At the top of the list was the cost of our first night dinner at the bistro down the street; the one she had insisted was her treat. Scribbled at the bottom was:

> My dear Maestro,
>   I regret there was no opportunity to say, addio.
>   Enclosed is a list of my expenses. Our master classes were a great success, si certo? There is much talent in this country worthy of the best guidance possible. The onus is on you. Don't let them down. Until we meet again—
> Lana

I recently found this letter in the scrapbook where I had pasted clippings from my performing days. It was still in its envelope, glued beside the *Carmen* reviews, which I obviously had not burned. On the front I had scribbled, "Inside is a letter which afforded me the first good laugh in days; Usova at her conniving best."

Rereading the *Carmen* reviews, I was pleasantly surprised at how kind and understanding the reviewers had been. I had always walked over this disastrous episode in my life with heavy boots. In one paper, the copy ran down the full left-hand side of the page.

"If ever a young artist had her work cut out for her, it was she. Only last Friday night the company opened with a seasoned Carmen from the Metropolitan Opera who pumped so much gypsy temperament into the part that anyone coming after her would seem pallid. When Miss St. James first appeared in the door frame of the cigarette factory and sauntered down the steps, I thought, 'Yes, here is another Carmen to be reckoned with.' She oozed sex as she wended her way through the groups of soldiers gathered about the square. Her first notes were full and sensual. She stopped in front of a portly dragoon, circled him and began the well-known "Habanera." What happened from then on is a mystery to this reviewer. The electrifying confidence displayed in her entrance vanished. Instead of sweeping everything before her as the part demanded, she was caught up in it. She obviously was scared, and if there's one thing Carmen isn't, it's scared. However, by the end of the second act Miss St. James seemed to sink her teeth into the role and began to project. Some of her toned-down acting incidentally was quite effective, and her dancing and castanet playing was excitingly coloured. The gowns she wore were outstanding. Their authenticity was clear in every act, ending with an exceptionally striking one for the final scene."

Another review was equally tolerant. Part of it was definitely a collectable.

"It's not easy for a local singer to share a starring role with an artist of international reputation, backed by many years of professional experience, but last night, the Opera Festival gave us a Canadian Carmen with Jessica St. James. Miss St. James's performance is certainly worthy of critical acclaim on its own merit. Her principal shortcoming is that she lacks vulgarity, but gentility is a quality that a good actress can quickly shrug off. With this testing performance under her belt, Miss St. James can now set about expanding and loosening up her part to the point where it will be truly vibrant and vital, earthy and exciting."

When I finished reading the reviews a sudden rush of nostalgia blanketed me and the words "'what if' flooded my psyche.—'What if my Carmen hadn't been as bad as I thought? On the other hand, what if I had taken that first stab at the role in Massachusetts instead of going to Salzburg with Usova? Or what if I'd listened to Arturo's instincts and realized Carmen was not for me? Surely Usova in all her wisdom should have known. In fact, what if I'd never met Irma Mensinger and Usova had been only a phantom? Did the hand of fortune gripping my wrist lead me in the wrong direction?

I prodded my remembrance back to the day after the performance and Joyce's paper bag. In it was Usova's discarded shawl. I recall picking it up with my forefinger and thumb as if it were contaminated and looking carefully to see what damage had been done. I would mend it if I could, package it, and get rid of it as soon as possible. I wanted nothing around to remind me of the previous night's disaster, nothing around to remind me of Usova. Now that she was out of my life and my first performance over with, I was determined to confront Arturo with the issue of my friendship with Victor before the problem intensified into irreparable damage. Fiery rumours were still spreading like flames on kerosene, fanning his jealousy.

Shortly before six, my husband phoned to say he wouldn't be home for dinner; he had to take over for the conductor of the CBC Orchestra, who was ill. There was a rehearsal from six to ten.

I waited up for him, even though I needed all the sleep I could get to make sure I was well rested for the next day's matinee. When finally he arrived home, it was midnight. I promptly challenged him. "We must talk."

"About what?" he responded offhandedly, walking to the kitchen to pour a scotch.

"About what's bothering you," I said, following close on his heels. "Please, whatever it is, let's get rid of it," I pressed on. He took a sip of scotch before walking back into the living room as though he hadn't heard me. He picked up Joyce's newspapers by the fireplace and sat down in his favourite chair nearby. I followed him, not letting up. "Come on, let's talk now, before there are more misunderstandings." I tried to sound amicable.

He had begun to peruse the front page when, in exasperation, he slammed the paper down on his knees. "Look, I come home tired, and all I want is a little peace." He again took up the newspaper. "Will you just leave me alone?"

I stood before him, glaring at the back page of the front section. I took a deep breath, trying to hold back the urge to tear the thing from his hands, to yell at him in frustration, "For God's sake, let me in. How can I get through that wall of stone you've built around yourself?" But I didn't, knowing it would only add another stone. I turned and retreated up the stairs to the bedroom. I'd find another way!

I sat on the bed, staring at the opposite wall with its weathered pink brick, which the architect had carefully exposed. How I loved this little house and our life in it. I knew I must do everything in my power to mend the crack that was widening each day between us. For over a month, we had had no physical contact. Up until Victor had loomed on the horizon, sex had always played an important role in Arturo's and my relationship. He wasn't affectionate in the usual sense; he didn't believe in holding hands or stroking my back unless it signalled a far more basic urge. It was as if only through the act of making love could he express his inner feelings. He felt safe in his sexuality. He was a man of few words, and words had no place for him in bed.

Where did Victor fit in? I stared hard at the wall, hoping it would give me the answer. There were moments when I didn't even like Victor, but strangely, in a way that people working together feel a kind of electrical energy derived from thinking and acting intensely in tandem, I felt exhilaration resulting in a strong pull; but that was all. When he disappeared south of the border. he would become an amusing memory in the merry-go-round of life.

My instinct told me speaking to Arturo about Victor would be as slippery as roller skating on ice. I would write him a letter, carefully searching out each word to make sure I got it right.

By the time Arturo came to bed, I was asleep.

Driving to the theatre the next morning, I realized if I was to give a credible performance, I must cast out all concerns over Arturo and our tenuous relationship. There was room for positive thoughts only. Self belief was uppermost.

Because I arrived early to get ready for the matinee, I was relieved the stage door was unlocked. They were setting up for the first act, the stage manager yelling out commands a là Fremstad.

My dressing room was as I had left it Monday night. My wig was on the form where Tanya Taylor's had been, my makeup box open in front of the mirror. My costumes were still on the rack and the other Carmen's in the far corner of the room. From now until my final performance, this space would belong to me.

I put my fur-lined coat on the floor and lay on top of it. For half an hour, I did a series of stretches, extending and relaxing my body as if about to run an Olympic race.

Sitting, I began breathing exercises, taking in air by extending my abdomen, then lower ribcage, then upper ribs for three counts, holding for six, finally exhaling slowly and steadily, emitting a humming sound for twenty counts. This deep breathing was followed by quick panting, like an over-heated dog, to relax the diaphragm.

Already feeling more at peace, I lay back once more. Commencing at the top of my head, I tensed then relaxed every limb, searching each muscle for any sign of rigidity. I moved down my body—brow, eyes, mouth, jaw, neck, shoulders, arms, fingers, back, buttocks, legs, feet, and toes. The intense concentration helped take my thoughts off of myself.

To keep my mind free of any unwanted swill, I summoned up an image of a sandy beach on the east shore of Lake Huron where I had spent my summers. It was a calm, clear, hot day. I was stretched out on a towel, the warmth from the sun caressing my body. I could hear the waves gently lapping on the shore, their steady rhythm lulling me into semi-consciousness. There was the occasional cry of a far-off gull. As long as I held this image, I was able to keep my queasy stomach at bay.

Half an hour before curtain, I began to work on my face, using darker makeup this time, hoping to look more gypsy-like. After putting on my costume, I stood in front of the full-length mirror on the back of the door. I sighed and shook my head. Would I ever be able to disguise the tall, slim, statuesque figure staring back at me? My features, too, still had the look of a well brought-up boarding school graduate under the thick layer of greasepaint. I certainly had my work cut out for me. I would have to gain at least another twenty pounds before the result was to my satisfaction. I was stuffing tissues inside my already padded bra and darkening the faint cleavage between my breasts when my reflection suddenly disappeared behind the opening door.

"*Merde*—I guess you got rid of the dragon lady, or am I squeezing her behind the door? By the way, your boobs look great!" Victor was in his costume and on his way to the stage. Before I could say anything, he was gone. The orchestra began to tune up. A last-minute look at my score, a few scales and arpeggios, and I left the room.

Waiting to make my entrance from the factory platform, I could sense the climate of the audience. There was a warm responsiveness which had been lacking Monday night. The Wednesday matinee house was carpeted with snow-white heads bussed in from retirement homes in the surrounding suburbs, and they were hungry for live entertainment.

When the men of the chorus began calling for Carmen, my nervousness disappeared, quickly replaced by excitement. The minute I stepped out of the cigarette factory, there was a low rumble of acknowledgment from the audience. This time, I would be careful to stay well out of the reach of the corpulent corporal. Instead, I selected the shortest, shyest soldier I could find to flaunt my erogenous wares before weaving my magic spell on Don José. The feared "Sequidilla," with its troublesome hurdles including a high *B* flat, floated from my throat with ease. All former problems evaporated into the air, flushed away by Bizet's glorious melodies. After each aria, there was a generous round of applause.

Though disagreements in tempi between Victor and Bartoletti made their appearance early in the first act duet with Micaela, I was not affected until midway through the second act.

The scene was in Lillas Pastia's Inn. Carmen was about to dance for Don José, who had just been released from prison, where he had been sent for letting Carmen escape. "*Je vais danser à votre honneur.*" My castanets rolled and my feet began to beat out their Spanish rhythms—toe-heel-heel, toe-heel-heel-toe. The sound of a bugle was heard calling Don José back to camp. He told Carmen he must leave. Losing her temper, she shouted at him to go. Throwing his sword and cap back at him, she cried out that he obviously didn't love her. Don José forced Carmen to sit and demanded she listen to him. He took from his jacket the flower she had thrown at him in the first act.

The minute the introduction to the flower aria began, Bartoletti slowed the orchestra to a Wagnerian crawl. At the same time, he turned the volume to full capacity. The aria is meant to be sung *sotto voce*, half voice. It should move along, the tempo marked *andante*. From the beginning, this had been a sparring point between Bartoletti and Victor, and this night was no exception.

Sitting, I was supposed to remain cold and indifferent to Don José's declaration of love, but watching the veins of Victor's neck begin to bulge and his face redden with exertion and rage, my apprehension mounted. I turned my back to the audience so no one could see the concern reflected on my face.

At the conclusion of the aria, Victor was supposed to sink to his knees, his head in my lap, but Victor just stood, glaring into the pit. There was a thunderous ovation, but he remained staring, his features signalling potent fumes of fury while the orchestra played on. Out of the corner of my eye, I saw the maestro gesturing for me to begin singing; he wanted the applause cut short.

Victor abruptly turned and began to leave the stage cursing loudly enough for the white-haired ladies in the front rows to hear him, "He can finish the fuckin' opera himself."

With alarm, I jumped from my chair, grabbed his arm, and tugged with all my might before he had a chance to go more than a few feet. Bartoletti flicked his fingers again at me and nodded his head. I began the duet: "No, you don't love me—you don't love me, for, if you did, you'd follow me away into the mountains." With my free hand, I reached for Victor's coattail. I heard it rip when I pulled myself around to confront him, blocking his exit, my face level with his: "You'd follow me with your horse, and we'd be free."

The duet remained a solo. His expression was frightening, his flesh a purpled-red, his eyes beads of rage, his teeth clenched under a curled lip. "Out of my way," he hissed, trying to get by me.

Bartoletti looked up, wondering why Victor wasn't singing. His heavy black brows were knitted together in a deep scowl, and the forefinger of his left hand was pointing at Victor.

I took hold of Victor's wrists and leaned against his chest. "Away you'd follow me. There would be no officer to command you. We'd be free to love; free to roam beneath blue skies." Our eyes met, locked in a battle of wills.

Finally, I felt the tension in his arms dissolve, and he began to sing as if by rote, "Carmen hush—Carmen, no more—Oh my God," then he growled angrily under his breath, "You can let go now. I'm not going anywhere!"

I nodded in relief but retained my grip, for, because of the look on his face, I wasn't so sure. The duet continued the way Bizet wrote it. Only when we were joined by the smugglers and gypsies did I let go of his wrists.

The minute Victor got off the stage, he bolted up the few stairs and disappeared into the hallway to his dressing room. I was too shaken to follow. Within minutes, he reappeared in his coon coat, a scarf around his neck, his fedora on his head. Underneath, he was still in costume and makeup. He had almost reached the exit from backstage when Fremstad appeared, breathing rage from his nostrils.

"Where'd ya think you're going?" he shouted. He had been watching from the front row and had heard Victor's threat.

Victor didn't answer and kept walking.

"You leave now, and you'll never set foot in this theatre or, for that matter, in this city again," Fremstad said, still shouting.

Victor hesitated, started again, and stopped. Without turning, he snarled, "If you want me to go back on stage, you get rid of that shit-head in the pit."

Fremstad walked up to him, barred his way, and, in a low constrained voice said, "You are a professional. Behave like one." He wheeled about to face the curious members of the cast gathered around them and yelled, "All of you, get the hell out of here. Go change for the next act."

Meanwhile, the stagehands were calmly going about their business of setting up as if nothing unusual was happening.

Whatever Fremstad said to Victor to convince him he should change his mind, I don't know, for I had to quickly change. I only know he was in his smuggler's costume at the beginning of the third act. Bartoletti was in the pit, arms raised, ready to signal for the orchestra to begin.

The rest of the performance proceeded without incident. At the end, my eyes clouded with tears when I heard *bravas* coming from the audience as I took my solo bow, but my greatest reward came from Fremstad when I was leaving the theatre. "You did well." That was all, but to me, it was as if he had bestowed on me all the superlatives in the book.

Oh, how I wished Arturo had been there!

20

A Burst Blood Vessel in the Throat

March 2, 1955

Arturo,
  Where were you when I needed you?
  I have just been through the most stressful time of my career, and you have wrapped yourself in an unpenetrable casing. Several times I have tried to get through its thick wall but have failed. We have become strangers. I hope this letter can cut through your unbearable silence.
  Since this recent problem seems to date back to the arrival of Victor Jubrensky on the scene, I can only assume this is what it's all about. Looking back, the minute I became aware of the rumours surrounding Victor and me, I should have realized that was what was upsetting you. I can assure you, your suspicions and doubts are totally unfounded.
  The trouble began after your set-to with Max. From that day on, he never spoke to me; I was excluded from all staging. When Victor arrived, he quickly sized things up and offered to help me by showing me, after each staging rehearsal, what Fremstad wanted in the way of interpretation and placement. Because these sessions were in Victor's allotted practice room at the academy, tongues soon began to wag. I was afraid if I told you of Fremstad's unprofessional behaviour, you would add more salt to an already festering wound.
  If our marriage is to survive we must start talking!
  I have heard the company plans to take Fledermaus *on tour with the same cast as before. If this is true, I will be away weeks at a time. You too will be taking more and more conducting engagements out of Toronto. Our future together is secure only if we keep channels of communication open and clear up misunderstandings before they reach gigantic proportions.*
  From now on, no sweeping things under the carpet, please. Let's clean house as soon as it needs it.
  You must never again doubt my loyalty and love.
Yours always,
Jess

This was the first of such letters I was to write to Arturo regarding marital problems. It took a long time before I realized it was impossible for him to reveal even a fraction of his inner self; the past scars had gone too deep. For him, emotions were to be felt, not discussed.

I had sent my letter to his office at the academy. I knew he must have received it because, a few days later, when he arrived home he suggested we have dinner at the fancy restaurant on the roof of the Park Plaza.

"I'm a mess. I'll have to change!"

"So? I can wait."

"What's the occasion?" I said innocently, hoping to get an acknowledgment of my letter, or at least to squeeze a hug and an endearment out of his obviously expansive mood.

"Does there have to be a special occasion to take my best girl to dinner?" he asked casually, pouring himself a scotch. "Do you want a drink before we go?"

With a martini in hand, I went quickly upstairs to change into something more festive, all the time wondering if, in the future, letters would be the only way to keep our marriage on track.

Throughout dinner, he was like he had been that first night we had met over a ping-pong table. He flirted with me in the most irresistible way, never once mentioning the context of my letter; but I gladly cherished the moment while hope for our future happiness curled around my heart like an unspoken promise.

Later that night, for the first time in over a month, we silently made love. The subject of Victor was never mentioned again.

When the opera season came to another successful close, Arturo announced he would resign as Artistic Director of the company. His excuse was that he was finding it difficult to give sufficient time to both the opera school and the company because of his increased conducting engagements. It wasn't until I read Tanya Taylor's letter years later that I realized how profoundly her accusation of nepotism had affected him. This haunted him as long as I remained with the company.

Spring turned into summer; summer turned into fall; and fall turned into a miserable cold settling on the vocal cords. Severe laryngitis is usually a condition I treat with great respect. This time, I threw caution to the wind. I forced my voice to be heard at parties, croaking over the smoky din. I yelled and cheered enthusiastically with the rest of the crowd at a soccer match, not caring that I couldn't speak for days afterward. Arturo cautioned me to treat my voice with greater respect.

"It's the only voice God will ever give you," he warned, but I was in a sulk, angry and hurt. I hadn't heard from the opera company and was convinced they were finished with me because of what I perceived to be my less-than-acceptable performance of Carmen, but I was wrong. Unbeknownst to me, Arturo had received a call in September from Max Fremstad, who had taken over as Artistic Director of the company. Fremstad wanted Arturo to conduct *Tales of Hoffman* the following February.

It wasn't until December I received a similar call asking me if I would sing Nicklaus in the same opera. After Fremstad's call, I hung up the living room phone and turned to Arturo, who was sitting by a dimly glowing fire which begged to be stoked. There was a glass of scotch on the table beside him, the evening paper propped up in front of him. "Why didn't you tell me you'd be conducting *Hoffman* in February?" I demanded of the thin ribbon of smoke drifting from behind the newspaper. "Did you know I'd be asked to sing Nicklaus?" I stared at the large ad on the back page depicting an ultra-modern dream kitchen. It never moved from its upright position.

"In answer to your first question, I guess I forgot; and to the second one, I wasn't sure." The ribbon of smoke became a chain of *S*'s as he spoke. He was famous for being able to carry on a lengthy conversation with a cigarette dangling from his lips.

"Could you put the paper down for a moment?" I asked. "It's hard to have a meaningful conversation with an Eaton's kitchen cabinet."

"Then why try? Besides, I thought you said you didn't care if you never sang another note."

"That's when I thought I'd never be asked to sing another note."

There was a pause. The paper dropped to his lap. He took the cigarette from his lips, replacing it with a mocking half smile. "By the way, did they mention your boyfriend would be singing Hoffman?"

"Which one?" I countered, genuinely curious.

"Victor Jubrensky." His voice had a flat, humourless sound. I couldn't believe it! Was he still wearing this empty baggage on his back?

"Oh, dear God, not that again; I don't even like the man," I said, immediately on the defensive.

"Oh?" He took a long sip of scotch. The paper went back up. In seconds, little puffs of smoke appeared above it. Subject closed!

The next day I ordered a score of *Hoffman* from the Frederick Harris Company in Oakville. When it arrived, I underlined the role of Nicklaus in red pencil and with enthusiasm started to place it in my voice. Like Rip Van Winkle, my vocal cords had been asleep for many months and had to be awakened slowly, nudged carefully and tenderly into action, a half-hour at a time. The *tessitura* was ideal; most of it lay in the comfortable middle of my voice. Soon, Nicklaus and I were close friends. A few weeks of coaching under my belt, and I had the complete role committed to memory.

Music rehearsals with Arturo began after the Christmas holidays. The first rehearsal was in his office at the academy. The acoustics were perfect. The room was spacious, with a high ceiling and hardwood floor. The only rug was a small one under the honey-coloured Steinway concert grand piano. At ten in the morning, the sun streamed through the four windows forming a large bay, facing east. Visible through the window was a coat of freshly fallen snow. On the wall behind the piano was a large semi-abstract painting of a snow-laden tree, which reflected the winter scene outside.

Arturo had called for all soloists, without chorus, for a run-through of the opera. The thirteen of us were standing around the piano with scores open, chatting with past colleagues, and introducing ourselves to new members of the cast while we waited for Victor.

"There's no point beginning without Hoffman as he's rather an essential character in the telling of the tales. We'll give him a few more minutes." Arturo's soft-spoken voice commanded instant silence, reflecting the respect he received from each one of us. "First of all, I'd like to welcome you all. We've a great cast, and I'm looking forward to working with you." He waited for the general buzz of appreciation to die down. "I knew of a prominent English conductor who took over an orchestra after they'd had a season with Toscanini. Before the first rehearsal began, he said to them, 'Now gentlemen, we've had enough of this sticking to the score; how about a little interpretation?'" There was a ripple of laughter before he continued. "However, I want to warn you, I encourage interpretation, but not at the expense of the score. Please, at all times keep Mr. Offenbach in mind. Another thing, *Hoffman* can be an exciting and arresting opera, but it also can border on the boring if no one can understand what you are singing about. We've a better than average translation of the French text which is worthy of being understood, but if it sounds like you're working your way around a mouthful of hot spaghetti, it might as well be Chinese, so always keep in mind words ... wor—Well, Mr. Jubrensky, you finally decided to honour us with your presence!" Sarcasm exuded from Arturo's voice.

"Sorry, Maestro. Had a hard time finding you. Now I know where you are, it won't happen again, I promise!" In his usual breezy way, Victor had blown into the room as if propelled by a stiff gale from behind, his coon coat casually draped over his shoulders, the fedora perched on the back of his head at a precarious angle. His hair was longer and bushier than the year before. He was sporting a trim moustache and beard plus a few extra pounds. Without greeting anyone, he headed straight for me and gave me a bone-crunching hug and a juicy kiss directly on my lips. The raccoon fell to the floor, where it remained the rest of the rehearsal. After pitching his fedora to the far corner of the room, where it adroitly landed on a large easy chair, he compressed his solid bulk in between me and my neighbour to the left. "Hi, sweetheart. I was hoping you'd be my Nicklaus."

It was as if an airplane suddenly flew betwixt Arturo and the bright winter sun outside, casting a fleeting shadow over his face. Was this because of Victor's late entrance or his effusive embrace? I couldn't tell.

"Victor, when it concerns others, being on time is something I take seriously." Arturo's voice mirrored the buildup of ice on the window ledge outside.

"Yah—so I've heard!" Victor's response was just short of rude. He had an annoying smirk on his face as he accentuated each word. He was obviously referring to the rift between Arturo and Max Fremstad over the latter's tardiness for rehearsals. If Arturo caught the innuendo, he ignored it.

"Would it be too much trouble, Victor, to ask you to turn to page seven in your score? We'll begin with the scene in Luther's cellar."

While Victor fumbled with his briefcase on the floor by his feet to get his score, Arturo signalled with a nod of his head for Lindorf to begin singing. We sang through the opera, leaving out the chorus bits, stopping only occasionally for minor corrections. I watched Arturo's hands move with graceful fluidity over the keys, amazed how his short fingers easily stretched beyond an octave. Near the end of the rehearsal, he asked Victor if holding a *B* flat a little longer would be too difficult.

"No, it's a cinch," Victor assured him and immediately demonstrated.

"Of course it's easy when you do it badly," quipped Arturo. Victor accepted the rebuttal with good humour, and we all had a hearty laugh at his expense.

Arturo was right, the cast was first class. Everyone was well prepared, and the rehearsal went well. Victor was awe-inspiring. Gone was the roughness from his voice; his singing was full of subtle nuances. His portrayal of the self-absorbed womanizer and hard drinker was masterful. Whoever he was working with now was obviously right for him. If he kept improving at such a rate, he was well on his way to the top.

Though Arturo said nothing to Victor at the end of the rehearsal, the look he gave him spoke volumes. "Well done," it said. I would love to have had a piece of the same look, but I knew I didn't deserve it.

Throughout the first two acts, the character of Nicklaus is on stage the whole time, shadowing Hoffman. The role calls for a sporadic use of the voice and is never taxing. The only *sostenuto*, or sustained singing, is at the beginning of the second act in the well-known Barcarole. Because most of it is sung in unison with the soprano, the mezzo taking the lower line, the sound should flow easily from the throat. Despite this, from the outset I could feel all was not right. The middle of my voice kept disappearing as if I was singing through a heavy blanket. The lower and higher registers at first appeared unaffected but by the end of the rehearsal, even they were fading, and my throat ached.

It was obvious Victor was aware something was terribly wrong because of his frequent questioning glances in my direction. "I think you need Usova," he remarked when we finished.

"No," I said huskily, "I think I need a doctor."

I didn't dare glance in my husband's direction for fear of receiving the remonstration I deserved. I was relieved when he excused himself because he was already late for another appointment.

Most of the cast was going to Murray's for a bite to eat, but I begged out. Food was the last thing I felt like facing, and I knew speaking would be difficult and harmful to my sick voice.

The sun had disappeared behind a thick covering of grey clouds, and it had begun to snow, the wet flakes leaving a layer of slush underfoot as I walked west on Bloor Street. The throat doctor shared by most of the singers had his office in the Medical Arts building, a short distance from the academy. I felt a mixture of melted snow and tears running down my cheeks as I splashed through the slush. I was worried and frightened. Like an athlete whose muscles had lain dormant for many months, I had nursed my voice with great care when learning the role. Even when working with the coach, I had sung *mezzo-voce*, never using full voice, singing an octave lower when necessary to avoid strain. Why, then, was I now in trouble?

The doctor could see me, but I would have to wait. There were several people ahead of me. Sitting in the reception room, I could feel my stomach tightening into a clump of knots. What if it was something serious—unredeemable? I knew of many careers that had been cut short because of abusive treatment of the voice. What was I doing wrong? Should I crawl back once more to Usova and beg for help?

The wait seemed interminable before the doctor could see me. When at last I was leaning back in his chair, his little mirror thrust far into my wide open throat, his nose almost touching my cheek, he said with raised eyebrows, "You have burst a blood vessel on one of your vocal cords. What have you been doing to yourself?"

I looked at him, disbelieving. "I couldn't have," I blurted out as soon as he removed his mirror from my throat.

"Please feel free to get another opinion," he snapped, taking my outburst to be a rebuttal.

"No, no—I only meant—" and I told him of the upcoming performances and how careful I had been when preparing my role.

"Think back, think back further," he kept repeating.

I began searching for facts, trying to reconstruct events in the minutest detail, but I could find no clue as to why.

"Have you had a cold, laryngitis in the past few months?"

"Yes, but that was some months ago, and I wasn't singing then."

"How bad was the laryngitis? Did you keep silent and not talk, or did you force through it?"

"Well yes—I mean, no, I didn't keep quiet, and, yes, I forced through it. In fact, I lost my voice for a week, but that was way back in September. It seemed okay when I began to vocalize in December!"

"You'd be surprised by the number of people who walk around with this problem. Particularly susceptible are men who frequent football, soccer, and hockey matches. They yell for hours encouraging their favourite team and wonder why they're hoarse for weeks, sometimes months. Nine times out of ten, they've burst a blood vessel. It's only when you have to use the voice professionally that you know."

I began walking back toward Arturo's office. It was snowing harder, and the temperature had dropped considerably. I pulled the collar of my fur-lined coat as high above my ears as it would go. I could feel a raw, damp wind swirling around my head. I was tempted to cross over to the academy and get out of the cold. Besides, the sooner I told Arturo the better; but what would I say? How could I tell him I was not allowed to sing? No, not yet! I was too upset, cloaked in a heavy blackness of despair, unable to collect my thoughts. I kept walking, this time faster.

Almost an hour later, when I reached Parliament Street, I was overcome with fatigue from battling the persistent wind against my face and heavy snow underfoot. I was cold, and pangs of hunger were gnawing at my stomach from the hours of intense rehearsing. At Wellesley and Parliament, I stopped at the little bistro on the corner where we had had dinner with Usova a year earlier. I ordered a big bowl of hot soup and took from my music case a notebook full of stage instructions from the past; it was the only paper I could find. I ripped a page from the back and began to write a letter to Arturo. I made at least three false starts, each time making the explanation longer and more convoluted. It was almost six o'clock when I sensed the head waiter hovering over me. The dinner patrons had begun to drift in, but I was still unhappy with my results. I made one last attempt, this time not bothering to rip the page from the notebook. Short and to the point with as few words as possible, I began once more:

I have just been to Dr. Hetherington.
I have a burst blood vessel on one of my vocal cords.
The doctor has forbidden me to sing, speak, or even whisper for a month. I am to go back to him after that to see if I can begin to work again. In the meantime, anything I have to say must be written down.

Shortly after six, when I walked in the front door, I was greeted with the pungent smells of beef stew mixed with cigarette smoke. Arturo must be home, and I was relieved it wasn't Maria's day off. Because of my increasingly busy life, Maria, the woman who had cleaned for us once a week, was now coming five days a week from two until eight to both clean and prepare dinner.

I removed my snow-caked boots, leaving them on the slate floor to shed their layer of slush and salt, hung my wet, snow-laden coat on a hook in the vestibule to drip, and resolutely headed down the steps into the living room to confront the source of the cigarette smoke. Arturo was sitting in his usual spot by a freshly lit fire.

"What happened to you at the rehearsal?" he asked. "Why were you singing *mezzo voce*?" His voice came from behind the customary propped up newspaper, and there was a hint of irritation in it. I went over and lifted the paper from his hands and dropped the opened notebook on his lap. I waited with fear and trepidation, his mask-like face revealing nothing while he read the few lines. There was a long silence. He slowly raised his eyes and stared at me through his thick glasses, his look reiterating "I told you so!" He must have seen the tears beginning to spill from my eyes, for instead of chastising me, his gaze softened and he said quietly, "I must tell Fremstad immediately."

He stood, handed the notebook back to me, and, shaking his head, gently put his hand on my shoulder. "Never mind, I'm sure something can be arranged."

What happened next? The events are buried so deep in the past they have disintegrated into oblivion. Did I sing the role of Nicklaus, or did I have a replacement? If so, who was she? I searched a book on the history of the Opera

Company for clues. I discovered a substitute sang the first two performances only. I was listed as having sung the last three.

I took from the same shelf my score of *Hoffman,* hoping it would help to further recharge my memory. Inside was a notebook that spelled out each character's placement onstage. Nicklaus' every movement, every gesture was carefully scripted in my handwriting. Studying it, I was gradually able to bring into focus a clear and consummate image.

Whether in the studio or theatre, I remember attending all rehearsals, tucked away quietly in a corner, copiously taking notes. After each stage rehearsal, I would hurry home and set up the living room furniture as if it were Luther's Tavern, using a small table and a few occasional chairs. I would act out over and over the scene I had just witnessed, mouthing all the roles, which by now I knew by rote. I was promised two rehearsals in the theatre with my substitute singing, while I went through the movements. These were the only rehearsals I would have before my three performances.

At night, waiting for Arturo to come home after orchestra rehearsals, I would prop myself up in our king-size bed and study the score, trying to digest and absorb every little subtlety which lay hidden in its pages. This time, I was determined not to let anyone down.

Throughout the preparation of *Hoffman,* I was fascinated by the strange relationship which gradually developed between Arturo and Victor, built on mutual admiration for each other's considerable talents. They seemed to be able to cast aside their differences and petty annoyances in deference to the music. It was obvious Victor's cockiness and lack of social graces aggravated Arturo, and Arturo's biting sarcasm, frequently at Victor's expense, pierced like an arrow through the tenor's thick hide; but all was quickly forgiven under the guise of artistic achievement. I watched Victor develop the character of Hoffman, finetuning each movement to perfection. His voice, too, had an added quality of warmth without losing its brilliance. I wondered anew if he had changed mentors.

During one rehearsal, he purposely sought me out in the far corner of the darkened theatre to tell me he had been working for the past year with Usova.

"So, that's it!" I mused silently.

Apparently, when he returned to New York after *Carmen* in Toronto, he had a call from Usova demanding he come to her studio. Grudgingly, he acquiesced. As bait, she told him the Metropolitan Opera was looking for a dramatic tenor to sing Don José the next fall because the tenor they had contracted to sing the eight performances was now permanently indisposed. She would like to recommend

Victor but, before doing so, wanted to make sure he was up to her high standards. She wanted "no eggs on her face." He began working with her immediately. He was so impressed with her teaching and the obvious improvement in his voice he soon became her slave. She must have had her kid gloves on to have won him over so quickly. Six months later, he auditioned for the General Director of the Met., who promptly signed him up for all eight performances, to begin after he finished *Hoffman* in Toronto. Victor added boastfully that we'd be able to hear him over the radio on Texaco's "Saturday Afternoon at the Opera" in early March.

Over the years, I have followed Victor's career with much interest, feeling in a small way responsible for his meteoric success because of Usova's connections. It wasn't long before we were hearing and seeing his name everywhere. Our festival had been lucky to have snatched him before he became a celebrity and financially out of our reach.

The final dress rehearsal went well. I watched Arturo cast his magic spell; saw his influence over musicians and singers alike. The fact was, Arturo never exercised authority. He radiated it, effortlessly, unconsciously, encouraging the players, relentlessly searching out the melody without sentimentality. "Well done," he said, laying down his baton at the end of the rehearsal.

Addressing the company at large while mopping his dripping head and neck with his white handkerchief, he told one of his favourite stories: "A few years ago when I was a *repetiteur* at La Scala, I remember an evening following the dress rehearsal of *Butterfly* when the conductor thanked the singers and members of the orchestra for their cooperation, attention, and patience in preparing the opera. 'There is one favour I would ask of you,' he said. 'You know your parts, and I know mine. Please, none of you look at me opening night; it makes me nervous.'" There was loud laughter and banging of the bows on the music stands from the string section. Arturo raised his hand for silence. "I want to assure you, I suffer no such phobia. You don't have to stare at me; a glance out of the side of your eyes will suffice. But please, always connect with me so I can keep everything together. I've enjoyed these past weeks working with you; you're a great group. One last thing! I can't stress enough—all of you, members of the orchestra as well—*canta*—sing, sing, sing. Remember, music becomes alive only when it has heart and soul. I'm sure it will be a great opening night. Good luck and God bless!"

He left the podium with the members of the string section again tapping the stands with their bows.

The night before my initial appearance, I remember having one of my particularly alarming nightmares. When I think about it now, its frightening moments still haunt me. In the dream, I was performing *The Tales of Hoffman*. It began with the second act "Barcarole." I had never sung through the whole opera before; I only knew the second act took place in Venice, at the palace of the courtesan Giulietta, whom Hoffman loved.

When the curtain goes up, I'm sitting with Giulietta in a gondola outside the palace. My eyes are closed, and we are both lazily singing the "Barcarole." Opening my eyes, I see the courtesan is none other than Usova, grotesquely made up. Her mouth is a huge vermillion gash over her prominent teeth; the heavy-lidded emerald eyes alive with flashing, glittering sparks; her halo of bright red hair flickering with flames. In her right hand, she holds a large silver hand-mirror, which she keeps shining in my eyes. She has an evil sneer on her ghost-like face. She sings:

"Through this glass I'll have your soul—you'll not sing again—no, never.
You will be mine, entirely mine, forever and ever and ever."

I try to answer her and tell her she is wrong, but no sound comes out. I look into her mirror, and my reflection vanishes. Terrified, I glance up at the gondolier behind her, hoping for assistance. He has a wicked leer on his face, his eyes blank white pools. With a start, I see the gondolier is my husband. I try to call for help, but it is no use, my voice has gone. In desperation, I struggle to get out of the gondola, but the gondolier pins me down with the end of his pole.

I awoke feeling a sharp poke in the small of my back and heard a sleepy muttering at my side, "For God's sake, will you stop thrashing about; I'm trying to sleep."

The rest of the night, I lay awake, frightened lest the nightmare return.

That morning during breakfast, the first thing Arturo asked was, "What was bothering you last night? You were flailing about as if fighting off a sexual predator."

To tell him would be to relive the whole petrifying nightmare, and I wanted only to erase it from my consciousness as soon as possible.

Strangely, I can remember nothing of my performance that night and, because it wasn't the opening, there was no review. I do, however, recall Arturo coming to my dressing room afterward, squeezing my shoulders, planting a kiss on my cheek, and saying, "Darling, well done."

21

Big Plans for an Opera Workshop

Soon after *Tales of Hoffman*, Arturo's career took flight. He received a call from New York City Center Opera Company; they were in the process of mounting a new work by an American composer; the conductor had collapsed of a heart attack during a rehearsal; the opening night was a few weeks away; could Arturo fill the ailing maestro's shoes? Usova had been at the rehearsal; one of her children was singing the lead. She had quickly gone into action. She told the general manager she knew of a brilliant Italian conductor now living in Toronto who, she was sure, could do the job. "He is an amazing musician and can read any score at sight no matter how complicated," she had said. City Center was desperate; they took Usova at her word.

This meant Arturo would be in New York for the better part of a month. In the meantime, I was in the midst of preparations for a spring tour of the eastern provinces. Fremstad had decided to take a chance on *The Consul* instead of *Fledermaus;* it would be cheaper. There was no chorus and only twelve soloists and two scene changes.

Because the tour had already begun, I was unable to get to Arturo's opening night in New York. I had no understudy. To save money, only the lead Magda was double-cast. I was in St. John, New Brunswick, when Arturo phoned at two in the morning to read me *The New York Times* review.

> Though this opera will probably never have another reading, it was well worth the gamble, if for no other reason than the discovery of the brilliant Italian conductor, Arturo Moretti. At the last minute, he was called in to take over for the ailing Gino Pertile. Maestro Moretti was able to make as much sense as possible out of a convoluted and inconsequential score. This reviewer hopes the City Center Opera Company plans on putting Moretti on their permanent roster. Given their lack of first-class conductors, they could well use him.

When my husband finished reading these words, my heart swelled with pride. Finally, I thought, he's on his way.

By the end of May, my tour had come to a close, and Arturo and I were together again in our Cabbagetown sanctuary. He was flush from his success in New York. I had never seen him so exhilarated and full of hope for the future. Many offers had begun to pour in from all over the States. For the first time in his life, he was able to select the assignments which interested him most.

One evening, when I was watching *Perry Mason* on television, Arturo casually mentioned that he had seen Usova several times in New York and she sent her love. When I didn't respond, he came over to the television and turned it off. It was obvious he had more to say and wanted to talk. This was such a rare occasion, I didn't object, even though Perry was about to tell me who the murderer was.

"Would you like a drink?" he asked, walking from the living room to the kitchen, empty glass in hand, to pour another scotch. Arturo loved his scotch before dinner, but as long as I knew him, I never saw him drunk and he never touched liquor before a concert.

"No thanks. What's on your mind?" I said loudly to his back.

"You know how the old girl is; the minute she saw me, she started attacking me about her infernal school," he called from the kitchen.

Returning to the living room, fresh drink in hand, he continued. "After my last performance, Lana asked me to come back to her place for 'r-r-refreshments'; Victor was with us." His rolling of the *R* in refreshments was masterful. There was a pause while he settled comfortably into the chair beside a dwindling fire and took a long sip. "You know, I'm getting to almost like that fellow.... Well, as soon as we sat down on her uncomfortable chairs and started munching our baba-rhums, she began her favourite subject, Lana's lyceum. She ended with, 'Dar-rlink, when Lana gets back from Europe next fall she weeell again come to Canada for more master classes. Zen we shall see.'"

I laughed, for I had never heard Arturo do an imitation of Usova before. He took another sip and went on. "Victor, God bless him, instantly jumped into the fray. 'Lana,' he said, 'what we really need on this continent is an opera workshop; something for the kids fresh out of opera school with no experience. There're no small opera companies around for them to get their feet wet like they have in Europe. God, would I have loved a chance to perform without a noose 'round my neck. It should be sometime during the summer in some little hick town. We'd end up mounting a production—even maybe taking it on tour around the countryside.' At this point Victor was getting all caught up in the sound of his own voice when her ladyship barged in, 'And where does Lana fit in?' she asked, her frog eyes at half-mast, her eyebrows raised to meet her hennaed turf. 'Lana darling,' I said, 'it would be up to you to make sure the voices don't get ruined. You would be their protector. We could draw from a world bank of talent and they could all become your slaves.'"

With Arturo, nothing ever got lost in the telling. While he talked, I realized Usova, aided and abetted by Victor, had finally unbuckled Arturo's reservations. Despite my resentment over her successful subterfuge, I couldn't help but be swept along in the wake of my husband's enthusiasm. My mind kept returning to Duxbury, Massachusetts, and my missed opportunity to iron out the *Carmen* wrinkles at the expense of a less exacting country audience.

Arturo's ideas were on a far higher plane. He had in mind to invite world-renowned singers to instruct and perform and to mount a highly professional production with a first class orchestra, all under the guise of education. Both Usova and Victor suggested that Sir Roland Dunn, general manager of the Metropolitan Opera, could help set it up, making use of his international contacts. I shook my head in amazement. Arturo's aims couldn't get much loftier than that.

"Okay, as Usova would say, 'Dar-rlink, and where do I fit in?'" I asked with my eyes at half mast and eyebrows raised.

"You, my dar-rlink, will be a most important cog in the wheel. Your parents know the president of the Great Lakes University in London. You remember when I lectured at their music school last year? At that time, the dean took me on a tour of the premises and it would be ideal. It's equipped with plenty of practice rooms and pianos; three large rehearsal halls; a lovely little theatre—too small for a full scale opera performance but perfect for master classes, concerts, and rehearsing. It has residences for the students—everything we would need!"

"You really are serious, aren't you?" I asked.

"Oh, yes, very."

I remember, the first thing I did after Arturo's and my discussion about the workshop was to write to the president of the Great Lakes University, outlining what Arturo had in mind, and why he felt the university would be ideal for the enterprise. This prompted an immediate reaction from the president by way of a phone call, to set up a meeting with the new dean of the Music School.

When I mentioned, at the meeting, that we had in mind to ask Sir Roland Dunn, general manager of the Metropolitan Opera Company in New York, to mastermind the project, the dean became so excited he told me he would be free to take charge of the whole venture. The dean then offered me the position of chair of the Advisory Council and told me I would be responsible for raising the funds. I could see that this dean was anxious to feather his new cap and could easily become a thorn in our sides. I assured him the position of general director was already taken by my husband and that all we wanted from the university was the use of their premises and secretarial staff.

In the meantime, Usova had begun her assault on Sir Roland Dunn.

October 8, 1956

Rolly, darling—we must have lunch!
I'm most anxious to tell you of an exciting venture which I know you will want to be part of. Before someone else hears of it and sweeps it from under my nose, I would like to discuss the possibilities of you lending your considerable knowledge and talents to my enterprise. I am convinced that you and you alone could help launch this intriguing project; besides, I haven't seen you since we both left for Europe in May, and we have much catching up to do. I have tried to reach you by phone several times. Because there was no answer, I presume you are not yet back from Scotland. Darling, call me the minute this reaches you.
Yours, Lana

Her next letter was written two weeks later, this time to Arturo.

October 27, 1956

My dearest Maestro,
Yesterday I had lunch with Rolly Dunn, and I hasten to bring you up to date on the latest development.
Yes, Rolly is very interested in our workshop, but of course will insist on doing it his way. He would operate from New York, with no more trips than were absolutely necessary, to Canada.
You will call him immediately to arrange a meeting. You must carefully work out a practical plan of operation at once. He will insist on knowing exactly what you have in mind. I'm sure Rolly is our man, but we will have to proceed with great care as he knows the value of his name—as do I.
Darling Maestro, this is turning out to be a most exciting adventure. I am greatly looking forward to working with you.
Rolly's telephone number is 212-555-0321. Make haste!
Yours,
Lana

By the time Arturo was able to arrange a meeting with Sir Roland Dunn, it was early November. The meeting was to take place at his apartment in Essex House; we would stay at the Barbizon Plaza nearby. Arturo decided it would be judicious to sound Sir Roland out in person first before preparing a complete dossier; he might have input which would alter the direction of the workshop. Arturo insisted I come along, for he wanted me to hear firsthand what Sir Roland had to say regarding the role the university should play. After all, I was the one dealing with them.

We arrived at the hotel in New York early on the evening of November 2 to find a message waiting for Arturo from Usova: "I plan to keep tomorrow free so I can be with you when you meet with Rolly. Call the minute you arrive to let me know time and place."

"Then you won't need me," I said churlishly.

"Of course we'll need you; don't be childish." Impatience edged the practiced calm of his voice.

"There's no room big enough for us both. She goes, and I don't; it's as simple as that." I slammed my overnight bag down on the bed to make my point.

With this gesture of defiance, his agitation mounted. "Look, sooner or later you're going to have to come to terms. She's as much a part of this as I am."

"Yeah, well, knowing her, she'll take over and be the whole part."

Arturo quietly picked up the phone and was about to dial. I realized anger wasn't getting me anywhere, so I went over to him and facing his back, put my arms around his waist, resting my chin on his shoulder. "Honestly, darling, at this point, we don't need her. We can sound Sir Roland out better without her. Believe me, I know."

He put the phone down. "OK, you talk to her! You tell her!" He picked the phone up again, dialed, and handed it to me. While it was ringing I tried to protest, but it was too late.

"Ello?" said that too-familiar voice.

"Hello, Lana, it's Jessica."

Silence! I could see I would have to open the lid gradually to let the steam seep slowly out of the pot. "Um—it's wonderful you could manage to have us meet Sir Roland."

Silence! I took a big breath before beginning again. "Arturo thinks I should be at the meeting tomorrow because I'm the one dealing with the university."

Silence! I could hear a dramatic soprano in the distance singing the aria from Verdi's *La forza del destino,* so I knew she was still on the other end of the phone.

"My parents are friends of the president, and Arturo thought I might have clout." I tried to sound noncommittal.

Silence! Obviously this wasn't working so I thought it best to immediately get to the core. "Lana, I don't think it's such a good idea for us both to be at the meeting. It would make it very awkward, don't you agree?"

I waited. Finally, in her customary dogmatic way, she said abruptly, "Is Arturo there? I want to speak to him."

I looked at my husband questioningly and mouthed, "She wants to talk to you". He shook his head vehemently.

"He said he'll be in touch with you after the meeting."

"What's wrong? Is he such a coward?"

I put my hand over the mouthpiece and whispered, "Are you such a coward?" He nodded his head slowly with a wicked grin on his face.

"Yes, he is," I said, but she had hung up.

Next, Arturo contacted Sir Roland, only to find out he'd changed his mind. He wanted to talk over lunch at Sherry's restaurant, as he would be at the Met all day. It would be more convenient.

We arrived early at Sherry's, on the second floor of the Metropolitan Opera. We were uncertain how long it would take from our hotel, and we hadn't wanted to be late. Sir Roland had made a reservation and we were royally led to our table by a head waiter. It wasn't long before an elegant, slim man in a black bowler hat, English Burberry coat, with the creases in his pants looking as if they could cut one's finger, appeared before us.

"I haven't much time. I have another meeting uptown. I can't tell you what a mess I inherited six years ago," he said, shaking his head and rolling his eyes upward. "How they functioned before is beyond me. The jealousies, the rivalries—they're all a collection of prima donnas." He sat down, motioning for the maitre d' to bring the menu. I detected a Scottish accent while he talked on, as if taking up valuable time for introductions was unnecessary. "Now maestro, I understand you had a great success at City Center last March. Would you ever consider a position as Generalmusikdirector? I haven't a conductor who will work for me longer than six weeks at a time. It's not the singers that are prima donnas, it's the conductors. There's not one ..."

During Sir Roland's diatribe, Arturo took a silver cigarette case from his breast pocket, helped himself to a cigarette, and put the case back into his pocket.

"My dear maestro, you might offer me one," Sir Roland interjected; his voice ripe with disdain.

You could have heard a crumb drop. Slowly Arturo's hand went back up to retrieve the case. "Excuse me," he said, ice dripping from each word, "Would you care for a cigarette?"

I could sense this didn't promise well for our future relationship, however, over a delicious lunch and under a cloud of smoke, discussions began. It was decided that, yes, Sir Roland was interested, naturally on his terms. Arturo was to send, as soon as possible, a complete outline of the project.

After telling Usova the good news, we took the first flight back to Toronto.

The outcome of all this was that Arturo's and my life radically changed. Though I still toured frequently throughout Canada with the company, the main focus of my efforts was to keep in constant touch with the Great Lakes University in order to fine-tune all arrangements and to keep them posted on the latest developments.

Arturo, on the other hand, conferred on a regular basis with Sir Roland and Usova while passing in and out of New York on his way to fulfill his ever-increasing conducting engagements. Victor was now enough of a superstar to be able to demand his own choice of maestros. If he disapproved of the one chosen for him, he asked for Arturo. Consequently, Arturo soon became known in most of the big opera houses throughout the States and Europe and was always on the go.

It was a busy time for us both, and our weeks together in Toronto were few and far between. Strangely, because of this, we became closer through distance, for Arturo was able to express his feelings more freely in letters than he ever could face to face. When we were together, he was always so careful to guard the place where his heart was hidden that he failed to see I was unarmed.

22

Plane Crash

Arturo spent February in Toronto conducting Puccini's *La Bohème* for the company while I toured with *The Consul* to every little city and hamlet in western Canada. A letter arrived addressed care of the National Opera Company, Moose Jaw, Saskatchewan, two weeks into the tour.

Toronto, February 20, 1957

Dearest wanderer,
    Don't know where to aim this, but will try Moose Jaw as Max said you'd be in the jaw of the moose by now.
    The opera performances are finally over, and Fremstad is slapping himself on the back for recently saving the company from oblivion by showing a profit.
    We had one near-fiasco when our tenor went down with a throat infection on the second performance of Aida. I suggested they bring in Victor as replacement. When I arrived at the theatre shortly before eight, I was immediately greeted by a long-faced Bartoletti. According to him, Victor hadn't shown up for rehearsal in the morning, the only time he would have been able to go over the score to check the tempi before the performance.
    Of course, Victor gave a superb performance and set fire to the whole show—company, chorus, orchestra;—even—or should I say particularly, old Bartoletti, in spite of his animosity toward Victor. Then, the next performance, which was last Friday, our tenor-designate, now with a cured throat, was stranded in New York at six in the evening, (What a helluva time to be leaving for a performance in Toronto at eight.) because there was a fire on the plane. Victor had left for San Francisco, and there was no understudy, so Max told stories to the audience (which he obviously loved doing), and the theatre served coffee and sandwiches until ten-thirty, when the tenor arrived, complete with police escort.
    How goes the tour? I've heard nothing so I gather nothing cataclysmic has happened.

Darling, I must go. I miss you, adore you, and long for you, and that's a hell of a lot for me to admit.

A

P.S. You'll be glad to know Max is still late for rehearsals!

My tour ended mid-March, and I arrived home two days after Arturo left for New York. Victor was singing his first *Otello* at the Met and had asked Sir Roland if his dear friend Arturo Moretti could be the conductor; he would feel so much safer in the hands of someone he knew and trusted. I received a letter a week later.

New York
March 25, 1957

Darling,

I love you and miss you, like hell I do! I mean, I miss you like hell—I do! This is a miserable business being away alone, even though one's busy all the time. Next time you come with me, whether you like it or not.

I'm taking this evening off for a few minutes with you and several hours with my bed. I'd much rather have a few minutes with my bed and several hours with you. Better still, lump them all together!

Lana, as usual, has been "an event." Yesterday I had a battle royal when I refused to go to the lioness's den (You, of course, would think I have my animals wrong and that it was a kennel) for the evening, but she finally settled for lunch instead.

When she turns her emerald, enigmatic eyes on you from across the table and in five minutes starts to misquote from whatever you might have said, if you're smart you keep your mouth shut and accept the fact that she is a fascinating person as long as you are a fascinated listener. We went endlessly over which opera we should choose that would best suit "her children." I kept insisting it was too early to decide; that it would depend on the talent we were able to scrape up. As you well know, her hearing diminishes according to how much you disagree with her!

Have been lunching frequently with Rolly Dunn at Sherry's between rehearsals. He's had some compelling suggestions re—the workshop. I must say, this whole venture is becoming increasingly exciting each time I meet with the man. You'd better be working overtime on the millionaires of London, for by the time Sir Roland is finished with us, it's going to cost a fortune.

Had dinner the other night with Victor at his home in Brooklyn. He lives with his mother and sister, and what a pair they are! His mother is very French Canadian, from Three Rivers, Quebec. She could play "the Medium" in the opera of that name by Menotti, without the aid of costume and makeup. She had bangles to her elbows, rings covering every knuckle on her fingers, long filigree earrings touching her shoulders, and a long, bright red knitted dress over a shape like a milk bot-

tle with big black Minnie Mouse shoes peeking out underneath. The flowered fringed shawl covering the ensemble bars description.

We began our conversation in French;—at least, I think that's what it was, but when Victor saw the look on my face, he quickly insisted we switch to English. I'm sure he thought I would come out with one of my unsavoury remarks. Actually, underneath this eccentric outer covering was an extremely intelligent, interesting woman, and we had a great conversation about the state of contemporary music and where it was headed. Victor told me later she taught piano at the Brooklyn Academy of Music. Obviously he adores her and is very proud of her.

Now, the sister is something else again! Svelte, slim French figure, jet black hair with a smashing short bobbed hairdo, a black satin dress she must have been poured into, and heels on her shoes that would compete with the Eiffel Tower—in other words, a dish! This all led to quite an evening!

Everyone here who knows you (meaning Victor and Sir Roland) is sorry you didn't come with me—and those who only know of you are just as sorry. As for those who have seen only the picture of you I carry around with me so devotedly—Wow! They can't even wait; neither can I.

A

When Arturo returned to Toronto on Wednesday, we had only a week together and he was off again, this time to Paris. Victor had requested he conduct his *Hoffman* at the Opera Comique. This worked perfectly with his other engagements, and he readily accepted.

At the same time, I left for Ottawa, Montreal, Kingston, Kitchener, London, and Windsor. The company was taking *Fledermaus* on a small tour; we would be playing two nights in each city. Hotel accommodations were paid for by the company; we were expected to supply our own transportation. Because I had the largest and most comfortable (recently acquired) car, a Buick Riviera, I was elected to drive four other members of the cast.

My father had had a mild stroke and was forbidden to drive. He presented the Riviera to my husband, saying it was a Thanksgiving present. When I asked my father why Arturo and not me, he countered with, "It's thanks for taking you off my hands."

I felt a little nervous driving the car because of its high-powered engine. When Arturo first picked the car up in London to take it to Toronto, he was barely past Woodstock when he heard the shrill, high-pitched sound of a police cruiser signalling him to pull over to the side of Highway 5. The cruiser had been chasing a speeding car when Arturo whizzed past him at an astronomical speed. The policeman immediately abandoned the driver of the other car and took chase in his Chevy, which, by the time it and the policeman overpowered the Riviera, were both shaking with undue stress. Arturo never told me how fast he'd been going or how much the fine was. He only said that when he talked to a lawyer afterward, his advice was for him to plead guilty to speeding. Otherwise they would get him on a reckless driving charge, and he'd lose his licence.

The car drove like a dream and, as long as I kept excessive weight off the gas pedal, I was fine. We dropped Arturo off at the airport, and we five headed for Ottawa.

After the performance in Kingston and before going on to Kitchener, we stopped overnight in Toronto. There was a letter waiting for me from Arturo.

April 19, 1957

"Paris in springtime,'" as the song goes. Is there another city in the world that does such strange things to one's libido; that can faster turn a young man's—sorry—this man's fancy to thoughts of Jessica?

Darling, I have begun so many letters to you these past few days, but unfortunately I haven't been able to finish them. They have all been written while the plane was bouncing around or the taxi was rushing me to another rehearsal. In other words, whenever in these ridiculously crowded days I've had a few moments to myself to think—all I could think of was Orlofsky. Wonderful but frustrating! Never have I been so impatient to get back to my monocled, bearded, long-stemmed beauty. Darling, I love you. I kept phoning our little "Shangri-La" in Cabbagetown, but no answer. Are you still touring Fledermaus *or is it antihistamine-induced sleep?*

I was thrilled to have your letter today. So much more of what I adore in you is in everything you write and say. For a few moments, it was almost as though you were here. Just go on wearing down your side of the bed; it'll make it so much easier when I get home to roll over into position for devoted and devotional action.

The endless dinners and receptions one must attend; there was a reception yesterday when, after an hour's hard drinking and conversation (and this was really hard), I thought I'd better meet the guest of honour and found out with a shock that it was me. Oh, darling, you should be here to share this nonsense with me. Not that you aren't. You know, or should know, that you are with me every day and night.

Yours always,
A

During my week away from Toronto, a miracle had taken place. The drab city streets had burst into soft varying shades of green lace. With the warmth of the last few days, the late spring had decided it was time to show signs of renewed life. When I left, my front garden was full of dead vegetation; now there were little green shoots pushing their heads through the rotted flora left over from last year's harvest. I was grateful there was work ahead to keep me occupied until Arturo's return in a few days.

Opening the front door, I was greeted with the usual mound of junk mail fanning out over the slate floor under the mail slot. Amongst it was an envelope with no postmark. It was addressed to Madame Arturo Moretti. Pasted on were carefully cut out letters from a magazine. I bent down and picked up the envelope with its ominous lettering. I turned it over several times, searching for clues as to what the inside might contain. Perhaps it was an invitation to something. With curiosity, I opened the envelope. Inside was a sheet of paper with the same cutout, pasted-on lettering:

Beware—when the cat at home does stay

the rat away does play

At first I was confused; it took time for the message to sink in. Was this some sort of a joke? What kind of person would send this? I was about to throw it into the fireplace to burn with the rest of the junk mail, but I hesitated. No, I'd save it and show it to my husband. Maybe he'd know what it was about.

Arturo had been home three days before I showed him the anonymous letter. It was during breakfast; he had his face buried in the morning *Globe*. When he put the newspaper down to take a bite of croissant, I pushed the envelope toward him. "This arrived in the mail while you were in Paris. What do you make of it?" I said, trying to sound indifferent and unconcerned.

He quizzically took the piece of paper from the envelope. Reading, he raised his eyebrows, then his coffee cup, but said nothing. His mouth did a curious twitch, as if words were having trouble finding their way out. He put his cup back down without taking a sip of the hot liquid; then, with complete composure, he casually folded the accusatory message, slipped it back into the envelope, and put it in the inside breast pocket of his jacket. As far as Arturo was concerned, that was the last of it, but I tucked the incident into the far reaches of my brain to be dusted off and pushed forward in the event he might again be suspicious of my loyalty and devotion. Also, it would be handy to have a little ammunition if his fidelity ever did come into question.

In mid-May, Arturo was off once more, this time to Milan to conduct Victor's *Otello*. I have seldom seen him so excited; he would be going back to La Scala, not as a *répetiteur* but as the maestro. This was an opera house he had always longed to return to, not to remain but as guest conductor. He was to meet Victor in New York at La Guardia Airport and together they would take a United Airlines direct flight to Milan.

"Please, come with me," he pleaded. He had only to ask, and my bag was packed.

The day before we were to leave, my father suffered another stroke, this time massive, and I knew Milan was out of the question, that my place was at my father's side.

The next morning it was teeming with rain, and a thick dark army blanket hung over Toronto; sky and ground ghosted together in a grey mist. There were low rumbles of thunder in the distance. I phoned Trans-Canada Airways to see if the noon flight to New York City would be taking off and was surprised to have an affirmative answer. By the time we left the house, a strong gusty wind had joined the rain.

I waited outside the terminal's departure entrance at Malton Airport while Arturo went in to again check to make sure the plane would be flying. He came back out, nodding his head. He went to the back of the car, took his suitcase from the trunk, handed it to a red cap, and got back into the front passenger seat.

"You should be coming with me, you know," he said. "Victor, I'm sure, will be most disappointed." This was said with gentle sarcasm, while one side of his mouth rose in a slight smile. He took my hand. "I think Giovanni and Mirella will be in Milan then, too. If your father rallies, you will join me, won't you?"

I assured him I would hop on the first flight as soon as things, one way or another, equalized with my father; but in the pit of my stomach was a shadowy feeling that my father might hover close to death for many weeks and, if he did survive, would end up a vegetable. I knew my place was at home. After all, there would be many trips to Milan in the future and many more goodbyes we'd have to face. It went with the territory.

Arturo reluctantly let go of my hand and, with a quick hug, lightly brushed a kiss on my cheek and left the car. Without looking back, he disappeared through the automatic door of the terminal.

From the airport, I drove to London, arriving in the early afternoon. I headed straight for the hospital without going to my parents' house first. There, I was met by the family doctor, the same one who had brought me into the world twenty-seven years before.

When I saw my father, an IV attached to his arm, a plastic tube coming from his nose, I was shocked. His eyes were closed. The halo of white hair on the pillow framed his ashen face; the left side of his open mouth was slightly drooping. With alarm, I looked questioningly at the doctor. He assured me my father was out of immediate danger, that his condition had stabilized. He was in a coma now but because he was in good condition otherwise, his chances of recovery were good. I mentioned I was hoping to join my husband in Milan, and he said he saw no reason why I shouldn't. "If your father takes a turn for the worse, you could be here in a day."

I remained by my father's side, holding his icy hand until my brother came to collect me for dinner. During the meal, my mother tried to convince me I should join Arturo; she would be fine and, after all, my brother would be there to take care of things. "Your father could remain in a comatose condition for some time. He will surely need you later to help keep his spirits up."

It had been raining on and off all day, and a gentle spring rain was still falling when I left London around 8 PM. I wasn't far out of the city when a large black cloud drifted overhead. The horizon to the west looked menacing, and there were intermittent flashes of lightning brightening up the blue blackness all around me. Soon the heavens opened up and sheets of water fell across my windshield, making it almost impossible to see. It was as if I was driving into the murky waters of a pond. The windshield wipers were shuddering from the strain. Many cars had already pulled to the side of the road, but the Riviera just kept plowing through the deluge. The slashes of zigzag lightning streaking across the sky were immediately followed by loud claps of thunder. I continued on at a crawl, straining to keep track of the dashes of white in the centre of the highway, which kept disappearing as though wiped clean from a blackboard by a school-teacher's brush.

Shortly before eleven, the Riviera coasted up the laneway beside our house and came to a much-anticipated stop. The rain had abated. Never was I so relieved to be home. I put my overnight bag at the foot of the stairs and headed for the kitchen. I was badly in need of a nightcap. I turned on the radio to catch the eleven o'clock news and began to pour a straight brandy. The news had just begun.

"A United Airlines plane leaving New York late this afternoon for Milan, Italy, crashed over the Atlantic Ocean. The airline believes lightning was to blame," the announcer said.

I felt the glass slip from my hand and smash onto the spinning tile floor.

From then on, things have become a blur. I try to fold back the skin of time but, alas, it all has become a tangle of underground streams struggling to find their way to the surface. In order to come to terms with Arturo's death, in the past years I have read over and over his letter, which arrived two days after the crash.

May 20, 1957
La Guardia Airport

Hi, darling, remember me?

There was a time, about an hour ago, when it looked as though that was all you'd be able to do. We have just landed at La Guardia, where I have a two-hour wait before heading out again for Milan.

When we took off in Toronto, it was bumpy for awhile, then the heavens blackened ahead of us and about us. We banked to the north and the south and in all directions. Trays were dumped, "Ceintures, SVP," and we were for it.

We should have been in New York in less than two hours, but over an hour later we were still banking to the north to avoid the storms. Finally we landed, and it was only then we found out that for some time they hadn't been able to make contact with airports at either Toronto or New York. They're still cleaning up here after a near cyclone hit shortly before we landed. I'm waiting in the terminal for Victor to arrive. Knowing him, he'll probably arrive late and miss the flight.

Because you are probably on your way to London and can't be reached by phone, I am dispatching this post-haste before I take off again so you'll know we weathered the eye of the storm and I'm still in the land of the living. You always complain you find it difficult to read my scribble. Now I've given you an extra challenge for I'm writing this on top of The New York Times, which is draped over my briefcase, so if you can't read the lines, read between them.

My greetings to your family—particularly your mother, who I'm sure will be glad of your strength and comfort at this time. I keep my fingers crossed your father is now out of danger and will soon regain his health—too wonderful a man to have to finish his life an invalid. And to you, my aphrodisiacal pal, (Don't look that one up—it might mean what I think it does) if you can't join me in Milan within the next few weeks, I shall soon be flying back to you and will have you all to myself for two magical months in the north country planning our future workshop and searching among the Muskoka pines for a gold mine to pay for it.

Missing you already and loving you always.
A

A letter arrived from Usova the next day.

May 21, 1957

My dearest darling little one,

Oh, how your Lana grieves! As I write, tears spill over onto my aging cheeks. That fate has dared to cut short the life of such an exceptionally gifted man at the beginning of a brilliant career is more than cruel, it is unforgivable. The only thing for us to do now is to fight to make sure his name lives on. We will strive to bring our workshop to fruition. You must now put all your young energy into this venture. You must turn your thoughts into something productive; to make your grief serve you instead of letting it defeat you. It's what your Arturo would have wanted. Everything is in place for us to forge ahead; don't let him down. It is up to you to make this happen! I have been in touch with Sir Roland, who too is overwhelmed with grief. He thinks we should now ask his assistant at the Met, who is an extremely capable administrator, to take charge. Victor will help in whatever way he can. He is devastated over what has taken place and is consumed with the thought that if his taxi hadn't been caught up in traffic on his way to the airport, he would have been in that plane as well. He was within minutes of catching it. He has cancelled his Otello at La Scala. He felt he couldn't face it in the wake of what has happened, convinced he was to blame.

I wish I could be there to comfort you and give you strength, but next week I leave for Vienna, Bayreuth, and Salzburg, for my children, as always, have need of me. Oh, my darling little one, you must join me in Salzburg, and we will work-work-work; we must sing to help drive out the pain.

Your Lana's heart truly aches, and she embraces you with deepest sympathy and love.

The rough draft of my answer was scribbled in pencil on the back of this letter.

May 25, 1957

Lana—As far as I am concerned, the workshop died with my husband; I have notified the university accordingly.

My father is very ill. I am going home to be at his side.

Jessica

When I returned to Toronto in the early fall after my father died, there was a letter waiting for me from Victor. It was the last letter in the shoebox.

August 15, 1957

Jess—Guilt has finally won over indecision. Believe me, you are constantly on my mind; I'm always wondering how you are coping. Are you okay? The reason I haven't written before this is because I didn't know what to say or how to say it. How do you tell a dear friend that you are to blame for the death of her husband? It was because of me Arturo took that fatal plane! If I hadn't insisted he conduct my Otello at La Scala, and if I hadn't been stuck in traffic, it would have been me on that plane, not him. You can't know how heavily this has weighed on my conscience these past months. I will never find another maestro who can inspire and direct me as he could—someone whose wisdom and sensitivity I had come to depend on and esteem. I had grown to love this extraordinary man for his wit, his quick mind, his incredible musicianship. I can't bear to think he has left us forever.

Her ladyship told me you are with your ailing father—God, is there no justice? It's not fair! You must get going and sing your way through this; fill the void with *music. How lucky we are to be able to lose ourselves in this all-consuming and rewarding profession!*

There—I've done it! I've written a most difficult letter. You can't know how much better I feel having said what had to be said and should have been said long ago. Now you know how deeply I feel over your terrible loss—our terrible loss.

Dear Jess, I cherish our friendship. Do keep in touch. I'm sure our paths will again cross. The opera world is a small, select club.

Hang in there, gal!
Yours always, Vic

23

June 1998—Return to Salzburg

Toronto, June 1998

When I finished rereading Victor's letter, warm tears began to slowly spill from my eyes, rolling down the imperfections and creases of my seasoned skin. I thought of those years before time had purged my soul of the all-encompassing grief which had bankrupted my spirit after Arturo's untimely death; the death that robbed him of the brilliant career he so deserved. At the time, I remember following the newspapers, the television, everything, in order to give his death a purpose.

The empty rooms of my Cabbagetown house have reverberated with loneliness for many years, and I still fight off moments of longing when I feel Arturo's strong arms encircling me from behind, pulling me toward him.

I let Victor's letter drop from my hand onto the dining room table. It landed on top of the pile of yellowed paper scattered around the empty shoebox. The image of Victor's face, with its expressive dark eyes, its broad cheek bones, its prominent jaw, its head surrounded by a heavy mass of curly black hair, suddenly appeared before me. I began to reflect on his meteoric rise to fame; the beginning of his vocal problems midway in his career; and finally, his gradual descent into history. The sound of his less-than-healthy voice filtered into my veins as I recalled the first time I was aware he was in deep trouble vocally. It was about five years after his performance of *Hoffman*. He was singing the tenor part of Mahler's *Das Lied von der Erde* in Massey Hall with the Toronto Symphony. He was halfway through the first lied when the middle of his voice became unfocused and breathy. By the end of the third and last song, he was barely audible. Not knowing what to say to him after the concert, I went home without joining the throng of young females waiting outside the stage door.

The next time I heard him was two years later in New York; he was singing *Otello*, and I was relieved he sounded more like his former magnificent self. I asked him, when we had a bite to eat together after the performance, what had happened to his voice when he had sung last in Toronto. He told me that, at the time, a drug he had been taking for high blood pressure had so affected his vocal cords that he'd had to refrain from singing for at least a year. The doctor treating him had hoped that forcing through his swollen cords for so many months hadn't done them permanent damage. Victor assured me it hadn't, for he was now singing better than ever. However, from then on, whenever I heard him on the Saturday afternoon Metropolitan Opera broadcasts, usually singing Wagner, I could hear the brilliance of his beautiful instrument gradually wane, eventually replaced by a hard, forced, metallic quality. A few times, he even cracked reaching for a high note. Rumour had it that he had developed nodules on his cords and had had an unsuccessful operation to remove them. In the end, all one heard was the infrequent replays of his many recordings over the radio. It saddened me that a talent such as Victor's should be cut short because of the abusive treatment of a strong healthy voice. His career, with astute care, should have spanned over four decades instead of a scanty two.

Suffused with nostalgia, I began to pick up the letters, painstakingly putting each one in its proper sequence before tucking them back into the fragile shoebox, the bank I'd been drawing my many memories from over the past hours.

On June 12, at 7:45 in the evening, I boarded a plane for Frankfurt, Germany; first stop en route to Salzburg. I was full of anticipation and excitement. Tucked into a pocket of my purse was my map of the city from the summer of 1952 which had marked on it old addresses of places I'd stayed, where I'd eaten, and people I'd met.

Six o'clock the next morning, we touched down in Frankfurt in the pouring rain. At most large airports the carrier arrives close to the terminal, but in Frankfurt, the planes land at the far end of the tarmac and passengers have to take a bus. Dashing from the plane to the bus, I got soaked through.

My bus was the leader of the pack. It began weaving in and out of the large expanse of pavement like a huge snake searching for a bush to hide in. Visibility was poor, heavy rain and mist covered our bus. All of a sudden, the terminal disappeared behind a black veil and the bus came to a standstill. For what seemed an eternity, we sat enclosed in a vacuum. Suddenly the veil lifted enough to see the buildings float into view. I wondered if the plane to Salzburg would take off in such weather.

I had never found the Frankfurt airport easy. Much of my time was spent trying to find the correct gate, which was usually different from the one marked on the ticket.

Sitting in the terminal, with the monotony of the overhead announcements dulling my senses, fog from outside seemed to have settled in my brain. The facts of my past were like moving shadows scurrying by me with faces I hadn't seen for years. Were they real or what I wished them to be? Would they still be alive? I was apprehensive yet strangely curious and excited to see what Salzburg would reveal.

It was three hours before the heavy mists outside finally dissipated enough for our plane to take off and I heard the droning voice announce, "Passengers for Salzburg, please make their way to the departure gate." By that time, I was shivering all over from my thorough drenching. When I stood to pick up my hand luggage, with dismay I saw that my usually well-pressed pantsuit looked as if I'd slept in it for days—and not alone.

I was grateful to again be in the air. For most of the flight, the Alps were covered in dark clouds with only the occasional tip peaking through. In two short hours we began our descent into Salzburg and I could feel my heart begin to pound. I could also feel an acute soreness which had found its way into my throat. My clothes were still damp and, with the help of the plane's draughty air conditioning, I knew I was in for it. I would arrive in Salzburg as I had left in 1952, with a cold.

Stepping from the plane, the only thing familiar to me was the rain pelting down upon my face and the angry-looking clouds swirling around the surrounding mountains, making them disappear and suddenly reappear again, dramatically lit by shafts of sunlight. In 1952, there was no airport; Salzburg was still recovering from the effects of five years of war. Although it hadn't been bombed, it had suffered food shortages and Nazi tyranny.

Since the festival first opened its doors to the world in 1920, the city had oscillated between a meeting place for the sophisticated opera buff in the summer and a sleepy Austrian town the rest of the year.

When my taxi drove under the Mönchsberg to the old part of the city with its narrow streets and over-hanging wrought-iron signs, I began to feel the warmth that comes from being with old friends. The past years began to tumble away like loose bricks. I was home.

Even shrouded as it was in dark clouds, Salzburg has an intrinsic beauty, for it is surely one of the most picturesque cities in Europe. To my surprise, even though it was the middle of June and the festival had yet to begin, the streets were crowded with the more adventurous sightseers willing to brave the soggy weather. Years ago, there would have been only the occasional local inhabitant with a shopping bag, dark green Austrian rain cape, and black umbrella.

I was told my hotel was within easy walking distance of the Festival Theatre. When my taxi crossed over the Salzach River on the Staatsbrücke, sped along the Rainerstrasse and up the Paris-London Strasse, the thought flashed across my mind that I wouldn't want to be striking out in high heels and a long gown over these cobblestone streets to attend an opera, particularly if it rained, which it frequently did. The hotel must be almost a mile away from the Festspielhaus.

The Mozart was a small hotel, owned and run by one family. The young man at the reception desk spoke perfect English and couldn't have been nicer.

The first few days in Salzburg were spent nursing my cold, which had turned into a heavy one. I wanted to get rid of it as soon as possible so I could enjoy the rest of my time wandering the streets, conjuring up old ghosts.

As pre-arranged, on the fourth day I would have to find another place to stay; the Mozart was booked for the rest of my two weeks in Salzburg. In the summer of 1952, I remember swimming in Fuschlsee, about a twenty mile drive from Salzburg. There was a grand Schloss by the lake. I remember, too, spending a cold, wet night in the parking lot shivering in the back seat of the car, licking my wounds over a disastrous love affair. I knew that the Schloss was now a five star hotel; I wondered if they might have space.

The day was warm and sunny with big white, fluffy clouds drifting overhead. I struck out for Schloss Fuschl with my trusty map in hand, hoping the hotel might have a room. In 1952, Highway 158 was only two lanes. Now, in 1998, it was a super four lane highway. Because of this I nearly missed the road down to the Schloss. Built on the corner of the turn-off was a new large Gasthof which looked very inviting. I stopped to see if they could put me up for the remainder of my stay. Like every place else, they were completely booked, so I continued down the heavily wooded lane, catching fleeting glimpses of the sun sparkling on Lake Fuschl close by. Soon, after passing the simple stone gateway, the majestic tower of the Schoss loomed into view.

Schloss Fuschl, with its large tower capped with a high, pyramid-shaped roof, rose like a huge sea monster from out of the end of the lake. It was an imposing edifice built in 1450 as a hunting lodge. It had been a favourite hunting ground of princes, archbishops, and nobility over its long history. In 1940, von Ribbentrop, Hitler's foreign minister, acquired it to entertain foreign VIPs and important Nazi officials.

In 1945, at the end of World War II, it was put under military control, and the Russians used it as their headquarters. My first introduction to the Schloss was the summer of 1950, while studying with Eva. I had spent a few evenings there as a guest of the Russians. The husband of one of Eva's students was a captain in the U.S. Army. It was his job to make sure the Russians didn't use force to entice the displaced behind the Iron Curtain. Whenever there was a special evening at the Schloss, I always tagged along with my friends.

One evening, in particular, surfaces in my memory. The Russians were showing a German movie, which had been made in the late nineteenth century. The story was Wagner's *Ring Cycle* condensed into two hours. I marvelled at the spectacular effects unfolding before my eyes in black and white, particularly as the movie was conceived at the dawn of filmmaking. Valhalla was truly a land of the gods with its mists, clouds, hills, and valleys. However, what struck me most about those evenings at the Schloss was the age of the officers in charge; none looked older than thirty. The colonel looked to have recently stepped out of high school.

When the Schloss came fully into view, I slowed down to a halt so I could thoroughly absorb the panorama before me. The former parking lot was transformed into a vast verdant lawn, surrounded by rose bushes. In front of the stone arch entrance into the Schloss was a patio with expensively dressed people sitting at white linen-covered tables sipping mid-morning coffee with their pastries. On top of the low stone pillars, bordering the patio, were large pots of brilliant yellow daisies. The tableau was enchanting. It was Cinderella turned into a princess.

When I parked my little Opal beside the Mercedes and Porsches in the parking lot, it looked déclassé indeed. I was sure the expensive cars in the lot must be an indication of the going rates inside the Schloss. I didn't care, I was desperate.

The studded heavy iron door was open, tucked back against the wide, arched entrance. As I entered the impressive, vaulted ceiling hall, everything looked structurally the same, yet grander. Though the day was warm, there was a welcoming fire burning in the stone fireplace in the bar area to the left of the hall. Above the mantle was a king-size elk's head with magnificent antlers. The beamed ceiling of the breakfast room, visible from the hall, had been gilded, and the room was now twice the size, having been extended out toward the lake. The new wall was all glass, exposing a dazzling view of Fuschlsee below.

There were groups of uniformed young men everywhere, eager to serve. It all smacked of money—a lot of money! If this was the only place I could get a room, so be it. I wouldn't even inquire about the rates. I would pay with plastic and worry about the cost when I received my Visa bill!

The price of the room included a full breakfast of sliced meats, cheese, rolls, hardboiled eggs, fruit, juice, and cakes, with plenty to tuck into my purse (hopefully unnoticed) for a picnic lunch later.

There were a few single rooms left, not in the main Schloss, but in the new building by the parking lot. The room was small but comfortable and beautifully appointed. There was a big bowl of fruit, compliments of the house, at the bedside. The bathroom was larger than the bedroom, with gold taps, a marble basin and tub, even tissues to match. For the rest of my stay in Salzburg, I planned to bask in the lap of luxury.

I spent the afternoon walking in the woods and sitting on a bench at the edge of the lake. Soon I was visited by a flotilla of ducks which came close enough to peck at my feet. I was sorry I had nothing more than my sturdy walking shoes to offer them. The outstanding thing about Schloss Fuschl was its seclusion. There must have been over two hundred rooms, yet I was never aware of people. I saw them checking in and out but seldom on the docks or at the lakeside. I never met anyone walking on the nature trails and saw few boating or swimming. I seemed alone in my reverie.

I found my mind drifting back to when I last walked by the lake, the rain pouring down on my misery. The handsome features of the Graf's beguiling face began to come into focus. Would he still own Schloss Augen? Was it still a Gasthof? Would his son now own it? Would Karl even be alive? All these questions were spinning around in my head as the ducks nibbled at the toes of my shoes. Those terrible last days at Schloss Augen had now faded into an indifferent memory.

That night I dined in the hotel's elegant dining room filled with distinguished-looking people. The maitre d', with an aloof air of purpose, led me to a small table in the centre of the room under a brilliant spotlight. There was a time when I would have relished such an honour, but eating alone dressed in messy sports clothes with dirty, uncoiffed hair in such refined company was an honour I would forgo in the future.

Before he disappeared, the maitre'd dropped the menu in front of me. I began to peruse its contents: ostrich, venison, grouse. I was hoping for simpler fare. Perhaps a glass of red wine would help me to make up my mind.

I looked up to catch a waiter's attention when, from out of the kitchen door at the other end of the dining room came a parade of white-gloved waiters in a line, each carrying on one shoulder a large plate covered with a silver dome. They marched in unison, like well trained soldiers in an army battalion, toward the large, round table at my side. The six encircled the table, and each stood behind one of the cosmopolitan-looking patrons. On cue, with a nod from their leader, they lifted the silver covers high over their heads and, with solemnity, put the plates down in front of the guests. I opted for cold salmon (without silver lid) and a salad. From now on I would make a dinner reservation at the Gasthof up the road and eat in contented obscurity.

The next morning I set off for Salzburg after a sumptuous breakfast. It was another beautiful day and I wanted to take full advantage of the good weather while it lasted. I parked my car on Rainerstrasse beside Mirabell Gardens. As I got out of the car my nose was immediately treated to the sweet aroma of hyacinth, mock orange, and Japanese lilac. The formal garden was ablaze with flowers. There were tulips, peonies, and poppies. When the Kurtzes first took me to these gardens over forty years ago, even the grass had difficulty growing, and the flowers were few and sparse. For half an hour, I sat drinking in the visual feast and reflecting on the many happy hours passed in the company of the g*emütlichen* couple. I remember always having to struggle to understand what they were saying, for they spoke no English. I decided to see if I could find their apartment, where I had spent those last days in 1952, with Frau Kurtz nursing me through a bad cold and broken heart. Though the Kurtzes were long gone, I remember they had a daughter. Could she still be living in the apartment?

The building was directly opposite Mirabell Garten, its entrance off an alley. The previously open archway leading into it was now glazed. There was a steel-framed glass door which I tried to open, but it was locked and I could find no buzzer in order to gain entrance. The inside hallway was painted white and brightly lit. Peering through the glass, I could see the eight mailboxes on the right wall, but they were too far away to read the names above them.

By this time, it was close to one o'clock, and pangs of hunger indicated it was time for lunch. I thought of Fritz's restaurant where the Kurtzes had taken me and the Tattles that evening when I first tried my wings in song. I remembered it was within walking distance of the Kurtzes' apartment, and Fritz's wife was a fabulous cook. I took from my purse the fragile old map and my indispensable bifocals, the companion of age. With my nose inches from the map, I could faintly see a small *X* in faded blue ink. It looked to be about three blocks from where I now stood. My stomach told me it was worth a try.

I was surprised to find the *Gasthaus* on Franz Josef Strasse, directly across from the Mozart Hotel. Strange I hadn't noticed it before; maybe it was because I had only seen it at night. The garden at the back was closed, but the main room was full of what appeared to be local people. Fritz's daughter was now the owner. I soon discovered her W*iener-Schnitzel, Sauerkraut,* and *Apfelstrudel* were as good as her mother's.

The upright piano was still in the far corner near the entrance to the garden. While sipping a white wine *Spritzer*, the sounds of that magical night when we had sung until well after midnight, enveloped me. The place had been full to overflowing and a thick cloud of cigar and cigarette smoke had hung heavily over the room. The sweet sound of Trish's voice mixed with that of the unknown tenor rang in my ears. Frau Kurtz had insisted I join them while Jack took over at the piano, playing all the arias and duets of *Carmen,* from memory. Piercing through my reverie were Usova's harsh words, after Richard Alexander had told her I had been singing in a tavern.

"Darlink, it is so cheap. You prostitute yourself and you are not ready to be heard by public. Never forget, you are my emissary and as such you will always do me honour." I smiled; she always took every opportunity to cripple my fragile confidence. That night was the first time since studying with Usova, I had actually enjoyed singing. I will never forget the ovation we received, our audience thumping loudly on the tables with fists and spoons, wanting more.

I have often wondered what happened to the Tattles. What a gifted couple they were! Trish could have risen to the top with the instrument God had given her, and Jack would have made a fine conductor. Did they end up producing babies like the maestro told Trish she should do? After that summer, I never heard of them again.

When I finished lunch, because it was such a beautiful day, I decided to cross Mozartsteg and wander through the old *Stadt*. I sat on a bench in the Mozart Platz remembering my first visit to Salzburg in 1948 with my mother. It was shortly after World War II when Salzburg was still occupied by the Americans. We had watched the Stars and Stripes being slowly lowered in silence at dusk. Today there were sounds of music everywhere, coming from the Festspielhaus, from open windows overlooking the Resitenzplatz and the Waagplatz. I saw phantom faces of old friends on every corner, their voices haunting me as I began wandering about the old historical sights.

On my way back to the car, I began to window shop. Years ago, all one saw was local fare displayed in the windows. Now the stores were resplendent with the latest, most extravagant finery from all over Europe. In one window, a particular item caught my eye. I stood staring for a long time at a pearl-grey silk cocktail dress—so simple, so elegant, I knew I must have it. Over the loosely fitted sheath was a delicately draped duster of iridescent chiffon that glistened like a cobweb in the sun after a day's rain. This dress would surely disguise the imperfections inflicted on me by age and the pull of gravity. I had brought with me the perfect multi-coloured lamé scarf to toss casually around my shoulders and neck, creating the right dramatic effect. Entering the store to inquire the price, serious doubts began to surface. My critical eye frequently failed to keep pace with my aging body. I was inclined to visualize myself in clothing meant for the young and svelte, and I was sure the shopkeeper wouldn't volunteer the truth because it would hamper her sale.

The dress was very expensive, but I bought it anyway. It was an extravagance I would enjoy once the guilt faded away. I could only hope this time my eye read true. Such a dress must have silver pumps or sandals. This took another hour of search and, when found, another bundle of shillings. By that time, it was six o'clock and I was ready for dinner. The Goldener Hirsch was nearby where, in August of 1954, Arturo and I had taken Usova to dinner and she had first begun her eventually successful assault on Arturo. It was when the germ of a workshop in Canada was born.

I expected the restaurant to be as full as it had always been in the past. To my surprise, it was almost empty; then I remembered there was yet no festival when the opera-goers eat early and the fashionable eat late. Because I was in slacks and a casual shirt, the maitre d' carefully put me in a dark corner in case I might be guilty of lowering the dress standard. By the time I had completed my luxurious dinner and the long walk back to the car with my purchases weighing me down, it was past nine o'clock and I was tired and ready for bed.

The following morning, during breakfast, I noticed it was getting increasingly overcast but as it wasn't raining, I thought I would again drive to Salzburg and take my chances. Before leaving, I searched my map to see if there was a mark indicating where Eva had lived. I found a faint capital *E* on Reitgutweg, a street not far from the centre of the city.

Half an hour later, I parked my car at the end of Reitgutweg and began looking for any house that looked familiar. I could hear the gurgling sound of water rushing through the culvert underneath the laneway. I remembered, a little brook ran beside the garden behind her house, but nothing else looked recognizable. I walked back and forth in front of the house on the corner. I stopped at the gate, wondering if I should go in and enquire if Eva had ever lived there, when a very Austrian-looking woman in her mid-fifties, wearing a *Dirndl*, came out of the door. She had obviously been watching me with curiosity.

"*Was machen Sie hier? Suchen Sie etwas?*" (What are you doing here? Are you looking for something?) she asked suspiciously.

"*Bitte schön.*" I tried to explain in my best German that I was looking for a house where Eva Stein had spent her summers many years ago. I had been a pupil of hers.

Her face lit up like the sun suddenly peeking out from behind a dark cloud. "*Ach, ja, die prominente Dame. Ich erinnere mich. Bitte kommen Sie herein, auf eine*

Schale Kaffe. (Oh yes, the famous lady; I remember her well. Please come in and have coffee.)" Her demeanor quickly changed to that of a close friend.

While sipping our coffee and munching our cakes, she talked of Eva in glowing terms. She said she had known and loved her when she was a little girl. Her family had owned, and rented the house next door to Eva each summer, for many years. She had sold the house after her parents died, and the new owner had demolished it. That is, I think that's what she said, having as usual guessed at most of it.

For half an hour, I struggled to understand what the woman was saying while she chatted on, but I was soon lost in a barrage of unfamiliar words. Finally I thanked her for her *Gastfreundlichkeit* and left. I took with me a vivid picture of Eva sitting in her garden in a pale blue *Dirndl,* entertaining her famous, adoring guests. It was there I had met the world renowned Elizabeth Schwarzkopf.

I was so full of rich cakes, the thought of lunch brought spasms of nausea to my stomach, even though it was now noon. I remembered Usova's studio was somewhere between where I now stood and the *Inner Stadt.* I was curious to see if the building was as unassuming and unattended as I remembered. I again searched my map. Sure enough there was an *X* on Arenbergstrasse, a few minutes drive away.

Going down Ernst-Grein-Strasse, I noticed dark clouds gathering around the surrounding mountains to my right. This wasn't promising for an afternoon of sightseeing but because the street was on my way to the centre of the city, it was worth a slight detour. I had never before entered Arenbergstrasse from the east. Everything looked so strange, I wondered if I was on the right street. On both sides of the narrow road were six-foot-high stone walls; behind them were wooded areas surrounding large, luxurious homes. Inching my way down the steep incline, I came upon a big square building that looked strangely out of place among the other imposing houses. It was definitely the ugly kid on the block. The stucco was painted a garish pink with white trim around the windows. It wouldn't have looked quite so tasteless if it hadn't been for the black shiny painted eaves and down pipes outlining the flat contours of the building. The double entrance doors were now painted black with white trim around the diamond-shaped windows, making it resemble more a commercial establishment than a domicile. It had looked better before, in its rundown state; at least it wasn't so invasive then.

Sitting in the car staring at the doors, I began thinking of that first day I arrived in front of them, not knowing which apartment to buzz in order to gain entrance. It had been degrees hotter than today. I recall being soaked through with perspiration. I couldn't help but be amused as I conjured up the image of Madame reclining on her chaise-lounge. She was still weak from her bout of illness in Rome caused by the "lions in her chest." It was those very lions which eventually ended her life.

Five years after Arturo's death, I had a phone call from Usova's husband, Wolfgang, in New York, telling me she was very ill. "She has forgiven you and wants to see you before she dies," he had said.

Thinking back, I recall being still very angry and bitter. My initial reaction was, she may have forgiven me, but I will never forgive her for doing her best to destroy my crumbling confidence. What does she want from me now? With Arturo gone, I'm no longer any use to her. I debated not going, but her husband sounded in such despair, for his sake I thought I should make the effort, and go to New York.

Entering her studio the next day, I couldn't help but ponder that first time I had sung for Usova. I was so frightened, so nervous that I wondered what I was doing there. I should have turned and retreated down the brownstone steps before entering the lioness's den. If I had, how different my life would have been!

When Wolfgang led me through the studio and into Usova's bedroom, even in the dim light I could see how ill, how vulnerable she looked. I suspected that, for the first time in her life, she was facing an adversary more formidable than herself and she had no power over the outcome. I tried not to look at her, to look at her bedcovers instead. With her defenses gone, she appeared naked. I felt as if I was spying on her, peeking through a keyhole. Her always carefully coiffed red hair had an inch of grey at its roots and was sticking straight up in clumps above her narrow forehead. Her closed eyelids looked unclothed without their cover of green eye shadow. Her prominent teeth were unnaturally exposed by her open mouth. My bitter heart began to melt, and I took the hand that was lying across her chest above the covers. Slowly, her heavy eyelids opened. A tired smile appeared on her grey lips and her fingers weakly encircled mine. "Darlink little one, you have come in time for the last act." Despite her weak and barely audible voice, her words were laced with irony.

The focus of her gaze shifted from me to her husband standing at my side. She took her hand from mine and weakly motioned toward a massive piece of furniture in front of the opposite wall. "Wolfie, take from the top dresser drawer the little velvet jewel box ..." Before she finished the sentence, her eyes closed and her head dropped back on the pillow, exhausted from the effort of speaking. She seemed to have stopped breathing.

"Lana, don't talk—rest. I'll stay here beside you," I said softly. I knew she heard me, for a spent smile reappeared on her ashen face.

When Wolfgang returned with the jewel box, he had in his other hand an occasional chair he had taken from beside the dresser. "Sit, stay a few more minutes. She'd like that." There was a long pause as if he knew he had more to say but wasn't sure what it was. Then he remembered the jewel box in his hand. "Here, she wanted you to have these." After handing me the box, he turned and shuffled out of the room. His stooped body was that of a defeated old man, and my heart went out to him.

I had no sooner sat down when Wolfgang came back and put his hand on my shoulder. "There are others out in the studio waiting to see her. The doctor said it would tire her too much if she saw more than one at a time," he whispered.

Before Wolfgang led me out of the room, I took Usova's hand once more and gave it a tender squeeze. I had made my peace!

Underneath the studio arch stood a familiar figure with a stunning brunette on his arm. "Stay," Victor muttered to me under his breath as if giving a command to his favourite puppy dog. "I won't be long. We'll have a bite later. I want you to meet the wife; I told her all about you," he said, brushing by me and entering the bedroom with wife in tow.

He looked even more commanding than before. His beard was carefully trimmed, and he'd lost weight. I waited a few minutes outside the closed door, then left. I didn't want to talk to anyone. I wanted to be free of this studio and all its unhappy memories as soon as possible. It unnerved me seeing Usova so near death. As often as she had fantasized serious illness in the past, I never believed ill health would eventually overwhelm her. I had thought her somehow immortal.

The sound of the rain on the roof and windshield of my car suddenly pulled me back to the present. I shivered. The temperature had dropped a few degrees since I pulled to a stop in front of Usova's studio. Unless I wanted to sit in my car all afternoon driving around in the rain, I might as well head back to Schloss Fuschl and make use of my marble bath tub, before having a simple dinner at the Gasthof on the highway by the entrance to the Schloss.

I put off my visit to Schloss Augen until my last morning. Not only was I thoroughly enjoying my stay at Fuschl, relaxing in the sun, swimming, boating, walking the *Fussweg,* and rediscovering the surrounding lakes and mountains, I was putting off a possible encounter with the Graf. The wound he had dealt me forty years ago left a deeper scar than I realized, but I knew if I didn't satisfy my curiosity now, I would always regret it.

I set off for Salzburg mid-morning, after the usual large breakfast. I carefully followed the directional arrows on my map, made in 1952. Nothing looked familiar until I reached Graf-Revetera-Allee, leading to the Schloss. The surrounding fields were as I remembered them: large green meadows that gave the feeling of country though still in the city. I marvelled anew at the chestnut trees lining the Allee. They were even more magnificent after their many years of growth, their huge leaves making a solid green roof, covering the lane in deep shadow.

Midway down the alley, I noticed a number of cars parked in the field to my right with metal framed trailers attached, some empty, some carrying what looked like long aluminum poles wrapped in brightly coloured cloth. Groups of people were standing around, looking heavenward. I was so curious to see what they were looking at that I pulled over, stopped the car, and got out. There was what appeared to be a mammoth bird high overhead, soaring in and out of the clouds. The sun glanced off its wings, creating lightning-like flashes. When it glided closer, I could see the body was separated from the wings by a metal frame. It wasn't until it floated directly overhead that the bird became a man. I watched spellbound while he glided to the ground at the far end of the field. Two people rushed from the group to guide him to a full stop a few yards from where I stood. They unhooked him from the huge V-shaped red and white wings. They dismantled the frame and the wings. Laying the wings out on the grass, they rolled canvas and poles together and secured them on a metal trailer. I remained fascinated until the cars began pulling out of the field one by one, disappearing back down Graf-Revetera-Allee. By then it was noon. It was the first time I had ever seen someone hang glide.

I continued on toward the onion-shaped bell tower of the ancient little rococo church, which peeked out high above the trees. I drove past the church, past the tall plastered brick pillars with impressive urns on top, and into the courtyard as a homing pigeon would fly to its nest. I parked beside the few cars in front of the old Schloss. When I opened the door to get out, a large white Mercedes convertible whipped around the curve in the lane by the church and sped past the pillars and through the courtyard, nearly clipping the back of my car before it came to a stop at the far end. A tall, middle-aged man with a bald pate stepped from the car and disappeared around the other side of the Schloss. He was taller and considerably younger than the Graf would be. He walked with such authority that I took him to be the present owner. The whole place seemed deserted. I walked around the Schloss and onto the expansive lawn, where I had last seen the Graf playing *boules* with his two children. To this day, I can see his stern features looking through me as if he'd never met me. How naïve and inexperienced I had been in those days! I retraced my steps back to the Schloss and peered into a ground-level window, trying to see past the thick veil of dust inside. It was full of litter, which was heavily coated in cobwebs. There were broken pieces of furniture, rusty appliances, and old dirty wine barrels, in strong contrast to the outside of the building, which looked as if a new coat of pale yellow plaster had recently been applied.

Tucked in between the Schloss and church was a large, new, yellow and white building with a black mansard metal roof. The shutters were all open, so I guessed there must be guests around somewhere. I became conscious of a din of voices combined with the clatter of dishes coming from across the courtyard, behind the stables where my room had been. I was puzzled, as there had never been a restaurant when I had lived there.

The stables had a new, imposing entrance jutting out from the front of the freshly painted yellow and white building. The whole place had the same country manor feel as before, however, now another two stars could be added to its sign. I walked under an ornately carved wooden arch at the far side of the stables, following the sounds and smells of food being served. Where the parking lot had been, there was now a large beer garden. At first glance, there seemed to be flowers everywhere, and there was a rose garden in full bloom on my left as I entered. There were large boxes of multi-coloured geraniums cascading from the many windows of the stable. There were flowers on top of the sea of pale blue-and-white-checked tablecloths. The cobblestones underfoot were dappled with shadows from the many large chestnut trees overhead, providing protection from the hot midday sun. The place was full of people. I spotted an empty table close to the entrance and sat down. No one came for my order so I was able to watch without being disturbed.

I noticed a stooped, white-bearded man dressed in grey Tyrolean *Lederhosen* with dark green braces over a blue-and-white-checked shirt, the same material as the tablecloths. He was wearing a green felt Tyrolean hat with what looked like a shaving brush attached to its side. The hat covered most of his long white straggly hair. He was weaving in and out of the tables loudly chatting people up. I was fascinated watching his outlandish antics. He gesticulated wildly with his arms, dancing around as if treading on hot coals.

When a waiter finally noticed me, I ordered a white wine *Spritzer* only, for my leftover breakfast of rolls, sliced meat, cheese, a boiled egg, and an apple was fast heating up in the car. I was planning to eat later, sitting on a bench under the trees farther down the road.

"*Bitte, wo kann ich die Geschichte von Schloss Augen kaufen?*" I asked the waiter, hoping there was a brochure or booklet available of the Schloss I could purchase. He shook his head and was about to leave when I again struggled for the correct words in German. "*Kennen Sie jemanden der etwas über Schloss Augen weiss?*" I hoped there was someone who knew a little of the history.

The waiter pointed to the man I had been watching and said in perfect English, "He owns the place. Ask him."

I finished my *Spritzer*, paid the waiter, and was about to approach the owner when he disappeared into the open French doors leading to the kitchen. I waited. When he didn't reappear, I decided to look for him. Where once had been the lobby and front desk area was now a large dining room with rows of simple wooden chairs and tables; a typical Austrian wine cellar. Entering the room, I saw immediately to my left the owner sitting in front of a dark green upright piano. He was absentmindedly picking at the keys as if trying to recall a familiar tune. I tentatively approached, not sure how to begin. "*Entschuldigen Sie bitte.* (Excuse me please)" I knew this was always a safe approach.

He looked up with glazed eyes, a slight frown on his face, annoyed I had interrupted his pleasant reverie. After a few false starts, I managed to ask him if he was the owner.

"*Ja, ja.*" He nodded his head with exaggeration.

In my best English-German, I began to explain that I had lived for a summer at the Schloss when the stables were a Gasthof. It had been owned by a *Graf von Scharnhorst*.

"*Ja, ich bin Graf von Scharnhorst.* The Schloss has been in my family for three hundred years," he said in German, his eyebrows rising with a questioning look. His voice had the shrill quavering sound of the elderly; gone was the mellifluous timbre which had seduced me when I was a young girl. A large white beard can hide all but the eyes. I looked hard into the eyes of this old man and could see nothing of the past charisma reflected in them.

"*Nein,*" I blurted out, shaking my head in disbelief. If he took exception to my rude outburst, it didn't show, for he only gave me a foolish smile and kept nodding. Could this man ever have broken anyone's heart? I tried hard to regain my composure before plunging on in my English-German. I began by telling him I had been a pupil of Madame Svetlana Usova. The name Usova had barely fallen from my lips when he jumped up from the piano bench, swept me into his arms, and gave me a big hug; that is, as big as his feeble arms allowed; then he planted a kiss on both my cheeks. In a flurry of excitement, he began dancing again on his hot coals, reciting over and over, "*Ja, ja, Ich kann mich gut erinnern. Wie konnte*

Ich die berühmte Usova vergessen. Viele ihrer Schüler haben hier über die Jahre gewohnt. (Yes, yes, I remember her well. How could I ever forget the famous Madame Usova? Many of her pupils stayed here over the years.)

From the way he brushed over the last statement, I was sure he had no idea which pupil I was. Perhaps I wasn't the only one to have suffered a loss of innocence at the hands of this piteous Don Juan.

He insisted on taking me to see his wife and to meet his son, who was now managing the Gasthof. I quickly declined; however, it seemed I had no choice. Before I knew it, he had taken my arm and was leading me through the dining room, into the lobby, and out the front entrance. Still tugging on my arm, he led me across the courtyard into the new building by the Schloss and up a flight of stairs to the first landing. The door to his apartment was open. Entering the hallway, I could see at the far end a tiny bird-like, shrivelled old lady standing on one foot and leaning against the wall. The minute she saw the Graf she began to moan. She stuck out her free, shoeless foot and pointed to it with a pained look on her face. *"Es schmertzt mich,"* she whined.

Ignoring her utterance of pain, the Graf gestured with his head in my direction and blurted out excitedly that I had been a pupil of *the* Svetlana Usova. For a brief moment, her eyes pierced mine like an X-ray machine. Did she know which pupil I had been? The stony look vanished instantly and reverted again to one of pain. She excused herself and abruptly turned and limped into an adjoining room; the Graf followed, protesting that she should stay to speak to this nice lady.

I left. I couldn't get away fast enough. I dashed to my car, frightened I might be followed. I drove through the courtyard and out the other end. I turned left onto Lotte Lehmann Promenade, wending my way through the back roads of Salzburg until reaching the highway leading to Schloss Fuschl. I never stopped to eat my sun-drenched lunch.

My thoughts began to whirl like a potter's wheel. How could I ever have contemplated spending my life with this pitiful man? Did the years totally strip him of the charm I believed him to have possessed? Had I been so vacuous as to have been smitten by his "window dressing" only? Had Usova been right when she said, "He's a dull, stupid man who knows only his own vanity"?

By the time I arrived at Schloss Fuschl, the sky had clouded over and little spots of rain had begun to appear on the windshield. It was now mid-afternoon and not the sort of day to walk on the *Fußweg* or drive around the mountains in search of new territory to explore. I had noticed a *Friseur* on the lower floor of the Schloss. Before returning to my room, I went below to see if they had time to blow-dry my hair and give me a manicure so I could arrive in Toronto looking respectable.

All cleaned up, I went to the reception desk to make a reservation for dinner. I had no intention of letting the rain ruin my freshly styled hair by eating at the *Gasthof* near the highway.

Epilogue

<u>A Stranger in the Mirror</u>

Shortly before eight, walking by the full-length mirror on the wall outside the bathroom, I stopped to make a final check before going to the dining room. I wanted to make sure the lamé scarf and Usova's large emerald earrings weren't in excess of the dress code! I stared into the mirror with a start. Who was that old lady in my beautiful new dress, wrapped in antiquity, and dusty with age? She looked like my mother, but Mother had been stooped and gnarled with arthritis in old age. This woman stood tall, her white hair shining like a halo around a face nesting in a tangle of wrinkles. Staring back at me was a stranger to the younger woman within. How could this have happened without me noticing its progression? What happened to those fast-flowing forty years, those years after Arturo's death?

At the beginning, I remember drifting in emptiness, stripped of all ambition, the future a blur. I cancelled all engagements, not caring if I ever sang again. I wandered from one incarnation to the next, desperately searching for a reason to go on living. The first year was spent looking after my ailing mother in London, until her constant nagging for me to sing again drove me back to Toronto to seek the protection of my Cabbagetown refuge. There I would spend long hours at the piano poring over my husband's opera scores, hoping in some small way to bring him back into my life. I would frequently muddle aimlessly around the empty house pushing a vacuum cleaner, trying to break the unbearable silence. Eating became an automatic chore; all food tasted like wood shavings.

It was almost two years after Arturo's death when fate came to the rescue. It seemed like yesterday when my accompanist, Lucy Jones, arrived at my Cabbagetown doorstep with a large, awkward sixteen-year-old in tow. The girl had a sullen expression on her plain, round face. Her mouse-coloured hair hung in uneven lengths around her wide shoulders. She was tall and had the lumpy figure of a teenager whose young fat would either drop off in a year or two or swell to a hefty size. She stood just inside the front door, not moving, her eyes staring down at her well-worn running shoes. When I approached her to say hello, she remained silent. There was an uncomfortable moment; then Lucy took charge as she usually did.

"This is Clara Davidson," Lucy said. "She's been a pupil of mine since she was eight. She's got no money, but she's got talent to burn. The silly girl could have a great career in piano, but she wants to sing. I've kept her under wraps until I thought she was ready to begin voice lessons. I want you to hear her."

Before I could ask Lucy why, she was leading the poor girl through the vestibule, down the four steps into the living room, and to the grand piano in the studio.

Lucy began to play the accompaniment to an aria by Giordani, *"Caro mio ben."* The girl stood in the crook of the piano, still looking at the floor with her arms and hands stiffly at her sides. The minute she heard the piano her head lifted, and her formerly dull eyes lit up as if street lights had suddenly been turned on. Her first words came out with such joy and feeling, I was aware of the hair on my arms standing on end. Though the tone was occasionally breathy from lack of focus and support, it was a strong voice with a lush, warm sound. The pitch was true and the phrasing that of a musician.

When she finished singing, I struggled hard to keep my excitement in check. It was as though my whole being had come alive after a width of vacant time. I walked to the piano bench and indicated for Lucy to move. "Here, let me take over." I struck a few chords and arpeggios and motioned with my head for the girl to repeat them; I wanted to see the range of the voice. It made no difference how complicated my demands were, she was equal to whatever I tossed her way. I took the voice down to *G* below middle *C* and up to the *E* above high *C*. No matter how much I stretched the cords, she sang every note with ease and clarity.

"Lucy, I want to talk to you. Clara, would you excuse us?" I led Lucy into the kitchen. I was so overwhelmed I could feel warm tears swelling up in my eyes. Such a natural talent comes along seldom. "Lucy, you know I've never taught anyone. This is an incredible talent. I don't think at this moment I'm up to the challenge."

Lucy took my reticence for indifference and was immediately on the offensive.

"Look, it's time you stopped wallowing in self pity and got off your ass. I think you need this kid more than she needs you. The only reason I'm bringing her to you is that I know you won't push her too soon; she's only sixteen. Will you take her on or won't you?" she pressed in her no-nonsense way, then added, "For free."

"Do you seriously think I'm equal to it?" But inside I knew wild horses couldn't prevent me from trying. I was ready to move on to my next incarnation, and it had come to me from heaven in the guise of this gifted child.

Lucy shook her head in exasperation. "Good God, girl; with the teaching you've had? Yeah, I know she's a rough diamond, but you're the only one I know who's classy enough to shape her and give her a little polish."

"I'd certainly like to give it a try," I said with mock diffidence. "Where'd you find her? Where's she from?" I wanted to know all about her.

Lucy told me that when she was a young girl she had spent her summers on her grandparents' farm in Saskatchewan near Regina. They had a piano, and she used to practice for hours when not helping out on the farm. Clara's family had a farm close by. When she was only six years old, Clara began visiting Lucy's grandparents' farm whenever she heard the sound of the piano floating over the fields between. She would sit in the parlour for hours, rapturously listening to Lucy practice. When she was eight, she begged Lucy to give her lessons. Her progress was so amazing that, when she finished high school six years later, Lucy took her to live with her in Toronto so she could concentrate totally on the piano. Whenever Lucy gave a vocal coaching lesson, Clara would sit outside the door on the floor of the apartment, absorbing every sound. She kept trying to coerce Lucy into finding a singing teacher for her. Finally, Lucy gave in and decided to pay her friend Jessica a visit.

As Usova would have said, I immediately welcomed Clara "into my clutches." Lucy was right, I needed her more then she needed me. Unless Clara fell into the hands of a charlatan, which I was sure Lucy wouldn't let happen, no one could prevent this gifted, responsive, and determined young girl from making it to the top. It was only a matter of time.

I spent the initial weeks introducing her to Usova's breathing exercises.

"First make sure the body is erect and slack, no tension anywhere. Ribcage extended, take in as much air as possible through wide open nostrils, the throat open as if in a yawn. Beginning deep, fill abdominal wall, lower ribs and back first, always keeping upper chest and shoulders relaxed and low."

Usova's accompanying growl and distorted facial expression I thought unnecessary as Clara's wide face had plenty of space without any extra help. The rudimentary thing for her to learn was how to use her diaphragm to support what would soon develop into a large and powerful instrument. She was quick to grasp everything I told her without questioning. I tried to tread slowly and carefully but, with Clara, it was like trying to rein in a thoroughbred race horse.

At the beginning, we worked mostly technique, concentrating on placing each note in the voice, making sure the resonance was well forward and the sound even. I put opera on the back burner for the present and began with the songs of Schubert and Schumann, as Eva would have done. If she could learn to interpret German lieder with understanding and conviction using a more intimate and refined sound, then using her large voice with the same imaginative energy, she could convincingly create an operatic role.

By the time Clara was ready to sing in public, I insisted she know each new song from memory before bringing it to a lesson. With Lucy accompanying her, I would have her walk to the piano, relaxed, head held high. She would then acknowledge me with a confident smile, assuring me, her audience, the concert was in capable hands. Standing in the crook of the instrument, she would nod to Lucy when she was ready. The interpretation of the song would begin with the first note of the accompaniment. Even when not singing, she must project with her eyes and with the expression on her face the story being told by the piano. This took some time for Clara to grasp convincingly, for though she was very musical, to translate the music into visual pictures was difficult for her. She was inclined to sing inwardly to herself rather than project outwardly to an audience. It is as important to know how to put across a song as it is to know how to sing it. By the time Clara was ready to give concerts, performing was second nature to her.

I chose her first operatic roles with great care so as not to exploit her young voice. The Verdi ones, which would eventually be her trademark, would come later. To begin with, it would be Mozart: both the Third Lady and Pamina in *The Magic Flute;* Susanna, Cherubino, and the Countess in *Marriage of Figaro.*

From the outset, the study of Italian, German, and French was a must. The more languages she spoke, the easier it would be for her in the future. If I forecast correctly, the globe would become Clara's home.

Her thirst for learning was insatiable. I took her to concerts, the opera, the ballet, museums, and art galleries. All forms of creative art feed off each other. I insisted she join me in yoga classes to learn how to keep both breathing and her body flexible and relaxed. I paid for ballroom dancing so she could acquire the art of coordination and grace of movement. Gradually, she began to lose her awkwardness and her teenage fat dropped off her like a heavy overcoat, replaced by the gentle curves of a woman. She became as slim as her large bone structure would allow. Over the next ten years, I watched with pleasure and pride as this incredibly talented, ungainly child blossomed into a cultivated, striking young woman.

By eighteen, Clara was on full scholarship with the Opera School and, at twenty, she was the big winner of the Metropolitan auditions in New York City. Finally, because of her phenomenal success wherever she sang, she brought many talented students to my studio, and I was in much demand for my services. I could pick and choose the pupils I felt I could help most.

It was almost forty years ago when Lucy brought Clara into my life and, though she is now in her mid-fifties, her career has not waned. I have retired from teaching but still she will phone me from faraway places to ask my advice. Should she accept a particular engagement? What should she do when a certain aria is giving her trouble? Would this or that medication harm her vocal cords? As long as one sings, one is always dependent on some trustworthy person to become one's mentor and outside ears.

How often in the past I've been asked, "Don't you miss singing, miss performing?" The answer is always no, not for a second. I perform through my wonderfully endowed *children*.

In the ensuing years, I have become a good teacher. I have made sure my pupils sing on the interest and not on the capital of the voice; no forcing, ever. From Usova, I inherited an uncompromising ear. I can detect the smallest problem before it damages the vocal cords, and I know how to correct it. But it was Eva who infused in me the heart and soul of the music, and from her, I learned to cut the umbilical cord when a student felt he or she was ready for release.

If one is robbed of confidence and self-esteem by a malicious thief, then one is very poor indeed. In hindsight, looking back on those early days with Svetlana Usova, I wonder why I continued to punish myself; why I put myself through such an ordeal. I know now there are less confrontational ways of acquiring the skills necessary to perfect one's art. It is so important for a teacher to know how to instruct without tearing apart the confidence of a pupil. As well, one must be careful not to enshrine a pupil in a strait-jacket of technique. Throughout my teaching career, I have been fortunate to have had many very talented pupils, most of whom are now singing in the prestigious opera houses of the world. Above the piano in my studio is Jessica's "wall of fame." Over these past many years, the spaces have been filled with famous faces; they are my harvest; through them I have been fulfilled.

The famous Italian baritone, Tito Gobbi, summed it up admirably in his autobiography: *Fortunate indeed is the person who is given the opportunity to plant in one decade the seeds which will flower in the next.*

When I look into the full-length mirror outside the bathroom at Schloss Fuschl, the shadows of my history finish their whisperings. Yes, the lamé scarf and

Usova's emerald earrings are perfect. I am ready to share the spotlight in the elegant dining room of the Schloss with my new dress and freshly coiffed hair.

978-0-595-43057-4
0-595-43057-0

Printed in the United States
87586LV00004B/1-39/A